UA7
12/19

DISTRICT VIII

who has covered Hungary and eastern
since 1990. He is the author of five novels and
eight non-fiction books, including *Hitler's Secret
Bankers*, which was shortlisted for the Orwell
Prize. His books have been published in fourteen
languages. He is the editorial trainer and writing
coach at the *Financial Times* and writes for the
Economist, *Financial Times*, *Monocle* and a
number of other publications. He divides his
time between Budapest and London.

By Adam LeBor

FICTION

Yael Azoulay series

The Reykjavik Assignment
The Washington Stratagem
The Geneva Option
The Istanbul Exchange (short story)

*

The Budapest Protocol

*

Balthazar Kovacs series

District VIII

*

NON-FICTION

City of Oranges
Tower of Basel
The Believers
Complicity with Evil
Milosevic: A Biography
Surviving Hitler (with Roger Boyes)
Hitler's Secret Bankers
A Heart Turned East

DISTRICT
VIII

ADAM LEBOR

HEAD
ZEUS

First published in the UK by Head of Zeus in 2017
This paperback edition first published by Head of Zeus in 2018

9 7 5 3 1 2 4 6 8

A catalogue record for this book is available from the British Library.

ISBN (PB): 9781786692719
ISBN (E): 9781786692696

Printed and bound by CPI Group (UK) Ltd, Croydon, CR0 4YY

Head of Zeus Ltd
First Floor East
5–8 Hardwick Street
London EC1R 4RG

WWW.HEADOFZEUS.COM

In memory of my father, Maurice LeBor,
a lover of Budapest.

'You cannot walk in a straight line when the road is bent.'

Gypsy proverb

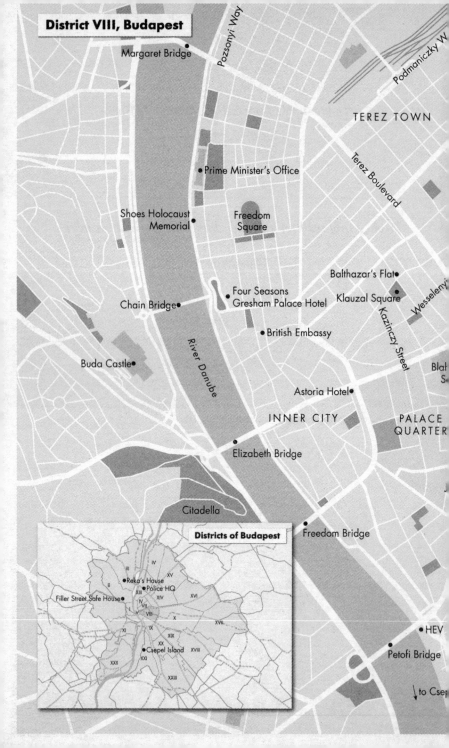

District VIII, Budapest

Margaret Bridge

Pozsonyi Way

Podmaniczky W

TEREZ TOWN

Terez Boulevard

Prime Minister's Office

Shoes Holocaust Memorial

Freedom Square

Balthazar's Flat

Klauzal Square

Wesselenyi

Four Seasons Gresham Palace Hotel

Chain Bridge

Kazinczy Street

British Embassy

Buda Castle

River Danube

Blah S

Astoria Hotel

INNER CITY

PALACE QUARTER

Elizabeth Bridge

Citadella

Freedom Bridge

Districts of Budapest

III

IV

XV

II

Reka's House

Police HQ

XIII

XVI

Filler Street Safe House

XIV

VII

IV

V

VIII

X

XVII

IX

XI

XIX

XX

Csepel Island

XVIII

XXII

XXI

XXIII

HEV

Petofi Bridge

↓ to Csep

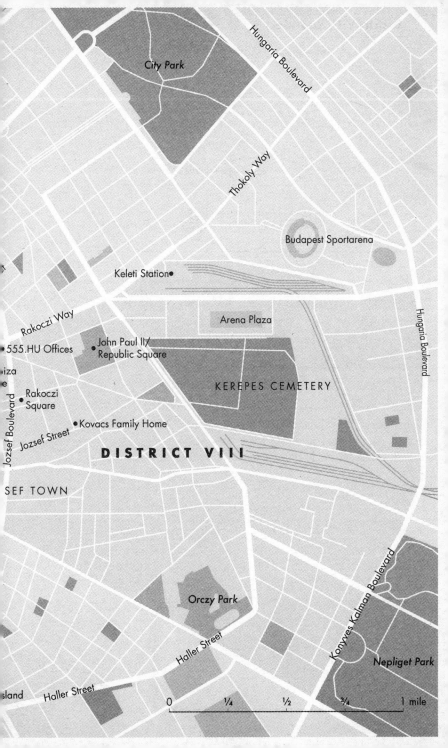

PROLOGUE

Keleti Station, 6.05 a.m., Friday, 4 September 2015

He lay on his back, his sleeping bag tangled between his legs, the nylon damp against his skin. A loudspeaker crackled for several seconds, paused, fired a long burst of jumbled vowels and consonants, fell silent again. His mouth was thick and dry, his T-shirt drenched with sweat. *Where was he?*

He turned on his side, looked around and remembered. A thin-faced boy, twelve or thirteen years old, was curled up under a brown acrylic blanket, his dirt-stained hand holding a torn backpack. A mother and baby lay on a sheet of corrugated cardboard at his feet. The child whimpered softly while the mother snored, oblivious, her chubby features serene in her sleep.

Simon Nazir rested his hand on his wife's back, felt her chest rise and fall, slid his fingers through her black, curly hair, felt the warmth of her skin against his, and closed his eyes. In his head he was still in Aleppo: he could hear the laughter of the shopkeepers in the bazaar, the siren call of the muezzin, smell the ancient dust, coffee and cardamom. He breathed in through his nose. The warm bovine reek almost made him gag. He opened his eyes, reached for his bottle of water and took a deep draught. The drink was stale and tasted of plastic. The sun was already up and the turquoise sky, streaked with fine white clouds, was about to deliver another day of heat and dirt and waiting.

Nazir tried in vain to get more comfortable, to stretch out without banging into another prone body. The human tide spread in every direction, filling the plaza in front of Keleti Station's main entrance, spilling along the sides. A busy intersection in a European capital was now a giant open-air refugee camp. The ground was covered with discarded food wrappers, cigarette ends, half-eaten sandwiches, rotten fruit, empty bottles of spring water, pairs of shoes taken off for the night. The lucky ones had tents, donated by tourists and music fans who had attended Budapest's Sziget Festival a couple of weeks earlier in mid-August. Half a dozen white vans were spread among the sleeping crowd, television network names emblazoned on their doors, giant antennae and satellite dishes pointing skywards. It was too early for the journalists but by ten o'clock there would be dozens of reporters here. Nazir watched a middle-aged man, an engineer he knew from home, twitch in his sleep, his arm around his ten-year-old daughter, a small suitcase in front of them.

The robo-voice was still droning in the background – the Hungarian language station announcements were a constant backdrop – but human sounds had pierced his sleep. A voice that he knew, one that he never wanted to hear again. Nazir glanced rightwards. Twenty yards or so away, there was movement, a male crouched, muttering.

Nazir told himself not to panic; to be calm, collected, *clever*. He was safe here. He was surrounded by people, police, reporters were coming. Nothing bad could happen, except more long days in transit. He and Maryam had been stuck at Keleti Station for five days, a halt in a journey that had lasted three weeks. They had fled Aleppo at night,

2

crossing the frontlines, taken a taxi to Damascus, another to Beirut, flown to Istanbul, then travelled overland by bus and foot through Bulgaria, Serbia and Hungary.

And here at least, nobody was trying to gas or shoot them, or even arrest them. They had made it to Europe, not quite the west, but certainly central Europe. The terminus's yellow paint was fading, its waiting room was dark and gloomy, its roof cracked. But Keleti was still a symbol of empire, and Budapest's place at the heart of the continent. A couple of days ago, he and Maryam had spent an hour staring at the departure board, dreaming of a new life in the west. On a normal day trains left here for Berlin, Vienna, Paris, Munich. But these were not normal times. Twenty-four hours ago the government had closed the western border to the migrants. All international trains were cancelled, although the local lines were still running. That didn't matter to the migrants, as they were not even allowed inside the station building. A line of riot police stood in front of the entrance. Every few minutes they moved aside to let the early morning commuters through, then stepped back into place, their arms crossed, their faces impassive.

Nazir drained the water bottle, heard the man's voice again, and then lay very still. The fatigues and pistol, his long beard, were gone. He was clean-shaven now, wore jeans, blue Nike trainers and a T-shirt, held an iPhone, could have been any one of hundreds of middle-aged men from Syria or Iraq or Afghanistan camped out at Keleti as they trekked through Europe. But it was him – the puckered scar above his right ear, a burn from an incendiary bomb, decided the matter.

Maryam stirred, as if sensing Nazir's unease, muttered something, then returned to her sleep. Nazir slid deeper into his sleeping bag, hiding his face. He tried to listen, focusing hard, could catch the inflections of the man's Aleppo accent, but not the words. Nazir watched through half-closed eyes as the two men to whom he was talking sat up and gathered their rucksacks. Where were they going?

Nazir looked at the line of taxis that stood by the side entrance to the station. The ride to the Austrian border cost 500 euros. He knew three families who had paid. Two had been dumped in the countryside thirty miles from Budapest, picked up by the police and promptly sent to a holding camp. The third had been left fifteen miles from the frontier. They had also been arrested but were released after paying another 500 euros to the police and had made it across. Two days ago the elder son had sent an SMS from Vienna.

For now, there was nothing to do at Keleti except wait and watch. One of the taxi drivers, he saw, was also looking at the three men. Nazir had noticed her on the second day. Firstly, because she was a woman, and seemed to be the only female working the station. She was in her early thirties, Nazir guessed, tall, with shoulder-length dark-blonde hair, brown eyes and an easy smile. Secondly, because she never seemed to have a fare. Every time Nazir looked, she was there, smoking, laughing, chatting with the other drivers. And she was friendly, unusually so. Nazir had exchanged pleasantries a few times with her when he'd gone for a walk. Her name, she said, was Ildiko. Nazir had been a silversmith in Aleppo. The cheap jewellery – rings and bangles – that Ildiko wore somehow did not suit her. The last time they chatted he realised that she was also surprisingly well informed about what was happening at Keleti, the territorial divisions between the Arabs, Africans and Afghans and even the squabbles between the Syrian opposition groups.

4

The three men were standing now, rucksacks on their backs, he saw. Nazir reflexively brushed his left hand, touched the scar where his little and ring fingers used to be, felt the flush of fear. He watched them turn and start to walk out of the station concourse. He unzipped his sleeping bag, still lying on his side, focused now, no longer wondering about Ildiko the taxi driver, and put his mobile phone inside the pocket of his jeans. He leaned over to Maryam, quickly scribbled a note on a piece of scrap paper with a trembling hand, took a roll of banknotes from his pocket and placed them both inside her sleeping bag.

'Simon,' she murmured.

'I'm going for some food. I'll be back soon,' he whispered in her ear, and quickly kissed her head. Maryam reached for him in her sleep. He embraced her through her sleeping bag, his chest against her back, her fingers entwining with his. Even now she smelled the same, of soap and lavender, her breath still sweet in the morning. All he wanted to do, all he had ever wanted, was to hold her and never let go. He kissed the back of her neck, then looked up at the three men. They were walking away from the station now, across Baross Square now, towards Rakoczi Way.

His heart thumped, his left hand throbbed. He closed his eyes for a moment, drank in the smell of her, swallowed hard, and stood up.

Thirty yards away, the blonde taxi driver dropped her cigarette, ground it out with a swift twist of her foot and began to follow him.

ONE

The body was gone.

Balthazar Kovacs stood in the middle of the lot and scanned his surrounds again. The ground was covered with smashed bricks, broken slabs of concrete shot through with rusty metal spars, and jagged lumps of plaster. Flies buzzed over a pool of greasy, stagnant water, the remains of a party nearby: blackened wood, an empty condom packet and a quarter-full plastic bottle of *Voros asztali bor*, red table wine that rarely saw a table. Charred sheets of typewritten paper, yellow with age, and mouldy books were scattered among the rubble. The only thing left standing was the lower part of the back wall, covered with graffiti.

He picked up a large black hardback book. Its binding was cracked and the pages were curled, but the embossed gold letters on the front were still legible: *Proceedings of the 26th National Congress of the Communist Youth Organisation, 1983.* He leafed through the stiff pages, filled with photographs of earnest youngsters in big collared shirts and wide flares, standing proudly under the banners of Marx, Engels and Lenin, between long articles about the role of youth in building Communism.

He put the book down, feeling the sweat drip down the back of his neck. A peaceful September Friday morning

6

in the backstreets of Budapest, although the temperature already felt like it was off the scale. Birdsong sounded from the trees. A woman in her sixties walked by in a pink leisure suit, cigarette in one hand, yapping terrier on a lead in the other. Children's laughter carried across the park from the playground. There was a new opposition billboard, he saw, covering two storeys of the side wall of a nearby apartment building. '*Kirugjuk a komcsikat!* let's kick out the commies!' it proclaimed above a photograph of the prime minister, his cabinet and business allies bedecked in red flags and linked together in a spider's web.

The SMS had arrived at 9.05 a.m., in the middle of his first cup of coffee. There were three words: 26 Republic Square, and a photograph. So he was in the right place. But where was the dead man? The photograph showed a thin, brown-haired male, in his late twenties or early thirties. He lay on his side, half-covered with bricks and dust, either dead or unconscious. If he was dead, which seemed likely as his eyes were open, had he been killed here, or brought here? The covering seemed a botched job, as though someone had been interrupted.

Balthazar glanced at the half-demolished wall, stepped closer. It was definitely the same wall. The graffiti was so fresh that the spray paint was still shiny. '*Bevandorlok haza*', it declared, 'Migrants go home', next to a picture of a man wearing a headscarf, hanging from a tree. The tree had been skilfully rendered, its trunk gnarly, black branches spreading like veins. A red tongue lolled from the mouth of the hanged man, his eyes bulging. Three letters underneath, painted in red, white and green, the colours of the Hungarian flag: MNF. *Magyar Nemzeti Front*, Hungarian National Front.

7

He took another step and bent down to peer at the ground. There were track marks in the dust, as though a heavy weight had been dragged through the dirt. He took out his telephone and quickly shot a video of the scene, panning from side to side, zooming in on the place where the man had been, then snapped a panorama of several still shots. He slipped the handset back into his pocket when something caught the edge of his vision, glinting in the morning sunshine. He knelt down and looked harder. A SIM card, large, old-fashioned, half covered in dust. He peered inside his shoulder bag: one evidence bag left, and a pair of tweezers. He used the tweezers to pick up the card, dropped it into the bag and stood still for a moment while he pondered his next move.

Each of Budapest's twenty-two districts had their own local force. This was the edge of District VIII, one of the city's largest and best known for being home to Budapest's main Gypsy quarter. In most murder cases the local beat officers found the body. They sealed off the area and called in the crime-scene and forensics team, who would then look for evidence. Then the case was passed to the district police's investigation team. They naturally wanted to investigate murders themselves, but nine times out of ten they were passed on to the city-wide murder squad, which made for a perpetual turf war. That was good news for killers, less so for their victims. Complications made for mishaps. Files went missing, reports were delayed; sometimes evidence was even 'accidentally' destroyed or lost in transit. But had there really been a murder here, or indeed, any crime? So far all he had was a text message and a photograph. Maybe the man was not even dead, just unconscious or drunk; maybe he had recovered and limped home. He certainly was not here any more.

Balthazar watched a bearded hipster on a old-fashioned white bicycle whizz by, heading down Luther Street to Rakoczi Way. He was about to put the evidence bag into his rucksack when he thought better of it. Just as he'd jammed the bag and the tweezers into his back pocket, he felt a pair of eyes on him. He turned around to see a wiry lad, eleven or twelve years old with street-smart eyes, staring hard, instantly calculating whether he was a threat or a potential source of benefit. 'You're a cop,' the boy declared confidently.

Balthazar knew there was no point lying. And who else would be picking up a piece of plastic and placing it in a bag? In any case, Gypsy street kids could smell out a policeman at a hundred yards. The boy had unkempt black hair, coffee-coloured skin, light-brown eyes and a brick in his right hand. He wore an oversized and grubby blue T-shirt, dirty cut-off jeans and a pair of worn-out Nike trainers. Balthazar smiled; a version of himself twenty-five years ago, but the pang in his stomach was something more than memory.

'Guilty.' Balthazar looked at the brick. 'Are you going to hit me with that?'

The boy looked at his hand. 'No. No, of course not.' He seemed about to run, paused for a couple of seconds, and tilted his head to one side as he looked Balthazar up and down. Confusion registered on his face. 'But you're a *Rom*.'

'Two out of two,' said Balthazar. He extended his hand, introduced himself in the Hungarian fashion, surname first. It was an old trick and nearly always worked. Hungarians were very polite, felt no embarrassment about introducing themselves. Indeed it was considered rude not to do so when meeting new people. Not responding to a person introducing themselves would be a very hostile gesture.

The boy solemnly extended a small hand. '*Szia*, hi, *Jozsi vagyok*, I'm Jozsi.'

'You can call me Tazi.' Balthazar lightly squeezed his thin palm. The boy's fingers were covered with red-brown dust. Balthazar pointed at the brick. 'Show me that.'

Jozsi frowned. 'I didn't steal it from anywhere. It was just lying around.'

'It's fine. I just want to take a look.'

Jozsi handed over the brick. Balthazar smiled as he ran his finger over an embossed cogwheel in one corner. Jozsi had a good eye. Communist-era building material, the detritus of the old regime, was now highly prized by interior designers. The brick could perhaps fetch 300 forints, the equivalent of a euro, before it ended up in a villa in the Buda hills or decorating a trendy loft conversion downtown. A pre-1989 street sign for Lenin Boulevard or Karl Marx Square, both since renamed, was worth hundreds.

This was a good place to hunt. The wreckage was all that remained of the former Communist Party headquarters. It was hard to imagine now that this building, which once covered half a block, had once been one of the most important sites in the country. Republic Square, like many landmarks, had been renamed, in this case for Pope John Paul. Hungary's governments had a mania for renaming streets and squares, as though a change of title could wash away what had happened there. But whatever it was called, this was a haunted place. Revolutionaries had tried to capture the party headquarters during the 1956 uprising. The fighting then, like all civil wars, was brutal. Mobs lynched officers in the AVH, the hated secret police, hanging them upside down from lamp posts and setting them on fire. Local toughs hurled Molotov cocktails at Russian tanks, burning the soldiers alive, leaving their charred corpses on the streets. After a long siege, a group of teenage AVH recruits had emerged from the party headquarters with their hands up. A British photographer had captured what followed, frame by frame.

Balthazar carefully put the brick on the ground, placed his foot on top of it.

'Hey,' said Jozsi, indignantly. 'That's mine.'

'I know. You'll get it back.' He took out his telephone and showed the photograph of the dead man to Jozsi. 'Did you see him? Do you know anything?'

Jozsi looked at the screen then back at Balthazar, juggling his deep suspicion of the police with his desire to get the brick back. 'He's gone.'

'I can see that. When? How?'

Jozsi looked down at the ground. '*Nem tom,* dunno.' 'I don't know' in Hungarian was '*Nem tudom*'. Street slang compressed it.

Balthazar crouched down so that he was at eye level with Jozsi, moved the brick up and down with his right hand. The boy knew something, he was sure. '*Kez kezet mos,* hand washes hand.'

Jozsi frowned, thought for a moment. 'The men came to take him away. They had a van.'

'Which men?'

'Men. I don't know who they were. Really.'

'Uniforms? Were they cops? Gendarmes?'

'No.'

'What kind of van?'

Jozsi shrugged. '*Nem tom.* A white van.'

'When?'

'Just after breakfast, around a quarter past eight.'

'How do you know all this?'

Jozsi stepped back, his eyes narrowing in suspicion. 'I live nearby.'

'Where?'

The boy stepped back again. 'Nearby.' Jozsi gestured at the brick. 'Can I have it back, please?'

Balthazar said, 'Sure. Just please tell me where you live. Don't worry. You are not in trouble. You can take all the bricks you want.' A suspicion of the authorities, generations old and seared into his people's collective memory, meant Jozsi would not say much more here. Balthazar would get his address and question him further later, with his parents present.

The growl of vehicle engines sounded across the square. As Balthazar stood up and turned to face the noise he felt Jozsi's nimble fingers on his right hand. He smiled, did not resist, as the brick began to slide out of his hand. A black van pulled up in front of the pavement and parked. 'Gendarmerie' was written on its side.

The vehicle was polished to an obsidian sheen, with thick wire mesh over the windshield and rear windows. The back door opened and six men emerged. Each wore black combat trousers, a black long-sleeved T-shirt and anti-stab vest, and a black ski helmet. Handcuffs, batons, pepper spray and heavy Maglite torches poked from pockets on their utility belts.

Balthazar turned. Jozsi had already vanished. He watched the squad walk towards him, their commander holding a long, metallic baton in his hand, black wraparound sunglasses covering his eyes.

Balthazar could walk away whenever he wanted, of course, by showing his police identity card. But he was in no rush. Quite the contrary. Even with his sunglasses, he instantly recognised the man with the baton.

The Gendarmerie had only been in operation for a month. The re-formed national police force was charged with 'special tasks for the protection of national order' and guarding the 'dignity of the government and Hungarian nation'. Protests by lawyers, human rights groups and opposition parties that this was a blank cheque to arrest anyone politically inconvenient had been brushed aside. So too had the pointed reminders from senior police officers that Hungary already had a national police force to deal with homeland security and terrorism. Jewish groups protested that the name awakened terrible memories – the original Gendarmerie had rounded up Jews for deportation during the Holocaust and had been disbanded in 1945. European Union diplomats and the European Commission had stated their 'concern' about the new force. The next day an article appeared in *Magyar Vilag*, a heavily-subsidised pro-government newspaper. The article reported that the ruling Social Democrat party was considering unilaterally rounding up all the migrants at Keleti Station, bussing them to the Austrian border and dumping them there. Ambassadors from EU countries issued a second statement that same afternoon, expressing their 'full confidence in Hungary's legal system and commitment to protecting human rights'.

Unlike the local police forces, who came under the authority of the Ministry of the Interior, the Gendarmerie reported directly to the prime minister's office. The usual oversight bodies, the parliamentary committees and the civil rights ombudsman, had no mandate to scrutinise its operations. In effect, the ruling party and the prime minister now had their own, completely unaccountable, paramilitary force. So why was the Gendarmerie interested in a dead man on a building site? Their very presence indicated that something had happened here. But what? There was only one way to find out. Balthazar stood and waited.

The six Gendarmes walked forward and positioned themselves around him: two squads of two on either side, and another standing behind him. All had their right hands hovering over their pepper spray and handcuffs. Balthazar did not move. The commander slid his baton back into the holder on his belt and took off his sunglasses. 'Hallo, Tazi,' he said.

'*Tiszteletem*, Attila,' replied Balthazar, his voice dry. Hungarian had three levels of formality. *Tiszteletem*, I honour you, was the most formal. Or the least, when used ironically.

Attila Ungar stepped forward, seemed about to shake hands, looked at his men, then thought better of it. Instead he asked, 'What are you doing here?'

'I could ask the same question. Why is the commander of the Gendarmerie out on the streets? Shouldn't you be in your nice office by Parliament?'

'I like it on the streets. That's where the action is. Where's the kid? Who was he?'

Balthazar shrugged. 'What kid?'

'The one you were talking to.'

'Who knows?' He turned around, pretending to look for Jozsi.

'Stop fucking about, Tazi,' said Ungar.

Ungar had been Balthazar's partner for three years, but they had worked together for a decade, rising up from beat officers in District VIII to the city murder squad. They had put away wife-beaters, muggers, violent armed robbers, barroom brawlers and at least one mafia hit man. Then one day, about two months ago, Ungar had invited Balthazar for a drink after work and announced he was resigning. Ungar had avoided all of Balthazar's questions, and claimed he just wanted a change of scene, to take a couple of months off. Balthazar had suspected that Ungar wanted to avoid a disciplinary investigation after several suspects had claimed he had beaten them up in the holding cells. Ungar denied everything but few believed him, especially as the suspects had substantial bruising and the CCTV system had suffered mysterious breakdowns each time he'd been in the holding area. Shaven-headed, thickly muscled, barely five feet six, Ungar was a weightlifter in his spare time. He seemed to have expanded horizontally even further since Balthazar last saw him. Black talons crept up the side of his neck.

'I'm not. Nice tattoo,' said Balthazar.

Ungar stepped closer. 'Isn't it? Tazi, we go back a long way. That's why you aren't lying on the floor, handcuffed. Or having a nice chat with my colleagues in the back of the van.'

'For standing in a building lot?'

Ungar smiled, a meagre movement of his lips that did not reach his eyes. 'Trespassing on state property.'

Ungar glanced at his watch. It was a Rolex Oyster, Balthazar noticed, quite a jump from the Casio plastic digital model Ungar had worn when they worked together. 'Tazi, you need to leave. Now.'

'Why?'

'I told you. Trespassing on state property.'

Ungar gestured at his men. They stepped closer. Balthazar did not move. Distant shouting echoed from the neighbouring apartment building. A window opened and the sound of the ten o'clock news on state radio drifted out. He could not hear all the headlines but several phrases carried: migrant flood, border overwhelmed, terrorist threat.

'What's in the bag?' asked Ungar, pointing at Balthazar's shoulder. His breath reeked of tobacco and coffee.

'None of your business.'

'Hand it over.'

'Why would I do that?'

'Because you were seen tampering with a crime scene.'

'What a busy morning I'm having. Trespassing. Tampering. And it's only ten o'clock. But I don't see any evidence of any crime.' He looked around at the Gendarmes. 'Apart from threatening behaviour.'

'If there's no crime, or dead body, then what is the Budapest murder squad doing here?'

'It's my day off.' Balthazar looked at the wall, pointed at the graffiti. 'I'm checking out the artwork. The red tongue is a nice touch, don't you think?'

Ungar's blue eyes turned cold. Balthazar was dissing him in front of his men. 'Always a smart-arse. Especially for a...'

Balthazar laughed. 'Yes, I was. Still am. Especially for one of those. Smart enough to know you don't have jurisdiction here.'

'I think we do. Don't you read government decrees? We have jurisdiction everywhere.' He pointed at Balthazar's shoulder bag. 'Even there.'

'I don't think so,' said Balthazar, shaking his head.

Ungar gestured at the Gendarmes standing around him. They stepped even closer, penning Balthazar in so he could feel their body heat. The Gendarme to Balthazar's right was tall and broad-shouldered with a knife scar under his right eye. He sniffed loudly before he spoke. 'Don't you notice it?' he asked of no one in particular. He sniffed again, triggering laughter among the other Gendarmes. 'That stink. Every time I step into District VIII.' He looked at Balthazar, his face sour. 'It's especially bad today.' He took out his pepper spray from his belt, held it in front of Balthazar's face. 'How about some deodorant?'

16

Balthazar said, 'Good idea.' The Gendarme with the scar exuded a powerful body odour, a mix of rank sweat and sour milk. 'Or maybe your uniform needs a wash? It's very hot.'

The Gendarme said nothing and put the spray back into his belt. His fingers curled into two large fists. There were calluses on his knuckles. His eyes lost focus and seemed to be covered with a thin film. Balthazar knew that look. He had seen it on Ungar's face many times when he'd had to drag him away from a suspect.

Balthazar could handle himself. He had grown up around here, not far away, on Jozsef Street, then and now the heart of the red-light district, his early years spent in a three-room flat without a bathroom that was home to ten people across three generations. He'd learned to fight his way home from school, as hard and dirty as he needed, and had eventually earned the respect of the neighbourhood toughs. When two skinheads had taunted Gaspar, his younger brother, he'd slammed their heads together and knocked them both out. After that, the pimps and prostitutes had taken him under their protection. Nowadays, he regularly worked out in the police gym and practised kick-boxing two or three times a week. But Balthazar also knew when he was outnumbered. Some battles were unwinnable. Especially against a new paramilitary police force with legal carte blanche.

Ungar shot him a look, one that said, '*Do you really want to do this?*'

Balthazar stepped back, slid his shoulder bag off and handed it to Ungar. The tweezers and the piece of laminated plastic in his trouser pocket suddenly felt larger and more conspicuous, pushing against his skin. What could he do if they searched him? Turned his pockets inside out? Not much. There were six of them and one of him. The Gendarmerie had already gained a reputation, well deserved, for lawlessness and unprovoked violence. Still, it was one thing to knock around left-wing protestors and human-rights activists – quite another to beat up a police officer.

Ungar peered inside Balthazar's bag, tipped it upside down. Nothing came out. The Gendarme's face creased in annoyance. He held his hand out. 'Phone.'

Balthazar reached into his trouser pocket, took out a small, blue Ericsson handset, at least a decade out of date.

Ungar looked at the handset. 'Very funny. Your proper phone.'

'That is a proper phone. Let me show you.' Balthazar pressed the speakerphone button, and called 112, the emergency number. 'This is Balthazar Kovacs of the Budapest murder squad. Code one. Yes, *code one*. Location: 26 Pope John Paul Square. Yes, the old party headquarters. Urgent. Yes, there are weapons involved. Yes, *now*.'

Balthazar held the handset in his palm. The operator's voice sounded from the loudspeaker, asking for immediate assistance, and for all cars in the area around Keleti Station to head immediately to Luther Street. A few seconds later, a siren wailed, getting steadily louder, another echoing in the distance.

Ungar stepped back, gestured at his men to return to their vehicle. He stared at Balthazar. He had been humiliated in front of his subordinates. This incident, it was clear, would not be forgotten. 'You remember your history lessons, Tazi. What happened to those AVH boys here in '56?'

'I remember that you copied my homework.'

'Like I said, a smart one.' His voice turned hard. 'Those AVH boys were just kids, simple boys from the countryside, raw recruits, drafted into the secret police. They didn't know what they were doing. They surrendered, came out with their hands up. They should have been taken prisoner.'

Ungar stepped closer. 'They were mowed down in broad daylight. One by one. Then set on fire. They didn't deserve to be killed like that. It was murder. But they were in the wrong place at the wrong time. And that's always a bad mistake.'

He paused, his eyes glinting. 'I'll be seeing you, Tazi.'

TWO

Sandor Takacs looked down at a freshly printed police report sitting on top of several manila folders. 'Code one?' he demanded. 'Officer in danger?'

'I was in danger,' said Balthazar. 'I was surrounded by six armed hostiles.'

'And whose fault is that?' Takacs said, exasperated. 'What were you doing there, anyway?'

'Investigating a murder.'

'No, you were not. You investigate murders here, under my command. You go where I send you. I did not send you to Republic Square, or whatever it's called nowadays.' Takacs put the report aside and pushed the folders across the desk. 'Do these look familiar, Detective?'

Balthazar picked the top file off the heap. 'Ildiko Nagy' was written on a white stick-on label. A photograph of a chubby teenage girl with frizzy brown hair was pinned to the cardboard. He checked the next in the pile. Marton Kelemen, a bald man in his late fifties, stared gloomily out.

Balthazar said, 'Yes. Why aren't they on my desk?'

'Because you never seem to be. I'm thinking of transferring you back to the beat. In District XXII.'

District XXII lay on the far edge of the city, a slice of quiet, immensely dull suburbia. Takacs continued, 'You can track down stolen bicycles. Arrest shoplifters. There might even be a burglary once a month.'

Takacs's annoyance was real, but would dissipate, Balthazar knew. Even so, form demanded that he show adequate obeisance. He bowed his head slightly. 'Please don't do that, boss.' He rested his hand on the folders. 'I am on these. Promise.'

Takacs looked doubtful. 'Really? Remind me, please, how many cases you are working on?'

Balthazar mentally counted for several seconds. 'Six.'

'And how many have we temporarily put on hold, due to lack of leads, witnesses and material resources?'

'About as many.'

'So that's twelve actual dead people that need you to find their killer.'

Balthazar reached into his pocket, took out his iPhone, called up the photograph he had been sent and passed the handset to Takacs. 'Thirteen.'

Takacs glanced at the screen. '*Twelve.*'

'There was a dead man on Republic Square this morning. It's our job to find his killer.'

'Not this one.'

'But—'

'But nothing, Tazi.'

'Nothing? Really?'

Takacs exhaled loudly, cutting him off. 'But... Attila Ungar.'

'Oh. The Gendarmes are on it.' Balthazar paused for a moment. 'So there is a case?'

Takacs put Balthazar's iPhone down and reached for the packet of cigarettes by his papers. They were Sobranie, the cheapest, roughest brand. He took a cigarette and held the end to his nose, closed his eyes, inhaled deeply and exhaled. Takacs had once been a forty-a-day man. 'Not here, in this building. And certainly not for you.'

Balthazar watched the shreds of tobacco fall on Takacs's papers. 'And we just let them do that?'

'So I am informed.'

'Why?'

'*Csak*,' said Takacs, brushing the brown flakes away. *Csak*, pronounced 'chuck', literally meant 'only', but used like this, it meant 'because I say so and that's the end of the matter', as a parent might inform a troublesome child. He stubbed the unlit cigarette in an large glass ashtray, adding it to an ash-free pile of crushed filters, paper tubes and chunks of tobacco.

The commander of Budapest police's murder squad was short and tubby. Two small brown eyes looked out from a round, pudgy face, under thinning grey hair, carefully combed over a bald spot at the back of Takacs's head. His face was shiny with sweat and his white shirt was already damp under the armpits. It was a sign of Takacs's displeasure that he was sitting behind his desk in his office on the tenth floor, while his subordinate was perched on a chair in front. They usually talked in the corner, where two armchairs nestled against a small coffee table.

As the commander of the Budapest murder squad, Takacs merited a corner office with large windows. The decor and furniture was standard government issue: light-blue walls, fake parquet floor and an Ikea adjustable office chair. But the view was spectacular: on one side, Arpad Bridge, a six-lane concrete ribbon with a tram track in the middle, spanned the Danube at the tip of Margaret Island; on the other, the green hills of Buda, studded with white villas, stretched away into the distance. Today the picture windows were not a bonus. The Budapest police headquarters were housed in a modern steel-and-glass tower block. The sunlight poured through and the room was steadily warming, had been all morning. The building's air-conditioning, overloaded by the *kanikula*, the summer heat wave, had finally given up. An upright fan in the corner turned from side to side, bringing little relief.

The thick heat of summer was not unusual for early September. What was unusual, Balthazar noticed, was Takacs's desk. The perennially teetering piles of reports, memos, files and torn-out newspaper articles had been replaced by an in tray and an out tray, both of which were near empty. Next to them stood a small, orderly pile of papers. What was going on here?

Takacs glanced at that day's edition of *Magyar Vilag*, which he made sure to always display. 'Terrorist Threat from Keleti Migrants' proclaimed the front-page lead, above a picture of a column of weary-looking male refugees trudging under a border-post sign proclaiming '*Magyar Koztarsasag*, Republic of Hungary'. The second story announced 'Prime Minister Welcomes Gulf Investors'.

He frowned, pushed the newspaper away. He thought for a moment. 'And actually, what do we have here? A photograph that may be of a dead man, and may not, a text message on your phone and some nasty graffiti. Who sent the message to your phone? Maybe it's your friends at Hazifiu.hu, stirring things up again. Forget about the Gendarmes. Focus on your existing workload. On actual real dead people.'

Balthazar often appeared on television news and chat shows, wheeled out by the police's press office as proof of the force's commitment to social inclusion. That made him a favourite target of Hazifiu.hu, the most extreme of Hungary's far-right websites. *Hazifiu* translated as 'patriotboy'. Last month the news portal had published his photograph, email address and mobile telephone number, prompting a deluge of hate messages and threats. Balthazar's home address, the website promised, would be next. The following day at dawn, the police had raided the website's office and the editor's home. Balthazar had not been featured since. Most of the threats were harmless, from the angry, embittered and unemployable who had been left behind by the change of system. But perhaps not all of them. Balthazar had enlisted the help of a friend in the State Security Service, a former hacker turned security expert. He had traced several of the emails' IP addresses back to servers in Parliament.

Balthazar thought for a moment. 'Maybe. But then they would run the photo of the dead man on the website to celebrate. The message came from a blocked number. I asked the mobile network. They said it would take up to a week to find out and then they'd need authorisation from the prime minister's office to release confidential information. Those are the new regulations, apparently.'

Takacs laughed. 'They need authorisation from the PM's office to take a piss in the morning. Like everyone else now.'

Balthazar leaned forward. 'Look at the video again, please, boss. There are track-marks in the dirt. As far apart as a pair of feet.'

Takacs picked up the handset and pressed the play button. 'That's not enough. A murder case needs a body. We don't have one.'

'Look at the graffiti, under the tree with the hanged man.'

Takacs swiped right, and enlarged the photograph, spelling out the letters painted underneath. *MNF*.

'Circumstantial. Could mean anything.' He shook his head and handed the telephone back to Balthazar. 'Were there any witnesses?'

Balthazar nodded. 'A kid. He said he saw some men take the body away in a white van.'

'What men?'

'I don't know.'

'Type, make of van?'

Balthazar shook his head. 'That's it. He was about to tell me more when the Gendarmes turned up. He scarpered as soon as they arrived.'

'Smart kid. His name?'

'Jozsi. A Gypsy.'

'Family name?'

'I didn't get it.'

Takacs sat back, splayed his fingers in a pyramid. 'So all we have, apart from your telephone message, is *Jozsika*, little Jozsi, somewhere in the backstreets of District VIII who says he saw some men take a body away. Well, that narrows the field.' He flushed and looked at Balthazar. Jozsi, short for Jozsef, was a very common Gypsy name. 'Ah. Er... Sorry, Tazi... I...' he muttered, a flush rising up his neck.

Balthazar laughed, 'Forget it, boss.' His voice turned serious. 'Actually, we do have something.'

'What?'

Balthazar reached inside his trouser pocket, took out the evidence bag with the SIM card inside and handed it to Takacs. 'This.'

As if on cue, just as Takacs peered at the evidence bag,

a knock on the door sounded. Balthazar watched Takacs's reaction with amazement. Not only had his boss turned into a neat-freak, he was also a speed neat-freak. Takacs did not answer. Instead he gathered the files and papers into a single pile, turned the code one report over, so a blank page was showing, placed all the paper in the in tray and dropped the newspaper on top. Balthazar watched Takacs's stubby fingers flow quickly and easily over his keyboard as he shut down his email and browser and called up a screensaver. For a man of his generation, his boss was surprisingly adept with computers and electronic communications. Only then did Takacs say, 'Come in.'

Balthazar turned to see a stout blonde woman in her late forties step inside. She carried a tray with two coffees, two bottles of mineral water and a plate of chocolate biscuits towards Takacs's desk. Balthazar glanced at Takacs. The evidence bag was still on Takacs's desk. Takacs had not noticed it. Balthazar understood instinctively that whoever this woman was, she should not see it. He stared at Takacs, who looked puzzled, down at the bag, back at Takacs, pulled a face to indicate urgency, then stood up to block the woman's view of his boss's desk and her path towards it.

Balthazar introduced himself. The woman wore a tight blue polyester two-piece business suit with garish gold-coloured buttons on the jacket and a knee-length skirt. She looked puzzled and faintly irritated – *Why was this person introducing himself now and blocking her path?* – but replied as custom demanded. 'Szilagyi Ilona,' she said, turning reluctantly to face him. She had brown eyes, heavy mascara and dyed blonde hair teased into an elaborate bouffant. She looked down at the tray as if to indicate she could not shake hands now.

Balthazar sensed movement at the side of his field of vision. He stood aside as Ilona stopped at the edge of Takacs's desk and greeted him as she put the drinks down.

Balthazar followed her eyes' sweep down Takacs's worktop. She stared at Takacs's computer monitor, frowning for a moment when she saw a bouncing screensaver of the Hungarian Parliament. The evidence bag was gone.

'Please excuse Detective Kovacs,' said Takacs. 'He is one of my best officers. When he obeys orders.'

Ilona smiled uncertainly, looked back and forth between the two men, puzzlement written on her face as she tried to work out their relationship. Was Takacs being funny? How could somebody defy their boss? She asked, 'Shall I add the milk and sugar?'

'That's very kind, Ilona,' said Takacs, 'but no thanks.' He stopped talking, let the silence build. Ilona made no move to leave, her eyes sweeping across Takacs's worktop for the second time.

'Thank you, Ilona,' said Takacs, with more emphasis. She hesitated for a moment as her smile faded, then left the room.

Balthazar waited until she had closed the door. 'Ilona?'

'Yes. Ilona,' said Takacs, sighing before he added three heaped spoons of sugar to his coffee and a splash of milk. 'Shall I be mother? Or I can call Ilona...'

Balthazar picked up his drink. 'No need. Black is fine. Why didn't you just switch it off when you heard her knock?'

'That would be a little obvious, don't you think?'

'Probably. Where's Erzsi?' Erzsi *neni*, Auntie Erzsi, had worked for Takacs for almost twenty years. Both men trusted her absolutely.

Takacs gestured at the tray. 'I didn't ask for this and I didn't ask for Ilona. Yesterday, at eleven o'clock in the morning, Erzsi was offered voluntary redundancy: six months' salary, plus a full-salary pension for life. One that would not count towards her personal tax allowance if she took another job. She had two hours to decide. She didn't want to leave.' He picked up his coffee, tasted the drink and grimaced. 'There were a lot of tears. I told her to take it. She did. We'll have a dinner for her in two weeks at Gundel.' Gundel was Budapest's most famous historic restaurant. Takacs continued talking, 'You will be there, of course. Ilona won't. She arrived today, at nine a.m. With a key to my office. Luckily, I had a tip-off that she was coming. I was here first.'

'A tip-off from who?'

Takacs smiled. 'A friend.'

'A friend in high places?'

'High enough.'

'And who sent Ilona?'

Takacs put the cup down. 'The same branch of government that offered Erzsi her retirement package. Ilona has been seconded from the prime minister's office. There is a new programme for long-serving state employees; it's called loyalty rewards. Like an airline. They get moved around different departments to broaden their work skills. Apparently, working for me is a reward.'

Balthazar laughed. 'I've always thought so, boss.'

Takacs inclined his head. 'I'm glad you agree. I could have said no, of course. But the virtue of Ilona, as you saw, is that she is not the subtlest operator. If I said no, then they would have sent someone else.'

Balthazar looked out of the window. A cruise ship passed under Arpad Bridge's concrete arches, a black-and-gold German flag fluttering at its prow. The boats started in Germany, wound through Austria and Hungary before heading south into Serbia and Romania and the Black Sea. The ship was long and white, three stories tall, and every cabin had huge picture windows. He could see the staff putting out lunch on the upper deck. Balthazar's stomach growled. He had eaten nothing that day apart from a banana, had drunk too much coffee and not enough water.

Balthazar asked, 'How do you know they didn't?'

Takacs frowned. 'Didn't what?'

'Send someone else as well? Maybe she's a diversion. Distracting you from the real spy.'

Takacs looked thoughtful. 'Maybe she is a diversion. And maybe you overestimate our prime minister.' He took the newspaper off the case files and tapped the pile. 'Meanwhile, you have plenty to do without worrying about Ilona. Or getting into turf wars with the Gendarmerie.'

Balthazar picked up the files and leafed through them. Ildiko Nagy, a seventeen-year-old school student, had been stabbed by her former boyfriend in The Dubliner, an imitation Irish pub near Nyugati Station. Marton Kelemen had been hit over the head with a bottle by his wife in their luxurious Buda villa after she found sexual texts from his secretary. The Dubliner had CCTV, and the cameras actually worked. The boyfriend was still using his Facebook account. A neighbour had heard Kelemen screaming at her husband, threatening to kill him, followed by the sound of broken glass. Mrs Kelemen was on the run. She had dumped her telephone but seemed to be using her own bank card. Balthazar knew he should be able to find both suspects in a day or two.

Takacs picked up a crumpled handkerchief, wiped his sweaty forehead. 'I never liked Ungar. He is a thug. Every time I tried to bring disciplinary proceedings or suspend him, it was blocked upstairs. Now he's found his place.'

With Ilona out of the room, the atmosphere had eased. Balthazar sipped his coffee. 'But we are the murder squad. The dead man in Republic Square should be our case.' The drink was tepid and slightly bitter, as coffee had been served in government offices for decades. He put the cup down. 'And anyway, what is the Gendarmerie's interest?'

'Tens of thousands of people, economic migrants, refugees, terrorists, who knows what, are pouring through our borders. Then one turns up dead near Keleti Station. Of course the Gendarmerie are interested. They need something to do. To justify their existence. Their equipment. Their budget.' Takacs looked into the distance. 'What we could do with that—'

Balthazar sat upright, alert now. 'He was a migrant? How do you know?'

'I don't, not for sure. He was found near Keleti, is one thing. But why else would the Gendarmerie be interested? They are taking over every case with any kind of international connection.' He paused. 'Are you sure you want this?'

'Of course. And I really don't want to be told what to do by Attila Ungar and his thugs. If the Gendarmes take the case, in six months' time we will both be out of a job. There won't be a murder squad. It will be disbanded and absorbed. There probably won't be a police force, in Budapest or anywhere else. Just the Gendarmerie. And we will both be applying to security companies for work.'

'Maybe. Meanwhile, there's something you need to see.' Takacs beckoned Balthazar to come around and stand by his chair. He pressed the space bar on his keyboard and his computer monitor switched on. The browser window showed 555.hu, Hungary's best investigative website.

'Take a look at this,' said Takacs. 'It was posted twenty minutes ago.'

TRAFFICKERS DISGUISE MIGRANTS AS GYPSIES TO EVADE BORDER CHECKS

By Eniko Szalay

Human traffickers are disguising refugees and migrants as Gypsies so they can easily pass Hungarian border checks and travel on to the west. The traffickers are working with Gypsy clan leaders, who loan the traffickers genuine identity cards and passports belonging to Roma men, women and children, as well as traditional Gypsy clothes, in exchange for a part of the fee the traffickers receive. The identity papers and clothes are returned once the migrants pass into Austria so they may be used again.

Many refugees, especially from the Middle East, have darker complexions and so can pass as Gypsies. The people-smugglers dress the women and girls in brightly coloured skirts and headscarves. The men are clothed in worn second-hand jackets and trousers. They are told not to speak in their native language while crossing the border. Some are even loaned musical instruments and carry violins and accordions to bolster their false identities.

Border guards at Hegyeshalom and other crossings to Austria have been ordered to be on alert for migrants and refugees. However EU nationals can still travel freely back and forth. As Hungary and Austria are both part of the Schengen zone there are no border checks, and cars with

Austrian, Hungarian or Romanian number plates are usually not stopped.

The people-smugglers operate freely in the side streets and parks around Keleti Station, which has now become the epicentre of Europe's refugee crisis. Yesterday, despite the large police presence at the station, which is now closed to international trains, the people-smugglers were operating openly and accepting payment in either dollars, euros or Kuwaiti dinars. Two well-known Roma figures in Budapest's underworld, both with connections to organised crime, appeared to be operating out of a café near the station.

A western diplomatic source told 555.hu: 'This is an organised network based in Vienna and Budapest, with links to the Middle East. The ringleaders are making vast profits from this trade in human misery. We have repeatedly requested that the Austrian and Hungarian authorities take action, but it seems nothing has been done.'

The rest of the article detailed how Eniko had asked three refugees camped out at Keleti to speak to the people-smugglers, then report back to her. They had all been quoted a price of 2,000 euros per person to get to Vienna, and promised a refund if they were turned back.

Balthazar read to the end. 'Great detail. She's a very good reporter.'

Takacs gave Balthazar a wry look. 'Isn't she? I liked Eniko. Are you still in touch?'

Balthazar shook his head, ignored the emotions that the sight of her name still stirred. 'Not directly. We have mutual friends.'

Takacs continued talking, 'Still, this must be the first time anyone has paid money to pretend to be a Gypsy. It's usually the other way around.' Alarm suddenly flitted across his face. 'Can I say that?'

Takacs had been Balthazar's patron for the last few years, had fought for him in inter-departmental battles, pushed for his promotion, stood by him every time. But Balthazar also accepted that despite his best efforts, and four days on a diversity-training course in London run by the Metropolitan Police, Sandor Takacs was a man of a certain age, who had lived his whole life in a very politically incorrect society, one never more so than where Gypsies were concerned.

Takacs was nudging sixty, could retire whenever he wanted. He had grown up in a village near the Serbian border, where smuggling was a way of life. He might easily have become a criminal himself, but a sharp-eyed Communist Party official had spotted his intelligence and sent him to Budapest to study. Balthazar had worked for him for five years, knew his moods and foibles, his weaknesses and his strengths. A display of photographs on the wall showed Takacs receiving a medal or award from every Hungarian prime minister since the collapse of Communism in 1990. Pal Dezeffy, the current prime minister, grinned at the camera, his arm around Takacs's shoulder.

Another array pictured Takacs at various seminars and international meetings with senior police officers, politicians and dignitaries. Next to that were framed certificates from courses Takacs had completed at the New York Police Department, the FBI and the London Metropolitan Police. But Takacs's greatest ability was born in four decades of police work reading the signs and portents that heralded a change of empire, government, ruling party, even ideology. Like the archetypal Hungarian, Takacs could enter a revolving door behind someone and still come out in front.

Balthazar laughed. 'Yes, boss. You can say that. There's a police station at Keleti. Why don't they just arrest these guys?'

'Is that a serious question, Detective Kovacs?'

Balthazar took another sip of coffee. The bitter sludge was really undrinkable. He put the cup down. 'No, boss. Not at 2,000 euros per person. What's their cut?'

'The usual. About fifteen per cent.' Takacs paused, thinking how to frame his next thought. 'Tazi, she writes about Gypsy clan leaders. Help me out here. Could they include...'

'My brother Gaspar? Maybe. He brings in some of his girls from the Balkans. He knows the traffickers. He knows the routes, who to pay off and where.'

Takacs picked up the packet of cigarettes, extracted one and twirled it between his fingers. 'Do you think he is involved?'

'In murdering migrants? No. But trafficking, probably.'

'Would he help?'

'Maybe. But you know how it works with pimps. Nothing is free. The vice squad are all over his patches, because he won't pay them enough.'

'Go and see Gaspar. If he is involved in the death of this man, he gets no favours. And if he is not and he knows something, we can think about trading. I'll have a word with the vice squad. Speaking of family, how's Alex? How old is he now?'

'Twelve. Thirteen, next month. It's my turn with him this weekend. He's coming over tomorrow afternoon and staying the night.' Balthazar picked up his telephone, called up a photograph and passed it to Takacs. The screen showed a skinny, brown-haired, green-eyed boy with a gap-toothed smile.

'Good-looking lad. Bring him in here to visit us. Maybe he'll also be a cop when he grows up.' He paused, 'If there still are any cops then...' He handed the telephone back to Balthazar. 'Sarah?'

'The divorce is finalised. I get him one day every other weekend and for two hours one evening a week. She made me surrender three weekday visits for the overnighter this weekend.'

'I don't know why these women behave like this. How can it be good for a boy not to have a father around?'

Balthazar gave a wry smile. 'Maybe Sarah thinks two mothers are enough.'

'Perhaps it's her...' Takacs looked at the ceiling for a moment, searching for the right word. '... partner. Turning her against you.'

'I don't think so. I get on fine with Amanda. Just not with Sarah. She's always so angry with me. She's still playing hard-ball, even though she left me. And that was almost three years ago.'

'There's no logic in these situations. Maybe you make her feel guilty, so she gets angry and she's taking it out on you. But watch yourself with Sarah. She's built a very good roof.'

Roof was criminal slang for protection. 'Who?'

'The American ambassador. Sarah had dinner there twice in the last month. It seems the ambassador went to college with Sarah's mother. They are still close friends. There's a $100 million Anglo-American investment on the table, for security equipment, staff and training for the new border fences. If the ambassador makes a request to the PM's office for help dealing with a troublesome police officer harassing an American citizen, it will be heeded. Especially after you had to be officially—'

'Yes,' said Balthazar, cutting Takacs off. 'So where are we? Officially?'

Takacs shrugged, slid the evidence bag across the desk. 'Expect an email from me informing you that the events at Republic Square are now a matter of national security and under the jurisdiction of the Gendarmerie. The email will be an official record of my instructions not to pursue it any further. Otherwise, what you do in your own time is your own affair.'

Balthazar smiled, placed the evidence bag in his shirt pocket. 'Meaning?'

Takacs's voice was deadpan but his eyes glimmered. 'No calls to or from this office, or my home or mobile numbers, no use of police email or databases, no requests to any colleagues, either verbal, on paper or by email. And no use of police communications, internet or telephone facilities. Find an internet café. And not the one nearest your house. You are on your own. Off the books. *Vilagos*?'

'*Vilagos*.'

Takacs opened a drawer in his desk, tossed an ancient Nokia at Balthazar. 'Catch.'

THREE

As Balthazar walked out of Sandor Takacs's office, three miles away, in the heart of downtown Budapest, in a secure, sound-proofed basement room, the newly appointed Second Secretary handed a Hungarian passport to a Hungarian civil servant called Akos Feher. Gold letters spelled out '*Europai Unio*' and '*Magyar Kosztarsasag*', on the top of the cover, '*Utlevel*' on the bottom.

'Open it, please, to the photograph page,' said Celeste Johnson.

Feher did as he was bade. The photograph showed a middle-aged man with dark-brown skin, jet-black hair, dark eyes, a curved, hawk-like nose and black eyes staring out at the camera.

'Who is he?' Johnson asked.

'As it says on the photograph page, Miss Johnson. Zsolt Szabo.'

'*Ms.*' She picked up the passport. 'Does he look like somebody called Zsolt Szabo to you?'

Feher sat back, shrugged. 'I don't know what a Zsolt Szabo looks like. It is a very common Hungarian name. He is dark, yes. Maybe he is a Gypsy. Or a Romanian Hungarian.'

'He is not.'

37

Feher looked at her before he answered. She was in her mid-thirties, he guessed, tall and well dressed in a white blouse and black trousers with distractingly large breasts. She was neither friendly nor unfriendly. No wedding ring. Two plain gold studs in her ear. Short, black, curly hair, very short indeed at the sides. A plain manila file on the table in front of her. He could not read her at all. He had never dealt with a foreign woman in a position of power over him before. Let alone a black one. But this was Hungary, his homeland, where his party ruled and his boss was the minister of justice. Be confident, be bold, he told himself. 'We have all sorts of Hungarians now. Immigrants get citizenship. Even *negers*.'

'Even *who*?' Johnson was incredulous.

Feher burned red. What had he said wrong? *Neger* was just the Hungarian word for a black person. What word should he use? 'I am sorry, really, I didn't mean anything bad. It's the Hungarian word for negro.'

Johnson raised her eyebrows, barely mollified. 'We don't use that word any more, either, Mr Feher.'

He looked down at the table. The red top was chipped and cracked. 'My English is not always the best. Excuse me. I apologise.'

So much for being bold, he thought. He was floundering badly. He was out of his comfort zone and the power dynamics were definitely not in his favour. There was something not right here, he sensed, at least not right for him. Definitely not right for his career. Diplomatic protocol dictated that if Johnson, or any diplomat, wanted to meet someone with his rank of assistant state secretary – a senior official – at the Ministry of Justice, they request an appointment at his office, a few minutes' walk away. The request would be granted, in three or four days, maybe a week, depending on who was asking.

Instead he had been summoned – there was no other word – on twenty-four hours' notice to the British embassy on Harmincad Street. That had made him uneasy. He had questioned the request with his superiors, asked for a trusted colleague to accompany him. But his boss had breezily said there was no need, promised there was nothing to worry about. Once Feher crossed the embassy entrance and walked through the security check, legally he was no longer on Hungarian soil. The power dynamic had shifted completely. He was not in danger, of course, but nor was he in charge. He was in Britain. And in trouble. That much was getting clearer by the minute.

Johnson tapped the edge of the passport on the desk. 'Apology accepted. Let's move on. This man, the so-called Zsolt Szabo, was issued with a Hungarian passport on' – she checked the file in front of her – 'August 30th. Two days later he was stopped at Luton airport attempting to enter the United Kingdom.'

'Why?'

'Because whoever he is, he is definitely not Zsolt Szabo.'

'How do you know?'

Johnson closed the file. 'The passport records that he was born in Budapest. But he cannot speak a word of Hungarian. He cannot tell us which school he attended in Hungary. He cannot name three cities in Hungary. He cannot name any, apart from Budapest. Which he mispronounces.'

'Then who is he?'

'We don't know yet. We were hoping you could tell us.'

Feher's sense of unease grew. Unease and guilt. Which was doubtless Johnson's intention. But what did she know? And how? He needed to hit back. 'How would I know? I don't work in the passport office. Maybe you should...'

He glanced at Johnson. She was surprisingly sexy in a strict, domineering way, with a blouse that was just slightly too tight. One button was undone. How would it be to undo another? Johnson caught Feher staring at her breasts. Her face was set in stone. He swallowed to cover his embarrassment. '... you could... ask them for help,' he said, his voice trailing off.

'We did. They did not know anything useful. They just produced the document. The necessary checks were carried out by the Ministry of Justice, they told us.' Johnson leaned forward, her brown eyes flashing. 'Mr Feher, I cannot emphasise enough how serious this matter is. There is a Europe-wide terrorist alert. Every day thousands of people pour across the border here and no records are kept of their arrival or departure. Many of them are fleeing, or say they are fleeing Syria and Iraq. Your government has no idea whose these people are. A non-Hungarian national attempted to gain entry to the United Kingdom using this document. That is bad enough. But it is not a fake, it is a genuine passport, with a correct serial number.'

Feher had been to the British embassy several times for meetings about cross-border cooperation and other legal issues. He had even attended a seminar here on human rights and the prison system. The building was magnificent, a former bank in the very heart of downtown. It had a marble-floored reception room with a glass-tiled roof and a sweeping central staircase. The last time he had been here, he was received by the ambassador in a grand office with views of downtown Budapest, served coffee on Zsolnay crockery and small pastries from the Gerbeaud coffee house, Budapest's most famous café on nearby Vorosmarty Square. He had even been invited, with his wife, to a reception marking the Queen's birthday.

Now he was sitting on a cheap office chair, across a worn table, in a small, windowless room. The space was about five yards long and five yards wide. It had grey walls, a grey floor and ceiling, and was accessed by Johnson placing her thumb over a biometric lock. There was a similar room in the basement of the ministry, daily swept for bugs, that was reserved for the most sensitive meetings. He had once seduced the most attractive of that year's crop of interns there.

Feher had refused to surrender his telephone at reception and it now sat in front of him, in a signal-blocking bag. None of his usual tactics – flirtation, promise of advancement, all-expenses-paid trips to the ministry's villa on the shores of Lake Balaton, or the Nokia box, a mobile-telephone box filled with 20,000-forint notes – would work here, he knew.

Feher asked, 'Could I have something to drink?'

Johnson nodded. 'Of course. Tea, coffee or water?'

Feher thought for a moment. A hot drink would need a few minutes to prepare, could buy him some time. 'Tea, please.'

Johnson stood up, excused herself and left the room. Feher sat back, tried to get comfortable, but his neck was locking up. He rubbed the base of his head, tried remember what he knew about his interlocutor from the ministry's files. He had skimmed her CV before the meeting. Perhaps he should have paid more attention. She had previously been posted in Ankara, Cairo and Islamabad. She seemed to have no experience at all in central or eastern Europe. So what was she doing in Budapest; quiet, sleepy Budapest?

He knew the answer, of course. Nowadays Budapest was neither quiet nor sleepy. Johnson had arrived just a month earlier, as the migrant crisis reached its peak. That told him plenty. She must work for MI6. He needed to consult with the minister. This was clearly serious. Not only serious, but *political*. For a moment he felt a flicker of fear, then banished it. He was on the fast track, backed up, hand-picked by the minister. An assistant state secretary at the age of twenty-eight, the promise of a place on the Social Democratic Party's candidate list at the next election. A lovely wife, a child, another on the way, and all the extra-marital partners he could wish for as long as he was discreet. He just needed to ride out this storm, this squall, and keep his head. Until then, he would use his usual tactics: offer to cooperate, but actually stonewall and stall. Yes, that was the way forward, at least for now. He felt better for thinking things through, for taking a decision.

He opened the bag, took out his telephone and tried to call the ministry. Silence. He checked the handset screen. No bars and no Wi-Fi. But what had he expected? He exhaled loudly, slid the handset back into the bag.

A few seconds later the door opened. Johnson came in with an aluminium tray on top of which were two glasses of water and two white mugs, each emblazoned with the words GREAT BRITAIN. A copy of that day's *Magyar Vilag* lay next to the mugs, folded over on an inside page, next to a brown envelope and a white plate with two biscuits. She passed a mug to Feher. A tea bag floated in the beige liquid, under a layer of milk. It looked revolting.

'Biscuit?' she asked, gesturing at the tray.

Feher looked at the tray. They were plain Gyori biscuits, the cheapest available. 'No, thanks.' He took a sip of the drink. It was tepid and tasteless.

Johnson sat back down in her chair. 'So, Akos. May I call you Akos, as it seems we will be working together?' She smiled as she spoke, a smile that almost reached her eyes, and leaned forward as if to display more of her impressive cleavage.

No, you may not, Feher wanted to say, even if you have undone that second button. I am not on first-name terms with foreign women who lock me in basement rooms in another country's embassy. But today it seemed, he was. 'Yes,' he replied.

'So, Akos, we were talking about the passport serial number. We would like your assistance.'

He sat back and summoned his courage. 'Firstly, I would like to thank you, Celeste, for bringing this to our attention,' he said confidently. 'It may be that this passport is a forgery. Our borders are overwhelmed at the moment. People-traffickers are ever more organised. They have access to extraordinary technology. You have doubtless read the Europol report that criminal gangs can even produce machine-readable passports with the new chip technology. I can promise you that we at the ministry will give this matter our *urgent* attention.'

Johnson smiled. 'That's a good start, Akos. But only a start.'

He looked again at *Magyar Vilag*: the newspaper had been carefully folded over and positioned on the tray facing him so he could read it. The headline on page three was clearly visible: 'State Secretary Arrested: Government Cracks Down on Corruption.' Clever. He would remember that trick, next time he was in charge in a meeting. If there was a next time. He continued talking, 'I am sorry, I don't understand,' he said, although they both knew he did.

'Oh, Akos, I think you do.' Johnson opened the passport, slid it across the table. 'Not only does the passport office say your ministry carried out the checks, the passport serial number starts with HM. That means it was issued at the specific request of the Ministry of Justice.'

Feher thought quickly. How did she know that? MI6 knew

everything, he supposed, and what it didn't know the CIA would tell it. Either way, there was no point denying it.

He opened the document at the photograph page. There it was: HM3097889. 'I will need to keep this.'

Johnson extended her arm and turned her hand over so the palm was face up.

Feher said, 'This is Hungarian government property.'

Johnson smiled. 'Maybe. But this is British sovereign territory. This passport was seized at Luton airport. The man using it is now being detained at a British immigration holding centre. We have offered him a deal: tell us how you got the passport and we will deport you, rather than imprison you.'

She checked her watch. 'He's been locked up for almost two days now. That's usually enough.' She smiled brightly. 'Of course, your government is welcome to make an official request for the return of the passport.'

Feher handed her the passport back. His instincts were right. This was worse than he thought. Much worse, especially if the man talked. 'Keep it for now.'

Feher read the headline in *Magyar Vilag* again. He had seen the newspaper that morning, of course, knew the man the story was about, a senior official in the Ministry of the Interior. He had made two mistakes: the first was to argue at an inter-ministry meeting that the government should provide medical services to the migrants. You did not need to be a liberal or an opposition supporter or a bleeding-heart activist to wonder why the government allowed such squalid conditions to continue. The scenes at Keleti were not only distressing, they were a public health hazard. Ten toilets and six taps for thousands of people. Foreign television stations – BBC, CNN, all the major networks – showed rolling footage of filthy, hungry children, queuing for food provided by volunteers.

The arrested man's second, and larger, mistake was to drive his Porsche convertible to work in Budapest. The rules were clear: government positions were opportunities for lavish self-enrichment. But never show your spoils in public. Sports cars were to be kept in the secret government garage on the outskirts of Vienna and could only be driven outside Hungary. Johnson's message was not very subtle. And what was in the envelope?

'How shall we go forward?' asked Akos.

Johnson picked up her mug, sipped her tea. 'By working together.'

'Meaning?'

'You use your contacts to find out who took the decision to issue this passport, how many others like it have been issued, when, by whom, and share copies of all the records with us.'

Feher almost laughed out loud. 'You are asking me to spy for you? On my own colleagues and ministry?'

'Of course not. I am asking you to cooperate with us on a matter of bilateral concern.'

Feher looked at his watch, a sleek, black Rado. 'I have noted your request.' It was almost noon. He was having lunch with the deputy minister today. He slid his chair back, was about to stand up. 'I would like to leave now. Unless I am being held prisoner.'

Johnson laughed lightly. 'Akos, you are free to go whenever you like.' She paused for a moment. 'Just one more thing.'

'What?'

Johnson passed him the white envelope. 'Take a look. You can keep the photographs. We have copies. Digitally stored.'

Feher took out a photograph and turned pale. He was sitting at the wheel of a silver Porsche convertible, the snow-capped Austrian mountains soaring in the background. The car could probably be explained away. But not the pretty, blonde young woman next to him, her arm around Feher's shoulder as she nuzzled his neck.

Number 8E bus, Thokoly Way, 12.00 p.m.

'I have to what?' demanded Balthazar, as the bus suddenly slowed. He held his mobile phone closer to his ear, not sure if he had heard correctly. A siren sounded in the distance. 'But it's nothing to do with the prime minister's office. Municipal CCTV is under the authority of the Budapest mayor. Why do I need a permit from the prime minister to get hold of this morning's footage from Keleti? When was this introduced?'

He sensed immediately there was no point continuing this conversation. The city official, usually cooperative, was merely relaying the news of the new requirement. Balthazar would have to use the *kis kapu*, the little gate, to get around it. Every Hungarian had their clutch of little gates, contacts across officialdom who sidestepped obstacles, sometime for a fee, but more often for a favour banked. Balthazar already knew who he would ask. Meanwhile, he called up the 555. hu website on his phone. Eniko's story was still the lead, but another, smaller article underneath caught his eye.

MAGYAR NEMZETI FRONT CLAIMS LATEST ATTACKS ON MIGRANTS

555.hu reporters

Eight migrants, including three women and children, were taken to hospital yesterday after they were assaulted by

thugs wearing masks. The group, composed of three families from Syria and Iraq, had crossed the border at Kelebia
and were approaching a line of taxi drivers when around half
a dozen men attacked them.

The article detailed how the assailants wore black trousers
and T-shirts and ski masks. They had pushed and shoved
the women and children and screamed abuse at them. The
serious violence was reserved for the menfolk, all of whom
were beaten, one until he was unconscious. Balthazar noted
how the article had no byline. The MNF had first appeared
six months ago, in the spring, as the migrant crisis grew.
Several reporters covering the group had received threatening telephone calls and emails. Balthazar had heard that one
journalist at 555.hu had been sent a video clip of his journey
home to his wife and young child. The article ended with a
quote from the government's spokesman: 'We ask our compatriots to channel their outrage at the daily breaches of our
sovereignty and territorial integrity through legal means
and channels.'

The siren was much louder now. Its howl filled the bus as
the vehicle pulled over to the side. It halted between stops,
halfway down Thokoly Way, two stops from Keleti Station.
The traffic on both sides quickly parted. Two motorcycle outriders sped down the middle of the road, flashing blue lights
mounted on their black fairings, in front of two Gendarmerie vans.

Balthazar looked out of the window to see if he recognised the riders. They were not wearing police uniforms,
but were dressed in black leathers with no insignia or name
tags. Instead of the usual open-face helmets, they wore the
full-face version with tinted visors. A motorcade followed

in the motorcyclists' wake: an S-class Mercedes saloon with blacked-out windows, two more Gendarmerie vans behind them and two more motorcycle outriders at the rear. Balthazar could just make out the number plate on the Mercedes as it swept past: MEH-005. *Miniszterelnoki hivatal*: the prime minister's office. Not the prime minister himself, whose number plate was MEH-001, but the fifth most important person in the building.

It was noon and the bus was half empty. The passengers grumbled at the delay. There was no air-conditioning and the grimy windows only opened inwards, at the top. No air circulated at all while the vehicle was stationary. It would have been quicker to take a police car from the police headquarters on Teve Street, marked or unmarked, and drive it to Keleti, but he had wanted some time to think, and to get the sense of the city. Balthazar had travelled by metro to Zuglo, a green suburb in the north of the city, then taken the 8E, which stopped right outside Keleti. His plan had been to call in station CCTV feeds, ask around among the migrants about the dead man, then check in with MigSzol, Migrant Solidarity, the charity that had set up shop in a row of unused offices in the Transit Zone. After that, he would walk down Rakoczi Way to Luther Street and Republic Square. Even if he could not get the municipal CCTV from the interchange at Keleti, or inside the station, there were a number of shops on Rakoczi Way that used street-facing CCTV, especially the Arab-owned moneychangers at number 46.

Balthazar reached inside his shirt pocket and took out the evidence bag that Sandor Takacs had returned to him with the SIM card inside. He turned it round in his hand. Whose SIM card was it? The dead man's or someone else's? Whoever the card belonged to, its call log and contact numbers needed to be stripped out. A crime had been committed, probably a murder. The SIM card and the photograph on his phone were the only evidence he had. The evidence bag was the smallest size. He folded it several times and jammed it into the ticket pocket of his jeans, pushing it down as far as he could into the tight space, feeling the edge of the SIM card against his finger. It wasn't ideal, but would do for now, until he got home.

Meanwhile, the traffic was solid and the bus was stuck at the side of the road. The passengers' muttering was getting louder and more bad-tempered. If the government wanted to use its tame television stations, newspapers and websites to pump out propaganda about the migrant menace and unsettle the population, it was succeeding. Tempers had been fraying all summer and the atmosphere was ever more febrile. The *kanikula* only made things worse. Slights, real or imagined, quickly turned into fights. Two young men had nearly come to blows in the metro over the last empty seat in the carriage. Balthazar had been about to intervene when one had backed down at the last moment.

Across the aisle of the bus sat a young woman in her early twenties, absorbed in her mobile telephone. She had dyed red hair, pencilled-on eyebrows and the orange remnants of a solarium tan. She wore a tight denim skirt and a red T-shirt with sweat marks under her armpits. Two large plastic bags filled with apples sat on her lap.

Balthazar watched as an elderly woman pointed at the fruit. 'Hallo, *draga*, darling. Those look like lovely Hungarian apples. Got one for me?'

The young woman looked up, smiled and handed her an apple.

'Thanks. What are you doing with the rest? Taking them to the market?' asked the elderly woman through a mouthful of chewed fruit. Her straggly grey hair was pinned up and she wore a stained floral housedress.

The young woman's smile lit up her face. 'I'm going to Keleti. They are for the refugee kids. I saw a report last night on television. All those children, living outside. No toys, no proper food.' She looked at the bags of fruit. 'These are from my uncle's orchard.'

The elderly lady stopped chewing. 'Does he know what you are doing with them?'

The young woman looked puzzled. 'Of course. It was his idea. It's so sad to see how these poor people have to live. They don't even have enough toilets.'

The elderly lady looked at the apple with distaste. 'No it's not. Nobody asked them to come here. Hungary is for Hungarians. Not all these Arabs and Muslims. They don't fit in here. They don't know our culture.'

The young woman frowned. 'But they don't want to stay. They want to go to Germany. They would all be gone tomorrow if the government opened the border. They are just human beings, like us.'

The elderly woman's face creased in sour anger. 'I told you,' she exclaimed, almost shouting now as other passengers turned to watch. 'Hungary for Hungarians. That's how it is. And always will be.' She took one more bite of the apple and threw the rest out of the window. A middle-aged man in a rumpled grey suit clapped enthusiastically. The red-haired woman turned away, embarrassed.

Balthazar looked at her. She caught his eye, her head bowed, clearly very unsettled by the exchange. He smiled encouragingly. 'You are doing the right thing.'

The redhead smiled gratefully and offered Balthazar an apple. He smiled and she threw it across the aisle. Balthazar caught it in one hand. The elderly lady watched and began swearing volubly. Balthazar stood up and walked over to her. She glared at him from her seat, wrinkling her nose in distaste. 'First the Arabs. Now it's the Gypsies. What next, the fucking Jews?'

Balthazar opened his wallet and showed her his police ID. 'The fucking police, actually.' The woman was blind in one eye, he saw. He softened his tone. 'Take my advice, Grandma, and give it a rest.'

She turned and stared out of the window, still muttering to herself.

FOUR

A brisk ten-minute walk south of Keleti Station, in a high-ceilinged, five-roomed flat of faded art nouveau grandeur, Zsuzsa Barcsy marched across the 555.hu newsroom and stopped in front of Eniko Szalay's desk, iPhone in hand. 'You're famous,' she exclaimed. 'Even more famous.'

'Thanks, but I'm also busy, Zsuzsa,' said Eniko, keeping her eyes on her computer monitor. She had three browser windows open and an email half-written. One window showed the 555.hu website. Her story on the refugees dressed as Gypsies was still the lead, with 687 comments and more than a thousand shares, a high feedback rate for a country whose population was barely ten million. The second, the in-house website tracker, showed the hits on her page, which were running at several thousand an hour. She was way out ahead of her colleagues. Her nearest rival, the football correspondent, had barely half as many. The third window showed the results of her Google news search for her article. Her story, she was pleased to see, had been picked up by the local correspondents for the Associated Press, Reuters and the BBC, which in turn had triggered a second wave of mentions around the world.

Eniko quickly wrote an email to all three, thanking them for the mention and offering to help if they needed more information. One question remained unanswered. Who was her source? An email had arrived three days earlier, tipping Eniko off. She searched her inbox now:

From: keletiwatcher@freemail.hu
To: szalay.eniko@555.hu

Who was keletiwatcher? Clearly, someone who spent a lot of time at the station. The text of the email was long and comparatively detailed, outlining how the people-smugglers operated from the nearby cafés and kebab houses and a particular set of benches in the centre of Republic Square, in front of the children's playground. Eniko had spent most of a day checking the locations, spending several hours simply walking around Keleti and its environs, people-watching, getting a sense of the place and its rhythms. All the details, she soon discovered, checked out. Without the email she would not have been able to write the story – or at least write it so quickly. Most intriguing of all, the sender knew enough to use a free email service that did not demand any personal details – but not enough to disguise the email's IP address. It traced back to the free Wi-Fi at Keleti that the volunteers had set up.

A hand holding an iPhone appeared in front of Eniko's screen. She looked up from the email to see Zsuzsa standing behind the monitor, her right arm extended forward. 'Don't worry about that,' she exclaimed, now waving her telephone excitedly. 'This is much more important. You're Date of the Day on Szilky. You and Tamas Nemeth.'

Szilky.hu was the country's most popular celebrity gossip website. It provided multiple updates every day on the doings of Nemeth, the best-known actor in Hungary. He had just won the lead role in a lavish new production of a play about

King Stephen, the eleventh-century monarch who brought Christianity to Hungary, soon to be staged at the National Theatre. News of the production had caused uproar in Budapest's cash-strapped artistic world. The playwright was a former press officer for the prime minister, not known for his dramatic talent. The director had previously made campaign videos for the ruling Social Democratic Party, the successor to the Communists. The play was heavily subsidised by the Ministry of Culture and sponsored by several companies known to be close to the government. None of the actors, hired at great expense, had seen the script. There were rumours it had not been written yet.

Eniko ignored her friend's telephone and continued typing. 'I'm a reporter. I write about the news. I don't make it.'

Zsuzsa laughed. 'Ooooh, pompous. Well, you are this morning. So you might as well listen.'

Eniko stopped typing. 'I'm all ears,' she said, dryly.

Zsuzsa's eyes dropped to her screen. 'You were more than ears last night, apparently. Szilky says you were wrapped in a black minidress, topped with a gauzy black chiffon wrap that that showcased your slim but curvaceous figure.'

Zsuzsa continued reading, 'The stylish couple were ensconced at a discreet corner table at Arigato, the city's newest and hottest Sushi eatery, where the star reporter shared a set meal for two, including the signature grilled octopus, with Budapest's hunkiest star of the stage and screen.'

Eniko was horrified to see that at least two other reporters had stopped working to listen to Zsuzsa, clearly enjoying the show. She turned pink and looked down, suddenly intensely interested in her keyboard, and started typing again, even more rapidly. '*Stop,* Zsuzsi. And I really need to finish this email.'

555.hu operated out of flat number 1 on the corner of Jozsef Boulevard and Rakoczi Way. The windows shook in their wooden frames when the number 4 or 6 tram trundled by below. The ornate plaster cornices, once bone-white, were chipped and grey. The black marble fireplace was cracked but still imposing, its shelf crowded with trophies and prizes. There was no air-conditioning and all the windows were open. Stand-up 1930s-style metal fans were positioned all around the newsroom, sweeping back and forth to little effect. A large poster of the famous American reporter H. L. Mencken took up much of one wall, together with his most famous quote: 'The relationship between the journalist and the politician should mirror that of the dog and the lamp post.' 'Especially in Hungary,' someone had added by hand underneath. But the shabby, bohemian decor perfectly suited the site's irreverent reporting, and the room crackled with energy.

The news department, home to half a dozen reporters and two editors, occupied the biggest of the five rooms. The commercial and advertising departments all had their own spaces, as did the editor, Roland Horvath, and the newly appointed news editor, Kriszta Matyas. The website had launched a couple of years before and its lively style had proved an immediate hit with Budapest's hipsters. But Bohemian urbanites, retweets, an army of Instagram followers, and Facebook shares of article links were a poor substitute for a proper business plan, adequate start-up capital and advertising. For now, the fifth room stood empty, waiting, so far in vain, for the massive expansion of advertising personnel that would drive new websites and other digital publishing operations.

The website had recently been bought out by Sandor Kaplan, a former business partner of the prime minister. Like Pal Dezeffy, Kaplan had been a leader of the Communist youth organisation during the 1980s. Both men had made a fortune in the early 1990s, a period known as *vadkapitalizmus*, wild capitalism, when state-owned assets and property were sold off for a fraction of their actual value to well-connected insiders. Kaplan had immediately appointed Roland Horvath editor of 555.hu. A paunchy, balding divorcee in his late forties, he had previously worked as a political reporter for the state news channel. He had excellent access to government politicians, and always seemed to be able to get ministers to answer a few questions – mostly, Eniko thought, because they were such soft questions.

Eniko finished her email, pressed send and glanced upwards. Zsuzsa was still standing behind her computer monitor. She grinned and raised her eyebrows. 'You really don't want to know what the rest of it says?'

Eniko said, 'No. It's hideous. Full of cliches.'

'What's full of cliches?' asked a third female voice.

Zsuzsa turned to see the news editor approaching. Kriszta Matyas was ten years older than Eniko, recently arrived from the state news agency, where she had worked on the foreign desk, much of whose coverage consisted of rote accounts of state visits and international cooperation agreements. A skinny brunette who was married to a senior official in the Foreign Ministry, she seemed to have little understanding of twenty-first century digital media and had provoked nervous laughter by asking what Instagram was. Her expensive business wardrobe and heavy make-up did not sit well with 555's bohemian image. Nor did her deference to authority. Her main contribution to the editing process seemed to be demanding ever longer quotes from spokesmen for the government or the ruling party whenever 555.hu exposed another scandal.

Zsuzsa said, 'Just some gossip on Szilky. Nothing important.'

'Then why are you spending office time on it?' Matyas looked Zsuzsa up and down. 'What are you working on now, *Zsuzsika*?'

Family and friends often added the 'ka' or 'ke' diminutive to names. It meant 'little' or 'small' and was a term of endearment. In a work or business environment it was extremely patronising. Zsuzsa blushed and stuttered.

'*Zsuzsa*,' said Eniko, 'is helping me out with my Keleti story. I have a lot to follow up.'

'Is there nothing else happening apart from the chaos at Keleti?' said Matyas, her voice arched. 'Can you please come and see me this afternoon, Eniko? There are some things I would like to discuss with you. Say two o'clock?'

Eniko nodded. 'Sure.' She and Zsuzsa watched the news editor walk away, her heels clacking on the worn parquet floor.

Zsuzsa glanced at Eniko. 'Thanks. What was that about?'

Eniko squeezed her arm. 'I'm not sure.'

'Why is she here? She's completely out of place.'

'I know. What worries me is that maybe soon she won't be. Kaplan isn't a philanthropist. He must have an agenda. I bet she knows what it is.' Eniko lifted her head towards the French doors. 'Let's go outside. You can tell me about the rest of the Szilky article. But keep your voice down.'

The two women walked out onto the apartment's balcony, and stood looking out over Blaha Lujza Square. Eniko watched the afternoon bustle as she listened to her friend finish reading the article. She could see all the way down to the Astoria Hotel and the Elizabeth Bridge that spanned the Danube. The traffic was locked solid but the number 4 tram trundled steadily along the main boulevard. Pedestrians hurried across the square, rushing to catch the 8E bus north along Rakoczi Way.

A harried-looking mother walked quickly towards the metro entrance, a toddler in each hand. An elderly lady was in her usual place, selling bunches of bluebells for 300 forints.

'Are you listening, Eni?' asked Zsuzsa.

'Yes. Sure,' she replied, focused on the scene on Blaha. 'Look at him,' said Eniko, pointing at a tall man in his early twenties, wearing blue shorts and a black polo top, who was walking back and forth, handing out leaflets. Two large pieces of red cardboard covered his chest and back, advertising the Bella Roma pizzeria.

'What about him?' asked Zsuzsa.

'What's he so happy about?'

The walking advertisement smiled at every passer-by, which among often glum-faced Hungarians marked him out as a potential lunatic.

'I dunno. Whatever. Don't worry about him. There's a photo of you and Tamas,' said Zsuzsa.

'Give me that.' Eniko snatched the telephone from her friend's hand. She stared at the screen. 'Oh, God, how did they get that?' The picture showed Nemeth, a very handsome man in his early thirties, with brown eyes and black hair, leaning forward as he offered Eniko a piece of octopus on chopsticks.

Eniko handed the telephone back to Zsuzsa. Her friend enlarged the shot, looked closer at Eniko. 'Considering that half of Budapest would kill to be sitting where you were, you don't look like you are having much fun.'

'I wasn't.'

'Eni, he's handsome, single, intelligent, straight, not mad or a druggie. What more do you want?'

'Yes. All boxes ticked. But he is kind of... boring. All he wanted to talk about was himself.'

'He is an actor. What did you expect? What did you want to talk about?'

'I was interested in who was backing the play. Where the money was coming from. The company sponsors. The government subsidies. How did the playwright get the commission? And had Tamas read the script?'

Zsuzsa's cornflower-blue eyes opened wider. 'You are joking? You had a dinner date with Tamas Nemeth and you wanted to know about government subsidies?' She stared at the photograph again. 'Where are your glasses?'

Eniko wore loose cream-coloured cotton trousers and a fitted pale-blue T-shirt. She took off her round brown-tortoiseshell spectacles and began to polish the lenses with the edge of her T-shirt. 'I didn't wear them. I don't on dates.'

'OK, I get that. How was the octopus?'

Eniko polished harder, rubbing at a non-existent spot. 'I don't know.'

'How? It was right there in front of you.'

'He missed.'

'He what?'

Eniko put her glasses back on and turned to Zsuzsa. 'I can't judge distances very well without my glasses. I leaned forward. The octopus went past my ear.'

Zsuzsa tried to stop herself laughing. 'Did he try again?'

'No. He was too embarrassed. Almost as much as I was.'

'Did he ask you to go on somewhere?'

'No. He called for the bill soon after.'

'Will you see him again?'

'On stage, maybe. Nah, Zsuzsika, I have to work. Have you seen the photo editor? I'm going back to Keleti this afternoon and we need some fresh pictures.'

Eniko gathered her long dark-brown hair into a ponytail,

swept it back off her face, and wrapped it in a plain black hair band. The style made her feel professional and business-like, but also accentuated her almost Slavic cheekbones, a remnant of a Tartar ancestor, and eyes the colour of sap-phires. She wore no make-up and her only jewellery was a tiny silver hoop in the top of her left ear.

'No, I have not seen the photo editor,' said Zsuzsa. 'Stop changing the subject.'

Eniko smiled. 'I can give you Tamas's number if you like. He wants to have lots of children. And a good, old-fashioned Hungarian stay-at-home wife.' Eniko turned to Zsuzsa. 'Do you want to be a stay-at-home wife?'

Zsuzsa lightly poked her friend in the arm. 'If he walks through the door every night, then maybe, yes.' Zsuzsa Barcsy was pale and pretty with long auburn hair, but self-conscious about her curves. She wore a long, flowery Indian-style skirt, a baggy pink cotton top and two dangly silver earrings.

For a moment Zsuzsa looked exasperated. '*Eni*, you have to move on. You're nudging thirty. You can't keep mooning over a month-long affair that happened half a year ago. And made you run away to London.'

Eniko looked down into the square again. The Bella Roma man stared upwards at the balcony for several seconds then turned away. Was she being watched? She was certainly stir-ring things up, and annoying some powerful and not very nice people, that much she knew. Everyone was on edge nowadays, especially after the threats and the video of her colleague. Or was she just paranoid? It was hard to judge. She would think about that later. 'I did not *run away* anywhere. It was a career opportunity.'

Eniko had recently returned to Budapest after a six-month internship at *Newsweek*, covering British politics. The House of Commons, with its bars, restaurants and long, alcove-filled corridors, and legions of male MPs who were flattered by the attentive interest of an attractive and occasionally flirtatious new reporter, had proved an excellent training ground. It was easy to extract information from male politicians, she soon learned. All you had to do was pretend to be utterly fascinated by what they had to say and occasionally brush off over-eager hands. There was no need to adopt different tactics in Budapest. Only seven of Hungary's 200 MPs were women and of them, only the minister of justice had any real power. Until last week, few Hungarian politicians took Eniko seriously as a journalist. They did now.

Eniko had brought down Bela Lidaki, the minister of the interior, by revealing he had set up an offshore company in the Cayman Islands to channel EU agricultural subsidies to plant apricot orchards on the *puszta*, the wide, flat plain in the east of the country. The orchards did not exist. The trees had not been purchased. In any case, the sandy soil of the *puszta* was completely unsuitable for growing fruit, although it seemed nobody in Brussels had bothered to check. The firm was registered in the name of Bela Lidaki's children's nanny, with whom he was having an affair. The minister, she had since learned, had merely been the frontman for the scheme, easily persuaded to take part with several Nokia boxes of 10,000-forint notes. He had been instantly sacrificed and was now under house arrest, while the police investigation was underway. The story had arrived in her inbox one morning, complete with documentation, receipts and video footage of the minister and his nanny on the balcony of a boutique hotel deep in the countryside, one known for illicit assignations.

It was all far too easy, she knew. So easy that she knew she had been used in some kind of internecine government power struggle. She had asked a hacker friend of hers to take a look at the electronic communications. The email address was fake and the sender's IP address, which logged its path through the internet, had been erased. But still, it was a story and had to be reported. Meanwhile, the refugee crisis had put Budapest on the international news map and hundreds of foreign journalists were in town. Eniko's phone had barely stopped ringing since she broke the story yesterday about the fake Gypsies. And there was so much more to report: increasing rumours that enough money – tens of thousands of euros – would buy an actual Hungarian passport, a genuine one with a serial number. A corrupt network of government officials, collapsing borders, thousands of people coming in every day, the refugee crisis was the biggest story she had ever covered in her career.

Her phone buzzed: a message had arrived. She picked up the handset, peered at the screen, frowned for a moment. A WhatsApp message: a photograph of what seemed to be a man asleep on a building site and an address: 26 Republic Square. The old party headquarters. She looked harder. Eeeugh. The man's eyes were open. He appeared to be dead. Eniko checked the number – not one that she knew and it was not registering as a contact in her telephone directory. Was this some of threat? The refugee crisis had unleashed all sorts of lunatics from the darker zones of Hungarian politics.

'What is it? Show me,' demanded Zsuzsa.

Eniko handed Zsuzsa her Nexus 6. The photograph seemed large on the oversized handset. Zsuzsa pulled a face. 'That's horrible. Poor man. He looks like he's dead. Who sent it?'

Eniko shrugged. 'I don't know. There's no name.'

Zsuzsa looked at the message again and sighed. 'Look closer. A letter in the message field.'

Eniko checked again. She had been so unsettled by the photograph she had missed it. A single 'B'. Eniko kissed Zsuzsa on the side of her face. 'You are very sweet and a true friend. But now I have to go.' She walked back into the newsroom and picked up her bag, a determined look on her face.

Bus 8E, Thokoly Way, 12.10 p.m.

Balthazar sat back down. The bus was still stationary as he bit into the apple, which was crisp and pleasantly sharp. He looked out of the grimy window. A new billboard was mounted on top of an apartment building. It showed the dates 1956, 1989 and the word '*Most?*', 'Now?', above the same picture of the prime minister, his ministers and business allies linked together in a spider's web that Balthazar had seen earlier that morning on Luther Street. Large letters proclaimed, '*Fejezzuk be a munkat!*', 'Let's finish the job!'. The posters were unattributed but were widely believed to be the work of a new conservative opposition party, which claimed that the governing Social Democrats were still Communists in all but name and another change of system was needed. Balthazar's eye wandered to a long queue of migrants which had formed nearby outside a pizza takeaway which offered a slice of margarita for 100 forints, around thirty pence. Next door, tables had been set up on the pavement outside a kebab restaurant. A large, overweight Gypsy male in his thirties was holding forth on his mobile phone. In front of him sat another man, dark, thin, hunched, a supplicant waiting. Balthazar did a double take. The obese man with the mobile phone looked familiar. Very familiar.

Was it him? Yes, it was. Viktor Lakatos. Fat Vik, as he was usually known. Second in command to Gaspar, Balthazar's brother. Lately Fat Vik had been branching out from prostitutes and hostess bars. He was often to be found sitting on an armchair outside one of Budapest's many BAV shops, the state antique emporiums, with several minions. Whenever someone walked towards the shop with a painting to sell, Fat Vik would send one of his guys to intercept them at the door and try to persuade them to sell to him instead. But there was only one thing being bought and sold in the streets around Keleti now – and it was not antiques. What, Balthazar asked himself, was his brother up to now?

The sirens finally faded but the bus, still stuck in traffic, did not move. Balthazar's mind drifted back to his conversation with Sandor Takacs. There was a chance, he supposed, that the dead man might have been killed in a robbery that had gone wrong. It was well known among the muggers and pickpockets of District VIII that the migrants often carried large sums in cash or valuables. But then why had the Gendarmes been there? They had no interest in everyday crimes, unless they affected the prime minister or the political elite. And where had the body gone? This was no bungled robbery, he was sure.

Meanwhile, there were more personal considerations. He had blithely agreed to talk to his brother, but what if Gaspar was involved in the killing? Balthazar's career had already cost him dear. His father, Laszlo, had been furious after Balthazar had joined the police. Balthazar's mother, Marta, had refused point-blank to countenance his demands that her eldest son be ostracised. Laszlo had called a meeting of the Kris, the Gypsies' communal court. This was a drastic step. The Kris was usually convened to resolve disputes between families, without the involvement of outside authorities, and not to mediate in intra-family feuds. Eventually, the Kris had handed down its judgement: Balthazar could see his brothers whenever he wanted, was allowed to return to the courtyard whenever he liked, but female relatives – including his mother living there – could only meet him with Laszlo's permission. In addition, Balthazar was banned from all family events and from entering the actual family home without his father's permission. Balthazar had to pledge that he would never, upon pain of full ostracism, divulge any information to the police concerning any criminal activity he knew about that was connected to any of his relatives. He had agreed.

Beyond family affairs, there was the whole business of the Gendarmerie. Takacs was right not to go to war with the Gendarmerie, at least for now. The ostentatious motorcade through the middle of the city was a message – that the Gendarmerie had the strongest and most solid roof: the prime minister's office. The police's roof, shared with the state security service, the Ministry of the Interior, was lacking several tiles nowadays, not least its minister, Bela Lidaki. His downfall had been swift, too swift. Balthazar called up Eniko's 555.hu story on his telephone and quickly reread it. It was detailed and accurate. The incriminating evidence was overwhelming. Lidaki was guilty and deserved to go to prison. But a similar dossier, he knew, could be released about several government ministers, and numerous MPs and senior civil servants. Somebody had fed the dossier to Eniko. But who, and why bring down the minister of the interior in the middle of a refugee crisis?

His phone buzzed, interrupting his reverie. The text message instantly banished thoughts of migrants and refugees, murders, and threats from the Gendarmes: 'Hallo, Daddy. I can't wait to see you this weekend.'

Balthazar smiled with pleasure as he quickly tapped out a reply and sent it. But his smile faded as he remembered the rest of his conversation with Sandor Takacs.

If the ambassador makes a request to the PM's office it will be heeded. Especially after you were officially...

Officially warned not to park outside the American school in a far-flung suburb of Buda, in an unmarked police car while off duty just to get a glimpse of Alex after his mother had cancelled two visits in a row, Takacs might have said. And doubly warned not to get out of the car when Alex saw his dad, run over with the world's biggest smile, pick him up and promise to see him the next weekend. Which was anyway unfair on the twelve-year-old boy, as thanks to Balthazar's lurking, that visit was quickly cancelled, and the next one after it. But then, Takacs was happily married with three grown-up children who still came home every Sunday for a family lunch, two of them with their own youngsters.

Takacs's advice needed to be heeded. Sarah seemed to delight in torturing Balthazar, randomly cancelling his midweek visits and weekends with Alex, often with just a couple of hours' notice, or even less. Three weeks earlier he had been standing outside the front door of her apartment building on Pozsonyi Way in District XIII, when the text arrived: 'Sorry, Alex has a fever. We have to delay.' It was all he could do to control his temper and not take the lift upstairs and force his way inside. He realised, of course, that nothing would have delighted Sarah more. Lately though, Balthazar had a new ally: Maria, Sarah's cleaning lady. Maria was a Gypsy, possibly even a distant relative. She had grown up around the corner from Jozsef Street and fed Balthazar a stream of information about Sarah and Alex, sometimes even telephoning him when she was at the house. Sarah could not speak Hungarian, let alone the rapid-fire mix of Hungarian, Lovari, the main Gypsy dialect, and street slang that Maria spoke, so had no idea what she was talking about.

Balthazar had met Sarah at Central European University in downtown Budapest. Founded by the philanthropist George Soros, CEU was a small postgraduate college. Balthazar was the first in his family to enter higher education. As the eldest of three brothers and two sisters, he had been expected to leave school at fourteen, or sixteen at the latest, and eventually take over the family business, a position now filled by Gaspar. But Marta had other ideas, as did a sharp-eyed teacher at his primary school. Marta had stubbornly insisted to Laszlo that her eldest son would not follow in his footsteps. Instead, he would go to university. Laszlo laughed, shouted, slapped her back and forth. But Marta also had her arsenal. After two weeks without conjugal rights, and the opportunity to cook his own meals, Laszlo surrendered.

The primary-school teacher arranged for Balthazar's transfer to Fazekas, the country's best high school. Despite Fazekas's location in District VIII, Balthazar was the only Roma pupil in his year. He had graduated with the highest grades in his class and studied law and politics at Budapest's Eotvos Lorand University. From there he had moved to Central European University where he and Sarah quickly fell in love. The Hungarian Roma and New York liberal intellectual had found each other exciting and exotic. They moved in together, sharing a studio flat in District VII, the old Jewish quarter. After a passionate few months, Sarah fell pregnant. They decided to get married in a quick civil ceremony with just a couple of friends as witnesses. Balthazar's family had been furious. Partly because he had married a *gadje*, a non-Gypsy, although Sarah was Jewish and Jews and Gypsies were traditional allies, but mainly because they had not been invited or allowed to hold the usual massive celebration.

After graduating with a Master's degree in nationalism studies, Balthazar was deluged with job offers. A lucrative and not especially taxing world beckoned, he realised, where he could build a career as a professional Roma. Charitable foundations, international organisations, government departments, multinational corporations were all desperate to hire intelligent, presentable Roma people, especially when they were fluent in English as Balthazar now was, to burnish their liberal credentials. Balthazar had been a talented student and his professor at CEU had made it clear that there would be an easy path to a PhD, followed by a lecturer's position, assistant professorship, then even on to department head. Balthazar started a doctorate, specialising in the *Poraymus*, the Devouring, as Gypsies called their Holocaust.

After a couple of years, Balthazar had had enough of libraries and archives and extermination. He also realised that he had no desire to be a *diszcigany*, a decorative, token Gypsy. In a region convulsed by change, riddled with corruption, run by a political class interested mainly in self-enrichment, the law, he believed, offered the only guarantee of liberty. The law had failed him – and someone very close to him – once before. He would make sure it did not do so again. So, at the age of twenty-nine, he joined the police. In the politically correct, uber-liberal circles in which Sarah now moved, a policeman husband was beyond the pale. Sarah, by then an associate professor of gender studies, decided she was a lesbian and moved in with Amanda, a German student from Tubingen, taking Alex with her.

Balthazar read his son's message once more and slid his telephone into his pocket. He stood up as the 8E bus reached the stop by Keleti Station, glancing at the scene at the side of the station, where several refugee families had set up an ad hoc camp. One elderly lady was even boiling water on a portable stove. A line of taxi drivers stood watching and smoking. One in particular caught Balthazar's eye: a woman in her early thirties, tall, dark blonde, with her hair tied back in a ponytail. Where had he seen her before? The bus jolted to a halt. There were several flyers on the floor by the door and he picked one up before he got off, breaking his train of thought about the blonde taxi driver. He stood still for a moment, looking at the sheet of A5. The flyer was printed on heavy, glossy paper in full colour. A banner headline across the top declared 'Defend our homeland' on one line and '*Magyar Nemzeti Front*' – 'Hungarian National Front' – underneath. A racist caricature of a black man groping a blonde, white young woman took up most of the rest of the page. 'Stop the migrant flood: Join the patriots' revolution' was printed along the bottom edge, together with an email address: info@mnf.hu.

He folded the flyer into four and slipped it into the pocket of his jeans. The MNF. Here it was again, the third time today – and it was barely lunchtime. And who was paying for these glossy flyers?

FIVE

Eniko Szalay looked down at the torn sheet of paper Maryam Nazir had just handed her. One word was written on it – in flowing Arabic script, she guessed, although maybe it was Persian – with a line of smaller symbols underneath. 'I'm sorry,' Eniko said, handing it back, 'I don't read...'

'... Arabic,' said Maryam, her voice flat. 'I found it my sleeping bag this morning. I woke up and Simon was gone.'

'What time was that?'

'Around 6.30 a.m. Seven hours ago. I have called him dozens of times. His telephone is switched off. He has never done anything like this before.'

Eniko scribbled rapidly in her notebook as Maryam spoke, shooting glances at her between sentences, trying to evaluate her state of mind, judge how far she could push her. Maryam sat still and composed. Her black, curly hair reached halfway down her back. She had olive skin, large, dark eyes and was very beautiful. She wore blue jeans, a crumpled white long-sleeved T-shirt and black tennis shoes. She seemed calm but that was clearly a coping mechanism. How could it not be? Maryam was stranded in a strange, foreign city. She could not speak the language, did not even want to be here. Her husband had disappeared. Simon Nazir knew nobody in

70

Budapest apart from his wife. He had nowhere to go. He had not called her all day, was not answering his telephone. Most of all, there was the photograph.

Eniko glanced at Maryam. She was staring into the distance, seeing nothing. Eniko gently touched her leg. 'What does the Arabic say, Maryam?'

Maryam started with surprise, blinked several times. 'Sorry. *Bustani*. It's Arabic for gardener.'

Eniko put the paper down on the coffee table in front of them. 'And underneath?'

'They are numbers. A mobile telephone.'

Eniko had gone straight to Republic Square after she received the WhatsApp message on her telephone with the photograph of the dead man. The whole area around number 26 had been sealed off by the Gendarmerie. She had tried to approach the square from two different side streets. Each time, she had immediately been stopped by Gendarmes and threatened with arrest. Their presence told her what she needed to know: something bad had happened there, something important and politically sensitive. From there she had walked down Rakoczi Way to the 555.hu office at Blaha Lujza Square. She spent half an hour typing up her notes, encrypted them, then walked back up Rakoczi Way to Keleti.

Eniko had checked in at the MigSzol offices to see if they knew anything about a missing male migrant, probably in his early thirties. The room was packed with people asking for food, water, medical attention, speaking a babel of languages. It was impossible to find out anything. She'd been about to give up when one of the volunteers had suggested that Eniko try the moneychangers on Rakoczi Way. A young Syrian woman had been in earlier, he said, asking for help to find her husband who had gone missing that morning. She had refused to get involved with the police, but had said she had a contact at the exchange office on Rakoczi Way. Eniko had walked straight there, and found Maryam.

Eniko took out her mobile telephone and loaded the camera app. 'May I?' she asked Maryam. She nodded and Eniko took several photographs of the paper, before asking. 'Why gardener?'

'It is his nickname.' Maryam paused for a moment. 'We had a garden, with olive and lemon trees. We lived in Aleppo, by the Citadel in the Old City. Have you been to Aleppo?'

'No, I always wanted to. I heard it's beautiful.'

'It is... was. It is ruined now.'

Eniko saw that Maryam was drifting off. She smiled and leaned forward, her body language encouraging. 'Maryam, who is the gardener?'

A shadow passed over Maryam's face. 'We knew him, before the war. He was a teacher. An art teacher. He taught painting. Now he is a different kind of artist. They called him the Gardener because he likes to use garden shears on prisoners. Simon told me it took him just a few seconds to take off two fingers. They sent his fingers to us, held him for a week, while we raised the money. Our families sold almost everything we had to pay the ransom. Then we fled. We are Christians. Our families were in Aleppo at the time of Jesus. But there is no future for us in Syria.'

'Where do you want to go?'

Maryam shrugged. 'Germany. Britain. It doesn't matter. Anywhere safe. Simon said there was a way...'

'There are several ways. Smugglers will take you on back routes through the forests. The Gypsies will dress you up and drive you across the Austrian border. But you will still be travelling on Syrian passports.'

'Not necessarily. We have money. Simon had a contact. Someone who could get us Hungarian passports. He was going to call him, set up a meeting later today. He said we might even be able to go tomorrow.'

'But he got diverted by the Gardener.'

'Yes. It looks like that.'

'Who was he going to call?'

Maryam shrugged. 'I don't know. Someone who could get hold of the passports. The number is on the bottom of the paper. He made me memorise it.'

Eniko processed what Maryam had said. This was the third or fourth time she had heard that Hungarian passports were for sale. But the details were always elusive. 'Did Simon say anything else about who this contact was? Or how to find him?'

'No. Just the phone number. Simon said he would make sure we are not stuck in Budapest, even if the trains have stopped. But we are stuck in Budapest.' She paused, stared at Eniko, her black eyes suddenly glistening. '*I* am stuck in Budapest. He is dead, isn't he? That's why you are here.'

'I don't know. Really, I don't.' Eniko thought quickly. That was technically, if not morally, correct. But she did know that she was about to wreck Maryam's life, perhaps forever. And when should she tell her, show Maryam the photograph of her husband? Whatever iota of hope Maryam still had would be instantly vaporised by a pixelated image on a mobile phone screen. But how could she not tell her? And then what – would she let Maryam go back to Keleti, newly widowed and traumatised, to sleep on the floor, waiting, alone?

On a human level, her heart went out to Maryam. On a professional one, Maryam had information that Eniko needed. Information about this morning. Why Simon might have left his wife at Keleti. Who he was following. Who might have killed him. Information that may help Eniko find out more about his dreadful fate. She glanced at Maryam. She was trembling now. Eniko had a sense for people. They told her things, made all sorts of confessions. Even Bela Lidaki, the disgraced minister of the interior, had made contact, wanting to meet. But Maryam would close down as soon as she saw the photograph, Eniko knew. So she would have to stonewall, and Maryam would have to wait a while longer.

Eniko steeled herself, her voice encouraging but firm. 'I am here, Maryam, because I want to find out more. Who is the Gardener? What is his name?'

'His name is Mahmoud Hijazi. He is thirty-six years old. He was born in Aleppo.' Maryam's voice strengthened a little. These, at least, were known facts. 'At the start of the war, he was with the Free Syrian Army. Then he went freelance. A freelance interrogator. Now he is with Islamic State.'

Eniko continued writing. 'But you think he is here?'

Maryam nodded, her hair tumbling around her shoulders. 'Yes. Why else would Simon leave me a note about him? And then disappear. He has never done this before. He must have seen the Gardener at Keleti. We both saw other fighters there, from Syria. Everyone is at Keleti. The Free Syrian Army. The Nusra Front. The al-Shams brigade. Even the Kurds. They made a truce not to fight each other while they are in Hungary. Everyone except the Islamists.'

Eniko ignored her rising excitement and focused hard, writing down everything as clearly as she could, the future headlines already spinning around her brain. This was a huge story – if she could prove it. *Syrian Militiamen Sign Ceasefire at Keleti*. The whole world's media would really be knocking at her door. But for now, she needed to focus on Maryam.

The two women were sitting in on a brown fake-leather sofa in the back room of the moneychangers' office at number 46 Rakoczi Way. The plastic had cracked open on the cushions, revealing yellow foam rubber. A faded poster of Damascus was affixed to the wall. The floor was covered in dark-grey linoleum and the walls were painted dark yellow. A dusty striplight hummed and buzzed overhead. Maryam's and Simon's luggage – two rucksacks and two sleeping bags – was piled up in the corner. Eniko's telephone lay on the sofa, surreptitiously recording the conversation.

A knock on the door sounded. 'Come in,' said Eniko. A slim teenage girl wearing jeans, a green T-shirt and a white headscarf walked in. She carried a tray of coffees in small thimble cups, and glasses of water.

'*Shukran*, thank you,' said Maryam.

'*Afwan*, you are welcome,' the girl replied, as she put down the tray. She turned to Maryam and spoke in Arabic. Maryam half-smiled and said, '*Shukran jazeelan*, thank you so much.' She turned to Eniko. 'Amal says I am welcome here as long as I want. I can stay here.'

'I'm glad,' said Eniko, feeling considerable relief. She had thought about offering to put Maryam up in her flat. 'It's much better than the Transit Zone. How do you know them?'

'I don't. But I knew to ask them for help if I needed it. Her uncle knew my father. My father is from Homs. So is her uncle, Asaf Shamsi. He came here as a medical student in the 1980s.' She picked up the coffee, sipped it and closed her eyes for a moment. 'Tastes like home.' She opened her eyes and sat up straighter, suddenly revived. She looked Eniko up and down, as if seeing her for the first time, wondering who she was, why she had agreed to talk to her. 'The Syrians run the moneychanging business in Budapest. But you must know that. You are a journalist.'

Eniko nodded. She had known about the Syrian money connection, but not that the Shamsi family was a contact point for refugees. It made perfect sense, of course.

'Now I have a question for you,' said Maryam.

'Go ahead,' said Eniko as she sipped her coffee. It was semi-sweet, scented with cardamom. She knew what was coming.

'Where is my husband?'

'I don't know.'

Maryam stared at Eniko, her eyes locked on her like dark lasers. 'But you know something, don't you? That's why you are here. Please don't lie to me. Tell me the truth.'

Eniko swallowed, looked down at the floor. She had learned her trade on the local newspaper in her home town of Nyiregyhaza, in the east of the country, near the border with Ukraine. The worst job in the newsroom, the one nobody ever wanted, was the 'dead-knock', visiting the victims of the newly bereaved. Usually the door had been slammed in her face. Occasionally the grieving relatives seemed glad to talk about the person they had just lost. On one awful occasion she had arrived before the police and inadvertently broken the news. Eniko steeled herself. She had chosen this profession. She owed it to herself, and to Maryam, to be professional. 'Yes. I know something. I was sent a photograph this morning.'

'Of my husband?'

'I think so.'

'Show me.'

Eniko hesitated. 'It's...'

'*Show me.*'

Eniko took out her phone and called up the photograph. She handed it to Maryam and braced herself. Maryam looked at the screen. She gasped, gave a small cry like a wounded animal, swiped to enlarge the image.

For a moment she sat very still, her mouth slightly open as she stared at the screen. '*Ya qalbi, ya hayi,* oh my heart, oh my life,' she chanted, rocking back and forth, her voice breaking, her whole body shaking. The phone slid out of her fingers. Her eyes rolled back in her head and she fainted.

Keleti Station, 1.00 p.m.

Balthazar stood on the station concourse watching the scene in front of him. On one level it was surreal, but now the only surprise was how quickly the city had adjusted to the new normality. Dozens of refugees sat in silent protest, arranged in orderly lines. A line of riot police standing in front of the station doors watched impassively. Many of the refugees held handwritten signs in English, scrawled on cardboard or pieces of ripped-up boxes: 'Freedom', proclaimed one; another, 'Syria loves Germany'. Television journalists wandered among the crowd, interviewing the migrants. Balthazar recognised the BBC correspondent, a skinny man in his forties, on the edge of the concourse, talking to camera. A young boy, aged perhaps six or seven, hovered at the back of the shot. He was a handsome child, with blond hair, large blue eyes and a bright smile. Each time a reporter crossed his path, he instantly held up a sign proclaiming, 'Let My People Go'. Families were camped out on grubby blankets and bedrolls, men smoking and staring listlessly into space, women busying themselves with their children, teenagers playing with their mobile phones. A municipal street-cleaner in a green day-glo jacket desultorily cleared up some of the rubbish with a long metal picker and dropped it in his mobile dustbin. Two Gendarmes stood by the side entrance, smoking and chatting.

The sun was overhead now and the heat seemed even more unbearable, beating down from the cloudless sky, radiating off the hot concrete. Makeshift cardboard signs pointed towards the Transit Zone, one level down. His rucksack was resting on the floor by his legs, the black fabric bulging with the contents. As soon as he alighted from the bus, Balthazar had gone shopping at the supermarket on the corner of Thokoly Way. It was the nearest grocery shop to Keleti and was packed, its aisles a babel of foreign languages. A sign by the cashier listed the currencies that were accepted: euros, dollars, Turkish lira and Kuwaiti dinars, and the day's exchange rates. It had taken Balthazar a good half an hour to buy eight half-litre bottles of water, a large bunch of bananas, six packets of sandwiches, biscuits, and a dozen bars of chocolate. He could stand on the concourse for hours, people-watching, but it was time to unload the groceries, and as fast as possible. The trick was to pick a target, ideally a family, walk over, give them the bag and leave quickly. Or donate the food and drink to MigSzol and let the volunteers distribute it. The previous day, a group of well-meaning CEU students had turned up with supplies and started handing them out to random people, almost triggering a riot.

The station concourse was a modern plaza on two levels. The main section, in front of the entrance, where Balthazar stood, was at street level, stretching to Baross Square and Rakoczi Way. Halfway along the street-level plaza, a staircase led down to the lower level and the metro station, now surrounded by the Transit Zone. Balthazar picked up his rucksack, hoisted it onto his back and walked down. Last year, when Keleti was just a train station, Balthazar had investigated a murder near here. An Arab property developer had killed his Iranian business parter in a dispute over money. The investigation had taken Balthazar deep into Budapest's small Middle-East migrant communities. He had a gift for languages, spoke English, German, Lovari and had picked up some Arabic and Persian.

Balthazar recognised the guttural vowels of Arabic, the softer sounds of Persian and Turkish. The exclamations of joy and annoyance that carried over the clack of backgammon tiles were universal. Despite the overcrowding, the migrants had somehow managed to keep an open space in the middle of the Transit Zone. A queue was forming in the centre, in front of the MigSzol offices, for the lunchtime handout of donated food. At first, the government had refused to provide any facilities for the migrants. Officials said that they had entered the country illegally and they would do nothing to 'legitimise' their situation. But the reality was that public health, if nothing else, demanded that the crowds be provided with rudimentary sanitary facilities. It was a fraction of what was needed. There were no official food supplies.

A gang of teenage boys was playing football on one side of the Transit Zone. A group of elderly men had set up a makeshift café on the other, sitting on the floor as they brewed coffee over a camping stove. Balthazar jumped back as a football flew past his face. It bounced off the rear wall, towards a second group of men nearby, who were playing backgammon.

'*Ya, shabab, shabab*, youths, youths, watch out,' exclaimed one of the players, a potbellied man in his sixties wearing a grimy yellow T-shirt. The boys held their hands up in a gesture of apology.

Balthazar kicked the ball back to them. Considering that hundreds of people were camped out here, it was a marvel that riots had not broken out. A rota of volunteer doctors and nurses provided rudimentary medical care, while the seriously ill were taken to nearby hospitals. He watched a young girl in a brown hijab, perhaps twelve years old, wash T-shirts under the standpipes, laughing as the water splashed against her baggy red trousers. There were several parks nearby, but nobody wanted to be too far from the station, in case the borders were opened again. The Keleti rumour turned continuously, blending lies with truths, wishful thinking with the deepest despair. Routes had been opened, were closed, were opened again in a blur of gossip and hearsay.

Volunteers had set up a makeshift kindergarten by the entrance to the metro station: some children drew pictures in chalk on the ground, while the lucky ones had sheets of paper and coloured pens. Nearby, Balthazar spotted an African family, sitting on a grey blanket, a mother, father, two children, a boy and a girl aged six or seven. The parents were in their early thirties, tall and slim. They looked exhausted and disorientated, their clothes covered with dust. The mother was braiding her daughter's hair. The boy lay fast asleep in front of them, stretched out, moving in his sleep on a flattened cardboard box. Balthazar knelt down by the family and slipped his rucksack off his back. He started unpacking the groceries.

'These are for you,' he said, addressing the mother.

Her eyes widened as he handed over the fruit, water, sandwiches and chocolate.

The father said, 'We cannot pay you. We have no money left. The police took everything.'

Balthazar said, 'You don't have to pay me. It's a present. Where are you from?'

The father stood up and extended his hand. 'South Sudan. The world's newest country. With the world's newest war. My name is Samuel.'

Balthazar shook Samuel's hand. His grip was firm and strong. 'Welcome to Hungary.'

Samuel looked down at the food, raw hunger, pride and shame in his eyes that his life had come to this, accepting handouts from a stranger in a train station in a country he wanted to leave as fast as possible, so that his family might eat today. 'Thank you.'

The girl's eyes widened as she saw the chocolate. She grabbed the bar and started to unwrap it. Her father took it from her hand, broke off a piece. 'Eat it slowly,' he said.

'That's good advice,' said Balthazar.

Balthazar said goodbye, stood up and started walking to the MigSzol office. The football bounced over towards him. He caught it with his right foot and flicked it towards one of the players – a boy in his late teens, wearing a Nike baseball cap back to front. The boy gave Balthazar a thumbs-up and the game resumed.

The MigSzol office was more of a shop, the third space in a glass-walled modern building on the edge of the Transit Zone. The space on the right was empty, that on the left occupied by two uniformed members of the local Polgarorseg sitting behind a desk and playing with their mobile phones. 'Polgar-orseg' broadly translated as 'Citizens' authority', a municipal quasi-police force of unclear powers, that reported directly to the mayor of District VIII. The nuances were irrelevant to those camped out at Keleti, who usually recoiled nervously when the two officials appeared.

Balthazar was about to step inside the MigSzol office, when a familiar – very familiar – profile caught his eye: an attractive woman with a notebook in one hand, a pen in the other, scribbling away as she spoke to a tall, thin man with long, scraggly brown hair. Balthazar knew him by sight and reputation: Arpad Pinter – known as Arpi – a radical political activist and one of the founders of MigSzol.

Balthazar watched Eniko for a second, nodding, coaxing, smiling encouragingly at Arpi as she worked, her brown ponytail bobbing. He had not seen Eniko since her return from London. But he was not avoiding her, he told himself. No, not at all. They would meet. It was inevitable that their paths would cross sooner or later. Budapest was a small city. The migrant crisis was generating all sorts of new networks and connections. Did he need a work-related reason to see her? Maybe, maybe not. He watched her flick her hair back, a look of fierce concentration on her face, and damped down the emotions that bubbled inside him. Did she sense him looking at her? He watched Arpi walk away from her. For a moment Eniko seemed about to turn in Balthazar's direction, but walked the other way towards a female doctor.

MigSzol office, Keleti, 1.10 p.m.

The space was calmer than on Eniko's visit earlier that morning. There were fewer people milling around, but the room seemed even hotter. The glass frontage offered no respite from the heat. The warm air smelled stale, as though it had been circulated too often. There was no air-conditioning and a solitary fan made no difference. Boxes of apples, packs of nappies, and cases of small bottles of mineral water were piled up against the walls. She watched Arpi and the volunteers, mostly young men and women in their late teens or early twenties, prepare the lunch bags. Each contained two white rolls, a banana and small packet of processed cheese. A female doctor was tending to a teenage boy who was lying on a mattress in the corner of the room. He was thin and drowsy, with shadowed eyes and a drip leading from his arm.

The Shamsis had called a doctor after Maryam had fainted. They had made it clear that Eniko should leave, which she was more than ready to do. She had walked back to the 555. hu office at Blaha Lujza, trying in vain to ignore the heavy lump in her stomach and the image of Maryam sliding off the sofa. Eniko downloaded the photograph of Simon Nazir onto her computer and cropped around his face, editing out the backdrop of the demolished building on Republic Square. She then printed it out. Nazir still had the startled look of someone in a police mugshot but it was a less disturbing image. Once she was done, Eniko had walked back up Rakoczi Way to the MigSzol office in ten minutes.

Eniko caught Arpi's eye and gestured for him to step aside. He did so, a questioning look on his face. She took out a folded sheet of A4 paper from her jacket pocket and handed it to him. The grainy image showed Simon Nazir's disembodied face against a white background.

'Do you know him?' she asked.

Arpi looked wary. 'No, but I've seen him.'

Eniko had known Arpi for several years. His gaunt face was covered in at least three days' worth of beard and he was dressed in a grubby pink T-shirt and ripped, black skinny jeans. Arpi was a high-profile activist, always in the centre of any anti-government or anti-globalisation protest. He had recently been arrested for chaining himself to a tree on Kossuth Square, the site of Hungary's Parliament, protesting in solidarity with the migrants.

Eniko asked, 'Where?'

'Where do you think? Around here. He helps out some-times. What's happened to him?'

'He's gone missing. Do you know anything?'

'I'm not sure. There is some stuff going on here. People are scared, especially the Syrians. Not just of the police and the Gendarmes.' He looked around. 'I can't talk now. It's lunch-time. Call me tonight,' he said, and walked away.

As Arpi walked off, Eniko glanced through the MigSzol window at the plaza and saw the side of a very familiar face. Her stomach did a little flip. What was he doing here? His job, she guessed. Balthazar Kovacs was a detective in the murder squad. And it looked more and more like someone had been murdered. Who else would have sent her the photo of the dead man with a 'B' in the message? So he wanted to make contact. Had made contact. Maybe he needed some help. She was sur-prised he had managed to work out how to use WhatsApp to send a message from an unknown number. In fact she had not known that was even possible. Balthazar was not a tech-nophile. He could send emails and browse a website, but that was about it. Maybe he wanted give her a story tip-off. Or he just wanted to see her. Or something of both. How did she feel about that? She wasn't sure. Untangling her love life – or lack of one – and her work life was not quite so simple.

Eniko watched the doctor step away from the boy with the drip. Just as she walked up to her, the door opened and a woman walked in. She wore a shiny blue shell suit and looked to be in her early fifties, with a lived-in face and dyed blonde hair with black roots. Eniko felt the ripple of tension run through the air, and slipped the printout of the photograph of Simon Nazir into her jacket pocket as she watched.

The migrants at Keleti had provoked strong reactions from the locals. The surrounding streets were a rough and poor neighbourhood, another world from the Budapest most tourists saw. The altercations were becoming more frequent now, as tempers and the temperature steadily rose. Local toughs would march into the crowds, abuse and provoke the migrants, knowing they would be too scared to respond. Three days earlier, a gang of skinheads had sprinted into the middle of the Transit Zone, screaming abuse and punching random people, including a teenage girl, who was taken to hospital, before hurling MNF flyers in the air and running off. The station was covered by CCTV but the police showed no interest in apprehending the troublemakers. Instead, they had detained the family of the girl who had been punched, only releasing her when 555.hu and other media reported the story.

The new arrival carried two large, bulging carrier bags. She glanced around, and walked up to Arpi. 'Here,' she said, her voice roughened by years of cigarettes. 'My friends and I saw what was happening on television. It's not right.' She suddenly looked embarrassed. 'This is not much, but it's something. Anyway,' she said, and started back to the door.

'Wait, please, a moment,' said Arpi. He carefully emptied the bags on to the table. Chocolate, Gyori biscuits, crisps, apples, bruised bananas, wrapped sliced bread, and packets of parizsi, the cheapest processed meat, tumbled out.

Arpi turned to the woman, took her hand. 'Thank you. Thank you so much.'

'There's no pork in there,' she said, now blushing bright red with pleasure and embarrassment, and walked out.

Eniko relaxed and stopped writing. She thought quickly: it was not enough for a stand-alone article but the scene would make a nice human-interest vignette in a larger reportage piece. Should she go after the woman, or focus on the doctor?

The latter, Eniko decided, and walked over to the corner, where she was tending the young man with the drip.

The doctor's name, Eniko knew from her contacts, was Dora Szegedi. She was a recent arrival on the roster of medical volunteers at the MigSzol office. Szegedi was a paediatrician who usually worked at the nearby Heim Pal children's hospital. She was plump, in her mid-forties, with dyed red hair, blue eyes and a gold Star of David on a chain around her neck. She glanced warily at Eniko as she stood nearby.

'What's the matter with him?' asked Eniko.

Szegedi looked Eniko up and down, her chubby face lined with fatigue. 'And you are?'

Eniko introduced herself and handed her 555.hu business card to the doctor. It would, she hoped, do the trick. Apart from a couple of bloggers and the sole remaining liberal daily newspaper and television station, 555.hu was a rare example of a mainstream media outlet that had not descended into outright hysteria over the migrant crisis. Eniko had written several articles about the situation at Keleti, and the website had run numerous editorials demanding that the government provide proper sanitation and medical care for those stranded at the station.

Szegedi turned Eniko's business card over in her hand. 'Eniko Szalay. I've read your articles.' The doctor looked up at Eniko. 'Why are you interested? He's not dressed as a Gypsy.' Her voice was not exactly hostile, but it was certainly wary.

Eniko's article had already triggered blowback on the liberal left. To write anything remotely critical of the Roma – even when they were committing criminal acts and working with people-smugglers – immediately placed the author in the right-wing camp. The comments were pouring in now against Eniko's article, accusing her of being a turn-coat, stooge for the right wing, even a paid agent of the government.

'You read my article?' asked Eniko.

The doctor nodded.

'And what did you think?'

'The details were accurate... It seemed interesting,' said Szegedi, rapidly correcting herself. 'Sometimes uncomfortable truths should be reported.'

Eniko thought quickly. How could Dr Szegedi know the details were accurate? Unless... Eniko held Szegedi's gaze. 'Yes. They should be. But it always helps when there's someone nearby who knows what's going on, someone really *watching* Keleti.'

Szegedi turned pink, stepped to the side, took two small bottles of mineral water from a case. She opened one and took a deep draught, handed the other to Eniko. 'OK, Eniko. How can I help you?'

Eniko opened the bottle and drank. She reached inside her jacket pocket and showed Szegedi the photograph of Nazir.

Eniko asked, 'Have you seen him? Do you know him?'

Szegedi looked Eniko up and down, as though assessing her for treatment or referral. 'Yes. And no.'

Eniko nodded enthusiastically. 'Can you tell me anything more?'

Szegedi said, 'He was here a couple of times. He helped out with interpreting. He spoke pretty good English. I think his name was Simon, from somewhere in Syria.'

'Do you know where he is now?'

'No. I have no idea. Where did you get that photograph? And why are you so interested in him? There are thousands of refugees here.'

Eniko was about to reply, when something tall and heavy slammed into the other side of the glass wall.

Transit Zone, Keleti Station, 1.08 p.m.

Balthazar watched Eniko address the doctor, then he found himself spinning on his heel and walking away. The African family, he told himself. That was the reason. No other. They had been here for several days, that was clear. Perhaps they had seen the dead man. It was certainly worth asking them.

He started to walk back, when his path was suddenly blocked by half a dozen burly men. Balthazar scanned the area, realised instantly what was happening, all thoughts of Eniko and the African family evaporating as the adrenalin kicked in.

The men encircled him. The Transit Zone itself seemed aware of the coming violence. The steady backdrop of chatter immediately faded. The boys who had been playing football picked up their ball and quickly backed away. The queue of people waiting for lunch rapidly dispersed. The children splashing by the taps quickly ran back to their families.

Balthazar's mind divided into two: one half processed the fear, rode the adrenalin that instantly surged through him. The second half planned his next moves.

Rule number one when facing multiple attackers: step out of the line, stay out of the line, keep moving, don't show your back and *never* let yourself be surrounded. He swerved to the left, around the thugs. They immediately regrouped, penned him on all sides, started to encroach on his space, forced him back against the glass wall of the MigSzol office.

Rule number two: if surrounded, smash your way through with the hardest, sharpest bone in your body. Balthazar wrapped his right arm around his face with the elbow facing out, clenched his left fist, flexed his legs against the wall and launched himself forward.

Rule number three: eyes or groin. The attackers were too many, and moving too fast for him to get near their eyes. But their lower bodies were in reach. Balthazar slammed his fist into the crotch of the man on his left side. He reeled back, grunting in pain. Balthazar pushed harder, his right arm still around his face, elbow out, left fist flailing again and again, scraping against fabric, hitting muscle and soft tissue.

For a moment there were two of them, one on either side. Balthazar's fists shot out low, right and left, ramming into their groins. The human wall wavered, was about to part. The punches slammed into him: his back, his shoulders, his face, he felt the shock shudder through his jaw, ignored the pain, heard his father's voice sounding, 'Hands up, son, hands up.'

He brought his fists up to his forehead, one arm on either side of his nose, protecting his face, forced himself forward, shoving, punching, kicking, wielding his elbows, fists flailing with hooks, upper cuts, jabs and elbow strikes, some going wild, landing nowhere, others hitting leather, denim, skin, bone underneath; adrenalin pumping, legs and fists slamming into him, panting, gasping, the rank stink of sweat and sour milk in his throat, when something slammed into the side of his head.

The world roared, turned black.

SIX

Transit Zone, Keleti Station, 1.10 p.m.

Eniko had seen punches thrown in bars, watched drunks push and shove each other, sudden outbursts of posturing that exploded then evaporated as quickly as they started. But she had never witnessed a sustained fight, the fierce concentration of violence inflicted to hurt and injure. She was horrified, nauseated and transfixed by the spectacle.

Grunts, gasps of pain and expletives resounded across the Transit Zone. Time seemed to slow down and speed up simultaneously. She watched Balthazar pivot on his left foot and lash out in every direction, arms and legs working methodically like a steam engine. One part of her wanted to rush to his aid, another to run for her life. The kicks and punches, the flurries of movement, arms and legs flailing, seemed to last longer than any human being could bear. But the limbs kept on moving, whipping through the air like demons.

She stepped outside, hovered on the edge of the fight. Someone brushed past her, but she was too anxious about the fight to notice. Balthazar appeared in the middle of the mêlée, a man went down, then he was absorbed again. Then, as suddenly as it began, the fight ended. The men dispersed. Balthazar lay on the ground, his shirt ripped, a thin, crimson trickle seeping from his mouth, his eyes half open.

Eniko bound forward, crouched down next to him and touched his face. Balthazar blinked, groaned, half-smiled in recognition, turned on his side and coughed, sending a gout of blood from his nose. Then Eniko realised. Her right hand, the one that had been holding her phone, was empty.

Prime minister's office, Hungarian Parliament, 3.00 p.m.

Pal Dezeffy sat back with his feet up on his carved oak desk watching state television's afternoon news on his computer monitor. The reporter, a rangy brunette in her early thirties, was standing by a large construction works on the southern border, next to a large earth digger, piles of razor wire and bags of cement. The fence, which would seal off the frontier with Serbia through which most migrants passed, would be finished in a week, she exclaimed excitedly. 'Then we will be free of the migrant terror.' The camera panned across the border to the edge of Serbia, where hundreds of weary-looking migrants waited listlessly in the afternoon heat.

Dezeffy switched the report off. The border fence – in fact a twelve-foot concrete wall – had provoked protests from human rights organisations, the European Union and the small liberal parties that were not part of his grand coalition. He ignored all of them. The polls, both public and private, showed overwhelming support for sealing off the frontier. He looked around his large corner office in the neo-Gothic parliament building. Hungary's prime minister had been in power for six months, and he still relished his workplace. The walls were half lined with varnished wooden panels. *The Bridge at Mostar*, by Csontvary, one of Hungary's greatest artists, hung over the white marble fireplace, the pale arch of the bridge and the bright colours of its surrounds shining in the afternoon sunlight. A closed set of double wooden doors stood on the far side of the office.

A row of portraits of Dezeffy's predecessors was hung on the walls' upper sections, each topped by a brass lamp, polished till it shone. Just one was missing: that of Gyorgy Kiss, minister of the interior in the early 1950s, when Hungary languished under a home-grown Stalinist terror, then prime minister for six months before even Moscow tired of his brutality. Soon, Dezeffy told himself, *Nagyapa*, Grandad, would be back in his rightful place. Kiss, who had ended so many of his countrymen's existences, was now himself a non-person, universally reviled. But that too could be fixed, Dezeffy knew, with tame historians promised lucrative jobs at a new think tank, sponsored television documentaries and lavishly funded commissions of enquiry guided in the right direction.

Dezeffy glanced out of the window. A police launch roared downriver towards Parliament, bouncing on the waves it made, white spray soaring in its wake. He watched the boat as it came nearer, a small part of him wondering if this might be ... was the day, when they... he banished the thought. There was no possibility of that while he remained in this office – and especially while the woman waiting outside was in charge of the ministry of justice. Nor would there be any trouble from the new minister of the interior, after Bela Lidaki had been so publicly humiliated.

With the news off, the only sound in the room was the steady ticking of an antique grandfather clock. The parquet floor gleamed in the sunlight. Dezeffy's favourite antique silk Persian carpet took up much of the floor space in front of his desk: a delicate pattern of blue and pink roses. An antique coffee set by Zsolnay, Hungary's most renowned ceramics firm, sat on a silver tray, the cups and jug a deep navy topped with immaculate gold trim, next to a manila file and a black mobile phone.

Dezeffy picked up the Nexus 6 again, pressed the power button on the side. The screen stayed black. He tapped it gently on the green leather panel in the middle of his heavy wooden desk. The sharp edge indented the leather but the screen stayed dead. The phone had been dead since it had been handed to him an hour ago. It had been bricked, on purpose, he was sure. The technicians were due to pick it up in half an hour, but he was not optimistic that they would recover anything of interest. The owner, he knew, was adept with computers and highly security conscious. Dezeffy put the handset down and glanced at the grandfather clock: it was ten minutes past three. The minister of justice had been waiting outside for fifteen minutes. Perhaps it was time to let her in.

His desktop computer pinged, indicating an internal email from his assistant. His PA had forwarded a message from Celeste Johnson. The British diplomat – if that was all she was – was requesting an urgent meeting. Dezeffy knew very well what she wanted to talk about.

Dezeffy sighed loudly, pressed a button on the double telephone set on his desk. 'Send her in,' he ordered.

He watched the minister of justice walk in, barely suppressing her evident annoyance at being kept waiting. She glared at Dezeffy and sat down in front of his desk, her slender figure carefully showcased in a fitted white silk blouse that was open to the top of her cleavage. She had a model's posture and wore a grey Max Mara trouser suit. Her body language was brisk and confident as she slid one long, shapely leg over another, knowing she had Dezeffy's full attention. He could see the red soles of her black Christian Louboutin shoes and the thin spiky heel.

The French designer's shoes cost hundreds of euros a pair. Dezeffy knew that she had a wardrobe full of Louboutins with heels of different heights. She had started out on seventy millimetres but these were clearly taller than that. 'How high?'

Bardossy glanced at her feet, smiled with self-satisfaction. 'I'm up to ninety. But I'm thinking about a hundred for the reception tonight.'

'That should get you plenty of attention. How do you keep your balance?'

'Practice. But did you call me here to talk about high heels, Pali?' Reka asked, her voice barbed. 'I cancelled my Krav Maga lesson for this. What's going on?'

'We have a problem, Madame Minister.'

Hungarians loved diminutives. Outside his family, Reka was the only person who called Dezeffy 'Pali'. He sometimes called her 'Doshi', but not today, it seemed. She brushed her shoulder-length blonde hair away from her cheeks. 'We?' she replied, supremely unconcerned. 'You're the prime minister. You'll solve it. That's what prime ministers do.'

Reka Bardossy seemed to have all the necessary credentials for minister of justice: law degrees from Budapest and Harvard Universities, a successful career as a partner in an international law firm with an office in Budapest, a husband who was a prominent businessman and philanthropist, a silver Olympic medal for sabre. As the daughter of a former Communist dynasty – now of course loyal Social Democrats – she boasted solid political lineage and excellent connections. Her good looks were extremely useful. Whenever the European Commission issued another press release expressing its 'strong concern' about the centralisation of political and economic power under Dezeffy's government, Reka was on the next aeroplane to Brussels, her large blue eyes open and honest in their gaze as her lightly glossed lips explained why, really, there was nothing to be concerned about. After eight years of right-wing rule, the Hungarian government had a clear mandate for change, and was indeed implementing it, she explained. Eurocrats melted. The politics were easy to fix. Less so was something Dezeffy had not anticipated: the extent of her greed.

'Clear your afternoon,' said Dezeffy.

Reka slowly crossed her legs, then glanced at his desk. 'Here?'

Dezeffy closed his eyes for a moment, forced himself to look away from her legs and focus. 'No. Not here. Not anywhere.' He paused. 'Not today.'

She shrugged, glanced down at her wedding ring, a two-carat diamond housed in a white gold band. 'Suit yourself.' She glanced at her watch, an oblong gold Patek Philippe. 'Anyway, I have to be somewhere else in twenty minutes.'

This was too much, Dezeffy told himself. He was the *prime minister*. He slammed his fist down on the table. Reka jumped.

'Do I have your attention now, Minister?'

'Yes, Prime Minister, absolutely,' Reka agreed, suddenly businesslike.

'Good. Then look at these. And explain them to me.' Dezeffy handed her the manila file. She opened the folder and leafed through several photographs of Akos Feher entering and leaving the British embassy, each stamped with a date and time.

'That is one of your senior officials, is it not?' asked Dezeffy. Reka nodded. Dezeffy was right. This was a problem. A potentially major one. 'Akos Feher. Deputy secretary of state.'

'What's he doing at the British embassy?' asked the prime minister.

She shrugged. 'I don't know. I can find out. But what's the problem? My officials often meet with foreign diplomats.'

'Not in an embassy's secure room.'

Reka put the photographs down. This was getting worse by the minute. She really would have to clear her afternoon. 'How do you know he was there?'

Dezeffy leaned forward, his shoulders tense, his voice tight. 'Because the reception rooms for receiving guests have windows onto Harmincad Street or Elizabeth Square. The Brits like to show off the view. We have them all under surveillance. But we cannot watch the secure room in the basement. Your *colleague*,' he said, his voice strained, 'went into the building but did not appear anywhere again until he left, forty minutes later. Why?'

Reka closed the file, the sinking feeling in her stomach growing heavier. There was no point dissembling. 'He is the contact man. For the passports.'

'I see. How much do you get for each passport?'

'Between 30,000 and 40,000 euros.'

'Of which how much ends up in your Cayman Islands account?'

Reka turned pink. But there was no point prevaricating. 'Maybe a third, depending on the timeframe, any other potential complications.' She glanced at the closed double door on the other side of the room. 'Pal, I'm not really comfortable with this conversation.' Especially as Dezeffy only had part of the picture. He knew about the passport-selling scam but not where the documents later ended up. Reka was also running a separate operation, providing cover for the Gypsies who were working around Keleti and disguising refugees as Roma people, by ensuring they crossed the Hungarian border with no problems. As far as she knew, he had no idea about that. Reka looked back at Dezeffy. He was staring at her, and not with lust.

Dezeffy said, 'I'm not concerned about your comfort level. Who does Akos Feher sell the passports to?'

Her unease deepened. Why did he want to know that now? Someone neither you nor I would ever want to meet, she thought, even with our security levels. 'I'd rather not say.'

'You're not comfortable, you're not concerned. You would rather not say. Madame Minister, I decide the parameters of this conversation. Not you.'

Reka held his gaze this time, her eyes cold. 'OK. We can keep talking. Perhaps your name will come up as well. At least twenty-five per cent of the time.'

Dezeffy paused. They both knew it was an effective gambit, no less so for being very obvious. His cut was washed through two companies and three straw men, but if this blew up, went public, some of the mud would stick. In the age of WikiLeaks and the Panama papers, nothing was truly secure any more.

Reka asked, 'What's Britain's interest here?'

'The Hungarian passports you are selling to the traffickers are ending up in the hands of known Islamic militants. Who are using them to take flights on budget airlines to Luton airport. Where, it turns out, they cannot speak Hungarian and barely know where the country is.' He paused. 'You told me this... arrangement was safe, locked down. That you were dealing with business people. Not running a travel agency for ISIS.'

She blanched. Terrorism? This brought things to a new,

and much more dangerous, level. Not least for herself. Corruption, bribes, dirty money, that was her world. She could handle that. But Islamic militants? The CIA, MI6 taking an interest in her business dealings? The potential blowback terrified her. 'How do you know?'

Dezeffy's voice softened. There was no point going to war with Reka; they had too much history and she knew too much about him – far too much – to make an enemy of her. 'Because the British border force has arrested at least three trying to enter the country on passports that they have traced back to your ministry. Celeste Johnson has informed us. She wants a meeting. As soon as possible. Today is Friday. I can stall her over the weekend perhaps, but no longer. What shall I tell her, Madame Minister?'

Feher had told Reka enough about his conversation with Celeste Johnson to know that this mess needed sorting out quickly. In cases like this, she followed Stalin's motto: no person, no problem. Feher would not be killed, of course, but simply removed from the scene, skilfully, she hoped, in a way that both defused the issue and dumped the blame on him. But before that, she needed to talk to him. How had MI6 traced the passports back to her ministry?

She stood up. 'Tell her that I'm working on it. That I'm clearing my calendar and I'll get back to you as soon as I can.'

Dezeffy nodded. 'By tonight. Before the reception.'

Reka gathered her papers and her bag and walked out.

Dezeffy put the Nexus 6 into a drawer in his desk. He pressed another button on the telephone handset on his worktop. The double doors at the far end of the office opened, revealing a small annex. A man who looked to be in his early sixties walked into Dezeffy's office. He was balding, with straggly grey hair combed over his shiny, flaking scalp, a pasty complexion and red-rimmed, blue eyes. He wore thick black glasses, one arm of which was secured by tape, scuffed black shoes, flared beige trousers and a brown suit jacket with wide, unfashionable lapels that slid off his narrow shoulders. He held a slim digital recorder in his right hand, a printout in the left. Both hands were mottled with liver spots. A cigarette burned slowly between two thin, damp lips.

Dezeffy glanced nervously at the machine. The grey-haired man pressed a button on the side of the recorder.

'How much do you get for a passport?'

'Between 30,000 and 40,000 euros.'

'Of which how much ends up in your Cayman Islands account?'

'Maybe a third, depending on the timeframe, any other potential complications.'

Dezeffy asked: 'What will you do with it?'

'Add it to her file, of course.'

And to who else's file? Dezeffy wanted to ask. But to that question he already knew the answer.

The grey-haired man slipped the recorder into his trouser pocket and placed the paper on Dezeffy's desk. 'The latest private poll results, correlated to people-flow and coverage of Keleti Station.'

Dezeffy put on his reading glasses, scanned the paper for several seconds. 'Each time state television runs a report about hundreds of refugees living in squalor and dirt, support for the government goes up.'

The grey-haired man nodded, took a drag on his cigarette, blew out a stream of pungent smoke. 'So your proposal that we install more toilets, a washing area for laundry, double the number of taps with drinking water, set up a rota for medical staff...'

Dezeffy coughed, was about to wave the smoke away, stopped himself. 'Is not going to be implemented, obviously.'

'Obviously.' The grey-haired man looked down Dezeffy's coffee cup. 'Keleti is under control. But your poll ratings are not. These new billboards, with you at the centre of a *komcsi* spider's web, are proving very effective. The terms of our deal were very clear. If your voter base keeps draining away, so will our support.'

The billboards are effective because they are true, thought Dezeffy. Almost all of his political allies and financial backers dated back to his time in the Communist Party or its youth organisations. The party had surrendered political power in 1989 to the opposition, but the price of the peaceful 'handshake transition', as it was known, was that the Communists, now reborn as Social Democrats, kept control of their extensive business interests. These had only grown over the subsequent decades, generously funded by EU subsidies. Dezeffy asked: 'What do you suggest?'

The grey-haired man stepped closer, fixed Dezeffy with his watery eyes. 'I suggest you fix it. Meanwhile, we have another, more pressing problem.' He paused, dropped the butt into the black liquid. It fizzed for a moment then floated on the remains of the drink. 'Which needs solving. Immediately.'

Dezeffy replied, 'I'm listening.'

'One, the dead man in Republic Square.'

'The body is gone. A unit of Gendarmes took it away.'

'Where?'

'A gravel pit, outside the city.'

'The cop who was snooping around? The Gypsy?'

Dezeffy beckoned the grey-haired man to his desk, pressed down on his computer keyboard. A window opened, showing a video feed: Balthazar surrounded, fighting, eventually over-whelmed, his assailants leaving him unconscious on the ground.

'I'll think he'll get the message,' said Dezeffy.

'And if he doesn't?'

'The next time he will be out for more than a couple of seconds.'

'OK. The third problem is the most pressing. Your minister of justice. This is no longer a money issue. Your government's incompetence has drawn the attention of the British secret intelligence service. What they know will be shared with the Americans, possibly the Germans and the French. The USA already knows. You can expect an email from the Americans soon.'

The grey-haired man stepped forward, his fingers grasp-ing Dezeffy's arm. His grip was surprisingly strong. Dezeffy winced, glanced down at the brown nails, stained with nic-otine, digging into his skin. The man's breath stank of tobacco. 'We warned you about Bardossy. But you wouldn't listen.' He released his grip on Dezeffy's arm. 'It's a shame you didn't think with this,' he said, pushing an outstretched finger against Dezeffy's temple, 'instead of this,' he contin-ued, dropping his hand and poking Dezeffy in his groin.

Dezeffy gasped as rods of pain shot around his lower body, his breath coming fast and shallow. He made no move to defend himself.

The grey-haired man looked Dezeffy up and down, like a naturalist on an expedition who has just discovered a mod-erately noteworthy species of beetle, then removed his finger. 'We thought you had potential. But obviously, we were wrong. Never mind. You can be easily replaced. There is too much at stake here.'

'You weren't wrong. I promise. What,' Dezeffy panted, 'should I do?'

The grey-haired man removed his finger. Dezeffy collapsed back into his chair.

'Solve your Bardossy problem. For good.'

Pest side of the embankment, near the Ministry of Justice, 3.30 p.m.

A quarter of a mile away, Akos Feher sat on an iron bench and watched the Danube flow under the Chain Bridge. The man sitting next to him said, 'That's everything that happened? The whole conversation you had with the British woman?'

Everything apart from the 'request' that I spy on my colleagues, Feher almost said. Instead he answered, 'Yes. They know the passports are connected to the justice ministry. They know they are genuine, not forged or stolen. And they know the people carrying them have no connection to Hungary whatsoever.'

The man next to him nodded, thought for a moment before he began to talk. Once he had finished, he sat back. 'We've made you a decent offer. You should consider it carefully.'

Feher almost laughed. *Decent.* It was anything but. Perhaps he could claim asylum at the British embassy. Throw himself on Celeste's mercy, rest his head on her capacious breasts and tell her everything he knew. Which was, it was now clear, way too much. And how was he going to tell Dorka, gorgeous, blonde Dorka, with her soft skin and slim, nimble fingers, that they could never meet again? He glanced at the river. The water was almost blue, flowing fast, carpeted with tiny waves, their peaks rippling silver in the blazing sunshine. Across the river, on the Buda embankment, a crane

102

was poised over a half-demolished building, its wrecking ball dangling over the roof. 'I will. How much time have I got?'

'We are reasonable people. Think about it over the weekend. Spend some quality time with your wife, your son, enjoy their company...' He paused, the implication unsaid. 'You have until nine o'clock on Monday morning.'

Feher glanced at the stone lions on pedestals that guarded the entrance to the bridge. Feher had grown up nearby in a large riverside apartment, had seen the bridge most days, but was still captivated by its grace and beauty. Every Hungarian schoolboy knew its story. The suspension bridge was the first permanent link between the then separate cities of Buda and Pest. Its designer, a nineteenth-century Scottish engineer called Adam Clark, had also built Hammersmith Bridge. But the Chain Bridge was his masterpiece. Clark had fallen in love with a Hungarian and eventually died in Hungary. On the Buda side, Clark had also built an oval-shaped tunnel under Castle Hill. When Feher had been very young, his father had told him with a straight face that each night the bridge was dismantled and put away in the tunnel for safekeeping. Feher had almost believed him.

An hour ago, when his life had still been whole, Feher had been sitting at his desk in the Ministry of Justice, pondering his conversation with Celeste Johnson, but nevertheless looking forward to the late summer weekend. He had planned to spend it with his wife and their six-year-old son at his newly acquired holiday apartment at Balatonfured, overlooking Lake Balaton itself. The flat was worth around 30 million forints, or a hundred thousand euros. He had bought it from the local municipality for less than half that, plus three Nokia boxes for the relevant local officials and politicians.

Feher was in trouble, he knew, but he still had his job and his salary, a BMW saloon here and the Porsche garaged in Vienna, a duplex apartment in District V, and the bank accounts in Zurich and the Cayman Islands. He had encountered *difficulties* before. They were inevitable in the life he had chosen. It was impossible to have clean hands. But *kez kezet mos,* hand washes hand, as the saying went. What mattered were allies, one's roof. He had the support of the minister. He would find a way through. Perhaps via the *kis kapu*, or, if not, with the help of more Nokia boxes. There was always a way, in Hungary.

Then the call had come from reception, informing Feher that he had a visitor, waiting for him in the VIP entrance at the side of the ministry building. That was a signal: the visitor was authorised. Authorised and bad news, Feher immediately understood. The visitor was tall and loose-limbed, his head shaved so close it almost shone. He had deep-set blue eyes and wore a black T-shirt that showed his well-muscled physique, shiny black track pants with a white stripe down the side and wraparound mirrored sunglasses. He introduced himself as Antal. No surname. Another bad sign. Followed by two others: they did not shake hands and Feher still had not seen his eyes. Antal had led him along the embankment for a couple of blocks downriver from the Ministry of Justice, to the bench.

'What happens if I agree?' asked Feher. He wiped his forehead. The shadow from the nearby plane trees gave meagre shelter and the breeze, a slow, erratic gust of warm air, gave no relief. Across the river the wrecking ball began to swing.

'Your family will be looked after. Your wife will receive your salary in an off-shore account. They will be safe. You have our word on that.' Antal paused, dug around in his mouth with a wooden toothpick. 'You pack a bag when you come to work on Monday. Toothbrush, soap, T-shirts, the essentials. Then you make the call. We will ensure you are comfortable. There will be family visits, even conjugal ones. You will be away for a while and we don't want you to have to get divorced.'

Feher looked to his right. A few yards from where they sat, rows of metal shoes were lined up by the river's edge; men's boots, women's high heels and children's sandals. Just over seventy years ago, in the winter of 1944, this had been a place of terror. The Arrow Cross, the Hungarian Nazis, had lined up Jews here, tied them together to save bullets, then shot them into the freezing water. The victims were forced to take off their shoes before they were killed. The footwear later fetched a good price on the wartime black market.

Feher asked, 'How long is a while?'

Antal flicked the toothpick away. 'Normally, not very long. A few months. Then you could come back to work. But the problem is, the Brits and the Americans are making a lot of noise. Facilitating terrorism, fake passports.' He paused for a moment. 'It's very bad timing, your mistake.'

I didn't make a mistake, Feher wanted to shout. I just did what the minister told me to. Even as he formulated the thought, he realised its stupidity. His mistake had been to take the job in the ministry instead of the one at his father's law firm. A memory flashed through his mind: he was six years old, and his father held him up to the lion's mouth, told him to put his hand in. 'Don't worry, it won't bite,' his father had said, laughing. The lion's mouth was empty. The sculptor had forgotten to include a tongue. In his shame, he had jumped into the Danube and drowned, the story went. Feher never knew if it was true or not. But at least he'd had enough sense to put an insurance policy in place in case of a day like this.

Antal continued talking. 'Especially now. You've seen the news, the terror attacks in London and Paris.' Across the river, the wrecking ball smashed into the top of the building. The tiles shattered and the roof collapsed. 'Unfortunately we will have to make an example of you.'

'How long?'

'You'll probably get ten years.'

Feher's stomach twisted. '*Ten?*'

Antal smiled. 'Maybe eight. But you'll be out in three or four.'

Feher felt his eyes well up. He forced himself to control his emotions. 'My job. My career?'

'Ask your father. He might need a clerk.'

Feher swallowed hard stared at the Danube. A plastic bag was caught in the current. It floated, drifted sideways, floated back, seemed to fight for a while, then suddenly disappeared, pulled under. 'And if say no?'

Antal stood up and walked over to the Holocaust memorial. He knelt down and ran his forefinger down one of the iron shoes. Feher tasted his lunch rising in his gut, felt the acid flush of pure fear. The shoe, he saw, was child-sized.

SEVEN

Balthazar's flat, Dob Street, 6.05 p.m.

The voice sounded distant at first: tinny, muffled, as though his ears were jammed with cotton wool. Fragments of words and disjointed sounds spilled back and forth, slowly coming nearer, morphing into fragments of sentences. A woman, speaking English, fluently, but with an accent. He turned on his back, half-opened his eyes. He sensed sudden movements on his left side – rapid, small gestures. The sounds stopped.

Balthazar fully opened his eyes. Where was the talking woman? And where was he? On his back on a bed. There was a long, narrow, damp patch on the peeling ceiling in the shape of Austria. So he was at home, at least. He was wearing a T-shirt and a pair of boxer shorts. He couldn't remember getting undressed. Someone was asking how he was, could she bring him anything? Another female. This voice he knew very well and could immediately identify. One that set off several emotions at once. What was she doing here? The question had barely formed in his mind when several kinds of pain attacked. A sharp ache in his ribs when he breathed in and out. The dull throb of his shoulders and thighs, where the attackers' blows had connected. The pulsing of the scraped skin on his knuckles. The sharper ache in his jaw. Most of all, the iron bar inside his head.

He glanced to his left. She was sitting up next to him, cross-legged, a thin silver computer on her lap. There was no sound, but moving images flickered on the screen, sending coloured shapes across the room. The curtains were mostly drawn. His mouth felt like it had been sucked dry by a vacuum cleaner. He tried to sit up. Starbursts of pain erupted across his body, the iron bar jolted around his head again, and the room slid back and forth.

A hand reached for his arm, rested there, fingers warm against his skin. 'Tazi. Don't. You need to rest.'

He stayed sitting up, closed his eyes for a moment, wincing as the iron bar slid back into place. He opened his eyes and the room slowly steadied. 'What time is it?'

She put her laptop aside and picked up a pillow. 'Sit forward.' Balthazar did as she bade. She slid the pillow behind his back then looked at her watch. 'Just after six o'clock. In the evening.'

She reached for a bottle of mineral water, handed it to him. He thanked her, steadily drank without opening his mouth too wide, leaned back and touched his nose. Lightning shot through his face. The bone was bruised, the cartilage extremely tender, but at least it was not broken. A memory flashed through his mind:

He is twelve years old, in the courtyard of the building on Jozsef Street, where he grew up. His first pair of boxing gloves feel heavy on his hands. His cousin, Rudi, two years older, heavier, faster, in front of him, relatives standing around him, his mother watching anxiously from the window.

He tries to remember what his father has taught him: hands up, head tucked in, feet moving together, jab left to get your range, follow with a right cross, keep moving to the side, stay out of the line of attack. But Rudy is a whirlwind, fists flying, dancing around him. An explosion of pain in his nose, blood pouring out, anger displacing pain.

Now he advances, arms pistoning forward, tight, controlled. Suddenly Rudi is reeling backwards, his lip split, his mouth bleeding. The two boys are circling each other when Balthazar's father steps in, holds his son's hand up, the relatives cheer.

He glances up at the window on the third floor. She is watching, a flicker of a smile on her face, as she brushes her long, black hair from her face.

Then the day flooded back to him: Republic Square, the missing dead man, the confrontation with the Gendarmes, his meeting with Sandor Takacs, the food for the African family; most of all, the fight.

He looked at her. 'How long was I asleep?'

'More than three hours.'

'You have been here all this time?'

She nodded, a half-smile flickering uncertainly on her face. 'Someone had to keep an eye on you.'

Now he remembered. The football-playing boys and Samuel helping to carry him into the MigSzol office. A female doctor examining him, shining a light into his eyes. Pupils that took a while to dilate properly, but did, eventually. Two words: 'mild concussion.' His right hand checking his pockets when he came round: telephone, wallet, the edge of the SIM card in his ticket pocket. Everything still in its place. Whatever this was, it was not a robbery. He sank back onto his pillow, trying to process everything that had happened. He glanced at Eniko, her hair loose and falling around her face in the soft light, sitting on what used to be her side of the bed.

Balthazar asked, 'What have you been doing all that time?'

Eniko glanced to her left for a second before she answered. 'Working.'

'On what?'

She looked down at her computer screen, still flickering. 'The usual. Keleti. Migration.'

Balthazar knew that look, the sudden reluctance to make eye contact. He touched his jaw, the pain driving away his suspicion as he remembered the blow. A left hook, hard and fast enough to take him down, but not enough to break his jaw. He'd seen it coming, dodged some of the punch, but not all. He opened his mouth wide now, fresh pain shooting around his head, closed it slowly. Bruised, sore, very sore, definitely, but no bones rattled and everything worked. He gingerly ran his finger along his teeth, top and bottom. None were loose. The punch was well-judged, he understood. It could have been much harder, in which case he would be in hospital, unable to speak or chew, his jaw held together with wire.

Balthazar glanced at her screen, which was moving again. 'What are you watching?'

Eniko's fingers moved across the keyboard. 'You, at Keleti.'

Once he was down and out they could have done some serious damage, he knew. A stomp kick or two to the head would have put him in a coma, might even have killed him. But once he was on the floor the attackers had all fled. There were gradations of beatings. Despite the pain, his headache and the bruising, this ranked low to moderate, with no serious damage. He would be sore and stiff for several days but it would fade. But the beating came with a message: we can do this, and much worse. So *stay away*.

He glanced at Eniko. Her appraising look was shot through with a kind of admiration. 'You lasted quite a while, considering how outnumbered you were. And you went down fighting.'

'Thanks. You can get into Keleti's CCTV?'

She laughed. 'Probably. But I don't need to. It's all on YouTube. You are famous,' she said, as she passed him the laptop. 'One of the migrants must have filmed it and uploaded it.'

He watched the footage. It was blurred and shaky, but still managed to capture the fight. He watched himself breaking out, surrounded, his arms and legs flailing before he was engulfed again. She was right. Considering the odds, he had defended himself well. He imagined showing the clip to his father, until he remembered that his father refused to acknowledge his oldest son's existence. For a moment he was back inside the mêlée, could still smell that rank stink, of sweat and sour milk. He watched the footage again, froze the screen about halfway through the film. A man's face, laughing. This time he was not wearing a ski mask. It was easy to see the knife scar under his right eye.

Balthazar handed the laptop back to Eniko, turned sideways, swung his legs over the bed, exhaled hard.

Eniko put her computer aside, looked alarmed. 'Tazi. What are you doing? Tell me what you want. I'll bring it. The doctor said you have to rest.'

He smiled. 'Doctors say all sorts of things.'

Eniko pulled a face. He crouched down, picked up a pair of grey jogging pants, and carefully inserted one leg, then the other. The walls wobbled and a wave of nausea hit him. He closed his eyes and breathed deeply. The room stabilised and he slowly walked into the tiny galley kitchen. He needed to clear his head, think for a moment. Without Eniko distracting him. He glanced down into the sink, took out a plate and a cup, turned on the cold tap, let it run for several seconds, then stuck his head under the water.

Balthazar lived in a two-bedroom flat on Dob Street, in the heart of the city's old Jewish quarter in District VII, overlooking Klauzal Square. The main bedroom was his, and a narrow space, once the maid's accommodation, had a single bed for the rare occasions when Sarah allowed Alex to stay overnight. The walls and window were still the same faded white as when he moved in. The parquet floor was dulled and loose in places. The kitchen and bathroom pre-dated the change of system in 1990. The heavy, dark wooden sofa and chairs pre-dated the Second World War. The only furniture he had added were the shelves that covered one wall and were filled with books.

He shivered as the blast of icy water woke him. The landline rang. There were three handsets: in the bedroom, the kitchen and a third in the lounge. Only two people he knew used the landline: his brother, Gaspar, and Sandor Takacs. He took the call. 'Is she looking after you, *batyam*, my older brother?' asked a gravelly voice. There was no point asking Gaspar how he knew. Gaspar's network of informants and contacts ranged far and wide across District VIII and its environs. It certainly included Keleti Station.

Balthazar picked up a crumpled tea towel and sniffed it. It smelled stale but would do for now. He rubbed his hair as he spoke. 'Yes, she is, *ocsim*, my little brother.'

'Not as well as my girls would. That one is too skinny. And too smart for you. Are you back together now?'

'No.'

'Then let me send Judit over, I know she likes you...'

Balthazar laughed, interrupted Gaspar. 'No and no thanks.'

'But you are coming over later? Or shall I send someone to get you?'

'Yes, I am. No need to send anyone, *ocsim*. I'll see you later. Let me get myself together.'

Gaspar hung up. Balthazar tried to straighten out the torrent of thoughts running through his head. The first priority was to divide the emotional from the practical. The sight of Eniko was stirring up a surprising amount of feelings he thought were at least buried, even if they had not dissipated. Reading about her date with Tamas Nemeth was one thing. Waking up to find Eniko sitting on his bed on a late summer afternoon was quite another. Balthazar had retreated into himself after the break-up with Sarah. The divorce had been surprisingly swift and hassle-free, at least on the legal side. She had moved out and moved in with Amanda. They had sold their flat and split the proceeds. He had used his share to put a deposit on the Dob Street apartment. Balthazar paid her 70,000 forints a month for Alex, a quarter of his take-home salary. Her salary from Central European University was three times his policeman's pay. He had offered more but Sarah was not interested in his money. But she was very interested in micro-managing his relationship with his son. Nonetheless, Alex knew his father loved him and even if he could not see him every day, they spoke and texted all the time.

But the break-up had also hit Balthazar hard on other levels. No man likes being left by his wife – but it's a double blow when she leaves him for a woman. What had he done wrong that his wife no longer wanted to sleep, not just with him, but with *any* man? Balthazar knew he was attractive to women. His dark good looks, muscled torso and ability to handle himself were combined with a sharp and perceptive intelligence. Once the word was out that he was single again the invitations to lunch, coffee and art exhibitions started coming in, several from single friends of Sarah. He said no to all of them, at least at first. The split had battered his sexual confidence. After several months of celibacy he had had a couple of brief flings, but there had been nobody with relationship potential until Eniko had come along. Slowly, he began to trust her, to open up. After a couple of weeks there was an extra toothbrush in the bathroom, women's underwear next to his, floral smells, a kitchen where meals were produced. It felt right.

After a month, they were virtually living together. Things were moving fast, perhaps too fast, a small voice told him. He listened and decided it was still too early to introduce Eniko to Alex. He knew his son would like Eniko and would approve of her. Alex had been nagging Balthazar for months to find another girlfriend. But what if he and Eniko met, and got along very well, as would likely happen, and then the relationship crumbled and Eniko disappeared? There had been enough upheaval in the boy's life. A week or so later, he decided it was time. But the very day when Balthazar finally planned to suggest that Eniko meet Alex, she had told him that she had accepted a job offer in London and that she wanted to break up. He did not quite understand why: the position was a three-month internship, extendable to six months. London was not Lima or Hong Kong. Several budget airlines flew there, sometimes for less than a hundred euros return. Distance was no reason to what was turning into – for him, at least – quite a serious relationship. He pointed all this out to Eniko, tried to explain how much she meant to him. She would not meet his eye, but was adamant. It was over. He felt numb at first, in a kind of shock. Then nauseous. But when he heard her say that it really was over, pride kicked in. He stopped trying to persuade her to do anything, silently watched her pack her belongings and leave.

In any case, she seemed to be dating Tamas Nemeth now, if Szilky.hu was to be believed. He certainly wasn't going to ask. Balthazar glanced through the kitchen door. The edge of the bed was visible in his bedroom. There she was, sitting on it, absorbed in her computer and some or other news feed. She was fully dressed, in a T-shirt and jeans. For a moment he imagined her there, wearing one of his white shirts, and nothing else, as she used to. He closed his eyes for several moments. This would have to stop.

A memory flashed through his mind: he was back at home on Jozsef Street, in the aftermath of the boxing match with Rudy. His mother, aunts and grandmother all fussed around him, pressed sweets into his hand, hugged and praised him; Rudy too, before serving him his favourite meal of *csirke paprikas*, chicken paprika, with home-made egg noodles, his father looking on, beaming with pride. He felt safe, loved, wanted. And now, when he could have used some TLC? He was alone, apart from an ex-girlfriend who had dumped him when he was falling in love with her. He turned on the cold tap again and stuck his head underneath, before rubbing his hair even harder with the tea towel.

Every man he knew – apart from Sandor Takacs – had woman problems. But Balthazar had something else to deal with. He was a Gypsy in a *gadje* world. A perpetual outsider. In his bleaker moments, he thought that Sarah had seen him as an exotic plaything, to be used up and cast aside when the novelty wore off. For all his education and the ease with which he moved among Budapest's hipsters and liberals, and the diversity-loving faculty of Central European University, he never truly felt at home there. Almost without fail, every time he met someone from that world, or someone new in the hipster bars of District VII, they gave him what he called 'the Look'. The Look had three stages. The first was an involuntary expression of surprise. Surprise that a Gypsy could speak fluent English, was not wearing a shiny tracksuit. The second was the awareness that the surprise was showing and a flash of guilt in the person's eyes. The third was a rapid over-friendliness, an eagerness to show that really, he or she had no problem chatting with a Gypsy. Eniko, to her credit, had never given him the Look. But part of him was still, would always be, the Gypsy boy growing up in a tenement flat on Jozsef Street, wearing hand-me-downs, eating *zsiros-kenyer* – bread and dripping – for dinner, longing to see the world, but scared it would not let him in.

On top of that, and another complicating factor, was his policeman's instinct. The voice from Eniko's computer had stopped very suddenly as he awoke. That was not a coincidence. Her nimble fingers had clearly switched off a sound file. Who was the woman speaking? He knew an Arabic accent when he heard one. Plus, there was the article about his brother. 'Two well-known Roma figures in Budapest's underworld, both with connections to organised crime, appeared to be operating out of a café near the station,' Eniko had written. One of those 'well-known figures', he knew, was Fat Vik, Gaspar's *consigliere*. What did Eniko know about Gaspar and how had she come by that information?

He walked into the bedroom. Eniko was sitting with her back against the wall, laptop on her knees, staring at the screen, her hair falling around her face. She glanced at Balthazar as he stood near her. A black-and-white terminal window was open on her laptop screen, lines of code scrolling down. There was no point asking Eniko to explain. Her knowledge of computers and secure communications was far beyond his, knowledge honed ever sharper as the government's campaign against troublesome journalists intensified.

Eniko brushed her hair away from her cheek. 'I owe you a thank you.'

'What for?'

'B is for...?'

Balthazar frowned. 'I don't know. What is "B" for?'

'And next time use Telegram,' she continued, only half listening as she stared at the computer screen. 'It's more secure than WhatsApp.'

'I really have no idea what you are talking about.'

Balthazar opened the curtains and sat back down on the bed, ignoring the various pains that shot around his body. Light flooded the room. 'Let's go through to the lounge.'

She looked up. 'But you need to...'

'Walk around a bit. To stretch my muscles. To move.' To get you off this bed, before one of us does something we will regret later.

Eniko picked up her computer and followed him through to the next room. They sat down on the sofa. She glanced at him, her eyes warm, a soft look on her face, her lips slightly open. For a moment he thought about drawing her towards him, moving his mouth to hers. And then he remembered their last morning together, on this same sofa. That was history now. And he had no desire to experience it again.

'I can offer you tea,' said Balthazar. 'No sushi though.' He realised immediately how petulant he sounded, but the words were out of his mouth before he could stop himself.

Eniko blushed, looked away. 'He's not my... I mean, we're not...'

'I'm sorry. Bad joke. Your private life is your own affair.'

'I don't have a private life. I just work.' She picked up a gold rope neck chain from the coffee table. 'This is new. Not your usual style.'

'Birthday present.'

'Gaspar?'

'Who else?'

Eniko ran the chain through her fingers. 'Do you wear it?'

Balthazar smiled. 'Not for work.'

Eniko put the chain down. A silver-framed photograph of a young woman lay on the table. She had long dark-brown hair, tawny skin, a wide, full mouth and bright-green eyes. Eniko looked down at the photograph. 'I've never seen her before. She is beautiful.' She stared at Balthazar for several seconds, then looked back down at the photograph. 'She looks like you, a bit. Same green eyes. But she looks sad. Who is she?'

'A relative,' said Balthazar.

'Close or distant? One of your zillions of cousins?'

'Something like that.' Balthazar's voice was abrupt.

Eniko watched him pick up the photograph, walked across the room and put it on the bookshelf. She got the message. 'How is Gaspar?' she asked instead.

Eniko had met Gaspar several times. He was a rogue, a pimp and a criminal, but also had a certain charm. She was fascinated by the ferocious loyalty Balthazar and his relatives showed to each other. Gaspar sometimes managed to appease his father, Laszlo, enough that Balthazar was allowed to appear at important family gatherings for a while. Eniko had attended Balthazar's niece's christening party with him. Laszlo had barely acknowledged Balthazar, but had formally welcomed Eniko. Gaspar had played the violin and danced with Eniko. There were vast amounts of food and drink but what she remembered the most was how the air was thick with love. Gaspar had decided that he liked Eniko, and after a couple of weeks she was declared an honorary family member. She was surprised at how pleased she was to be accepted into the colourful chaos of the Kovacs clan. And more, how much she missed it.

'Gaspar is fine, thanks,' Balthazar answered, his voice still curt. Eniko was the second woman he had introduced to his family. And the second to walk out on him. It was nice of her to watch over him this afternoon but he had no desire to talk about his relatives with her. He sat down on the sofa, making sure to keep his distance. 'What were you talking about before? What letter B?'

Eniko read his body language. Her voice turned brisk. 'Somebody sent me a WhatsApp message this morning on my phone. An address, 26 Republic Square, and a photograph. I thought it was you.'

'It wasn't. A photograph of what?'

'A man. He looked like he was dead.'

'Show me.'

'I can't. I lost my phone in all the excitement at Keleti. Someone stole it.'

Now it was Balthazar's turn to work out how much to trust her. Somewhat, he decided. She already had the photo of the dead man. She also had information he wanted, about Gaspar and the people-traffickers. He picked up his phone from the coffee table, opened the message with the photograph of the dead man and passed her the handset. 'Like this?'

Eniko looked down at the picture for several seconds. 'Yes. Exactly. Is this your new case?'

Balthazar nodded.

'Any leads?' she asked brightly.

Balthazar half-smiled. 'None I can share with the press. Who sent you the photo?'

She frowned for a moment. 'It came from a number I didn't know. I called it but it had been disconnected. There was a letter "B" as well.' She handed Balthazar his mobile back. His puzzlement, she saw, was genuine. But if he had not sent the WhatsApp message, then who had? And why had they added a 'B' to lead her to Balthazar?

Balthazar said, 'But you can track your phone.'

'Yes. I can. And I know where it is.'

'Good. Why don't you go and get it? Or at least call the police?'

Eniko opened a new window on her laptop and handed it to Balthazar. 'Maybe you could get it for me, Tazi.'

A map appeared, showing Kossuth Square and Parliament in great detail. A small red light blinked continuously on the side of the building overlooking the Danube.

He passed the laptop back to Eniko. 'Maybe not. What's on it? Dezeffy's people will strip it out.'

Eniko shook her head. 'They won't. I've already remotely wiped it. Everything is gone, except the GPS. It's not that big a deal. All the data, contacts, everything is backed up in the cloud.' She reached inside her handbag and took out a silver iPhone. 'And I have more than one phone.'

Balthazar knew that Eniko also used her phone as a digital recorder. 'All your interviews as well?'

'Yes, of course. Anyway, I immediately email them to myself and put them on my computer. Tazi, who attacked you? They weren't migrants or random hooligans. It must have been planned. They must have been following you.' She paused, thought for a moment. 'It was a warning, wasn't it? To stop investigating the dead man at Republic Square.'

Her quicksilver intelligence was one of the things that most attracted Balthazar to Eniko. And she had something, clearly. Something that could help his investigation. 'Maybe. Let's trade.'

She sat up straight, alert now. 'I'm listening. What have you got?'

'I know who attacked me. Or at least who they work for.'

'OK. And you want?'

'The sound file you were listening to earlier. The woman. The woman with the Arabic accent.'

'What Arab woman?'

Balthazar sat back, and exhaled loudly. 'Eni, let's stop playing games.'

Eniko was about to protest, stared at Balthazar for several moments, saying nothing. 'OK.' She picked up her mobile phone, flicked through the menus and pressed down on the icon of the recording. Maryam's voice sounded.

They both listened to Maryam talking about the Gardener, Simon's disappearance, and reading out the telephone number. As Maryam spoke, Balthazar took notes in a small black notebook, and wrote down the telephone number. 'Thank you. That must have been a tough interview.'

'It was. I felt like a vulture, preying on her misery.'

'What was she like?'

'Calm, composed, until I showed her the photograph. Very beautiful. Long, black, curly hair halfway down her back. She's a Christian, so she doesn't wear a headscarf.'

'Where is she?'

'At the moneychangers, 46 Rakoczi Way. They said she can stay as long as she wants.'

'Have you called the number?'

Eniko shook her head. 'Not yet.'

'Be careful. Block your outgoing number. Or use a burner when you do.'

Eniko rolled her eyes. 'Thanks, Tazi.'

'You're welcome. The Gypsies she talks about. These are the two "well-known figures in Budapest's underworld" that you wrote about?'

'Yes. They are.'

'How well known?'

'To you, very. That's one reason why I didn't name them.'

'That and because even gangsters have lawyers.'

Eniko laughed. 'Yes. That as well.'

'Can you please send the sound file to me?'

'Of course not. That would leave a data trail. I'm not even supposed to let you listen to it. Now it's your turn. Who beat you up?'

Balthazar smiled, said nothing.

'*Tazi*,' Eniko replied, her voice rising in indignation. 'We had an agreement.'

Balthazar thought for a moment. He could play the police card, accuse her of withholding evidence. But she would likely then walk out and break off contact. He glanced at her flushed face and her eyes shining with annoyance. It was kind of nice to have her around again. And she had looked after him all afternoon, as the doctor had asked. He rummaged in the bowl on the coffee table, under the layers of crumpled receipts, old bills and used tram tickets until his fingers found something small and hard. Plus, he wanted to know what she knew about Fat Vik.

Balthazar handed Eniko a memory stick. 'No data trail. Even I know that. Nobody will ever know.'

She pulled a face, sighed, inserted the memory stick into her laptop and pressed several buttons on her keyboard. Five seconds later she pulled out the stick, handed it to Tazi. 'You didn't get that from me. Now who beat you up?'

Balthazar put the memory stick on the coffee table. He looked at the skin on his knuckles. There were thin red lines where it had cracked open. 'The Gendarmes.'

'A name?'

'Attila Ungar. My former partner.' Eniko took out a small notebook from her handbag and wrote Ungar's name inside.

Balthazar said, 'Be careful. He is dangerous. And very well protected.'

A telephone ring sounded. Balthazar glanced at his handset, which remained silent. Eniko reached for her handbag, took out her iPhone, which was lit and vibrating. She took the call. 'Now? I'm in the middle of something.' She listened for moment, nodding, said, 'OK. I'm on my way.'

She turned to Balthazar. 'Tazi, I'm sorry, I've got to go. It's my editor. Something's come up. I'll call you later. Don't get up. I'll see myself out.'

She walked over to the door and left. Balthazar watched her depart, regret and desire and some emotions he could not even name all mingling with exhaustion.

The clothes he had been wearing earlier, his shirt and jeans, he saw, were folded on an armchair in the corner. He picked his jeans up and went through the pockets. His wallet was still there. He opened it up – credit cards, his police ID, picture of Alex, money, everything was in place. He put the wallet down and reached back inside the ticket pocket for the evidence bag. The pocket was surprisingly large, but it was empty. He quickly checked all the pockets of his jeans. Nothing. He checked all around the armchair, took out the cushion and slid his hand down the side, peered underneath, checked the pockets again. The SIM card had gone.

EIGHT

Dob Street, 7.30 p.m.

Balthazar stepped out of his apartment building. The warm, humid air was heavy with the summer smell of the city: car exhaust, cigarette smoke, the greenery of the park on Klauzal Square. A familiar soundtrack too: a tram trundling by twenty yards away on the Grand Boulevard, raised voices from the faux-Irish pub on the corner across the street, a stream of abuse involving farmyard animals conjoined with various relatives – nobody swore like Hungarians – and a long burst of laughter. Two young women, one blonde, the other brunette, in close-fitting tops and short shorts teetered towards him on high heels, on their way to one of the many nearby *rom-kerts*, ruin pubs. The pubs were a Budapest night-life speciality, ramshackle open-air bars set up in the courtyards of run-down apartment buildings. The brunette openly looked him up and down, eyes wide as she registered the scratches on his face and neck, whispered something to her friend. He watched them walk past, hips swaying.

He smiled as he glanced at his watch: a summer evening in downtown Budapest. It was barely 7.30 p.m. and his city was already getting into gear for another night of partying. Eniko had left just over an hour ago. Balthazar had bathed and eaten a tin of tomato soup he had found at the back of the cupboard. The bath and the food had revived him. The pain was manageable now, a steady ache, dulled by paracetamol. The iron bar in his head had not vanished but had definitely shrunk and stabilised. Even so, he knew that his respite and new-found energy were fleeting. He was now on alert, running partly on adrenalin, but that would fade in an hour or two. So would the paracetamol.

He looked across the street. A short, overweight man in his forties, wearing a stained vest and lurid yellow shorts, was leaning against the wall, cigarette in one hand, bottle of Dreher beer in another. He nodded at Balthazar in greeting. Csaba Kiss was the owner of the twenty-four-hour ABC grocery store on the corner of Dob Street and Klauzal Street. Balthazar nodded back. The shop served as an impromptu pub for those who could not afford to drink in the Irish pub, or any actual bar. Csaba's cronies would soon start gathering for an evening of carousing inside and out on the pavement. The nightly gatherings were technically illegal, but Balthazar had no intention of intervening. Csaba always shut down the party around ten p.m., considered the time when decent people were readying themselves for bed. He raised his bottle to Balthazar: 'Want one?' Balthazar thanked him, shook his head.

Balthazar checked the row of parked cars on both sides of the road: all were empty. There was nobody he could see who looked out of place, or trying to look like they belonged, waiting or lurking behind a newspaper, or playing with a smartphone. The door of his apartment building opened behind him and he looked back. The six-storey, flat-fronted building had been built in the 1930s, with a restrained, modernist elegance. Balthazar had bought his flat five years ago for the equivalent of €35,000. It was now worth three times that. In the last decade District VII had transformed from a rundown part of the inner city into a major European hipster destination. The quarter's narrow streets and tree-lined squares were packed every night with Budapest's bohemians and tourists. Csaba's ABC was one of the last bastions. No doubt, it too would soon be turned into an artisan coffee bar or street food eatery.

Balthazar's apartment building, untouched for decades, was now restored to its art deco prime. Each flat had a small balcony with curved railings. Stylised reliefs of workers and families marked each floor on the front of the apartment house. A plaque by the front door commemorated Laszlo Seres, the composer of 'Gloomy Sunday', who had lived in the building until he'd had too many Sundays altogether and jumped from his balcony.

Eva *neni*, Auntie Eva, stepped outside. Dressed in her usual floral housecoat, her grey hair tied up in a bun, Eva *neni* was barely five feet tall. She lived alone in a small flat on the ground floor, from where she was responsible for looking after the building. She guarded her territory as ferociously as any bulldog and even in her eighties, her eyesight – and street smarts – were as sharp as ever. Eva *neni* had lived in the building all her life. Her only daughter had moved to London a decade ago, taking her children with her. Eva *neni* didn't like aeroplanes and the daughter came home once a year at the most. Eva had since then more or less adopted Balthazar. She looked him up and down, taking in the plasters across his knuckles, the bruises around his mouth and scratches on his face. 'I hope you gave it back twice as bad,' she said, her voice sharp.

He smiled. 'I tried.'

She shook her head. 'Are you OK, Tazi? You look like you should be in bed.'

He looked at his watch. 'I will be soon. A couple of errands I need to run.'

Her face softened. 'You need something? Apart from a wife? Food? Soup? You know where I am.'

Balthazar laughed. 'Thanks. I'm fine. Let me know if you find any candidates.'

Eva *neni*'s bright-blue eyes narrowed. 'I saw your friend leave here before. She's very pretty. Are you...'

'*Friends*. Yes. We are.'

'Your handsome son. When's he coming over?'

'Tomorrow.' Balthazar's voice turned serious. 'Eva *neni*, can you do something for me?'

Eva *neni* nodded. 'Of course.'

'Keep an eye on the place for me. I'll be back in a couple of hours. Let me know if you see any—'

Eva *neni* finished his sentence for him. '... suspicious characters. What do you think I have been doing ever since I've known you, Detective Kovacs?'

Balthazar leaned forward and kissed Eva on her cheek. 'Thanks.' She blushed and pushed him away, her manner brusque but her eyes alight with pleasure. 'Get going, then.'

He turned right onto Klauzal Square. The open space was lined on all sides by apartment buildings, low-rise by downtown Budapest's standards, many just two or three storeys high, some dating back to the early nineteenth century. During the Second World War, Klauzal Square and its surrounds had been the heart of the Jewish ghetto. After the Arrow Cross took power in October 1944, Klauzal Square had been a giant open-air graveyard, where frozen bodies had been stacked up like logs. Eva *neni* had told him graphic stories of how she survived the war, hiding in cellars and attics from the Arrow Cross militiamen who had roamed here, rounding up Jews before marching them down to the banks of the Danube and shooting them into the river.

Balthazar glanced at the square. It was hard to reconcile the tranquil summer evening with what had happened here decades ago. A huddle of teenagers stood by the entrance, smoking and passing a bottle of wine from hand to hand, tinny rap music drifting across the street from their mobile phones. Half a dozen neat green Bubi bikes, municipal bicycles, were parked in their docks, waiting for their next riders. The square itself was now a green oasis, with lush grass, verdant trees, neat paths and flowerbeds, and a modern playground. A woman in her thirties, blonde hair tied back in a ponytail under a blue baseball cap, sat on a bench on the other side of the square, facing the street, reading that day's issue of *Magyar Vilag*. Balthazar did a quick double take. She looked vaguely familiar. Had he seen her before? He was not sure. And the baseball cap was obscuring her face.

He put the thought aside and walked onto Klauzal Street. Here, many of the buildings were still ramshackle, unrestored, their doors and entrance areas covered with graffiti. The tiny shops offered the services of watch-repairers, cobblers and denture-makers. The street was straight and quite narrow, which meant it was easy for any followers to track him. But easy too, for Balthazar to spot them. Just before Klauzal Street ended on the corner of Wesselenyi Street, he reached into his trouser pocket and took out a packet of chewing gum. He squeezed out a single piece then dropped the packet, turning to look back as he picked it up. The street was empty. No sign of any watchers or the woman in the baseball cap reading *Magyar Vilag*.

No sign, either, of the SIM card that he had found that morning. He had looked around his flat, checking the bed, the area around the chair, anywhere where it might have fallen out. The most likely answer, he knew, was that Eniko had taken it while he was asleep. Which was actually quite serious, and a crime. The SIM card was his main lead, although he had to admit that Eniko had found out more than he had so far. It was clear now that the dead man was Simon Nazir, and that Hungarian government officials were somehow involved in selling passports. As was Gaspar. He took his phone from his pocket, scrolled down the menu, called up Eniko's number and was about to press dial, when he stopped himself. This was not a conversation for the phone.

He walked across Wesselenyi Street, continued on Klauzal Street past the empty lots untouched since Allied bombing raids in the Second World War, and the modern glass-and-concrete office buildings that were completely unsympathetic to their surroundings, until the end of Klauzal where it met Rakoczi Street. There he turned left and walked up Rakoczi, crossing Blaha Lujza Square into District VIII and then further up Rakoczi Way, heading for the moneychangers' shop, where Maryam was staying. Deep in thought about how he could persuade his brother to get out of this business, at least while the refugee crisis continued, Balthazar did not notice the man handing out flyers for the Bella Roma restaurant watching him, then take out his phone.

Kovacs family residence, Jozsef Street, 8.00 p.m.

There were twenty-two districts in Budapest, and District VIII was one of the largest. Its lower edge touched the *belvaros*, the inner city, facing the Astoria Hotel, a historic landmark on the edge of the Jewish quarter that had served as Adolf Eichmann's headquarters in 1944. Under Communism, despite its central location, this had been a ramshackle, dilapidated quarter. Now the wide streets and elegant tree-lined squares of the southern part of District VIII had been renamed the Palace Quarter, to attract foreign investors who were buying up the fine old villas and mansion blocks here and turning them into boutique hotels and trendy cafés. The upper sector, a couple of miles away, was another world. Bordered by Hungaria Boulevard, it was lined with *panel-lakasok* estates, cramped tenements flats named for the slabs of concrete from which they had been constructed in the 1970s and 1980s.

The Gypsy quarter, sometimes known as 'Chekago', lay somewhere in the middle, concentrated in the narrow, nineteenth-century side streets that ran north from the Grand Boulevard, the inner-city ring road. Jozsef Street, site of Balthazar's childhood home, was in the heart of Chekago. The door to the courtyard at number fifteen was open when he arrived, and a small crowd milled around. They tried not to stare at the scratches and bruises on his face, and made way for Balthazar as he stepped inside. Gaspar, he saw, was in his usual place: sitting on an oversized white leather sofa in the middle of the courtyard, watching Fat Vik hand over an envelope to an elderly, grey-haired lady who was dressed in a shabby blue polyester blouse and worn slippers. She clasped his hand, bent over and kissed it, thanking him repeatedly, pouring blessings on Fat Vik, Gaspar and his family.

Fat Vik wore an oversized black T-shirt and a pair of loose grey jogging pants. His nickname was apt – he weighed at least two hundred pounds and had a substantial belly that preceded him. Vik gently moved the woman's hand and guided her away. Balthazar stepped forward and greeted Vik and his brother. Gaspar smiled, revealing two rows of mainly gold teeth, and tried, too quickly, to stand up. Defeated by his bulk, he sank back down into the sofa. Gaspar was even bigger than Fat Vik. Vik stood up and offered his arm to Gaspar. Gaspar raised himself again, this time successfully.

Balthazar winced as Gaspar hugged him. Steel bolts of pain shot around his chest and midriff. '*Batyam*,' wheezed Gaspar. 'How are you?'

'I'm fine, *ocsim*,' said Balthazar, gently disentangling himself from Gaspar's embrace. 'A few bruises. It's nothing.'

Gaspar stepped back, looked Balthazar up and down, stared into his eyes. He touched the side of Balthazar's face, his stubby fingers surprisingly gentle. Balthazar breathed in his brother's odour – tobacco and sweat, mixed with the tang of alcohol and something else, indefinable, warm and familiar: the smell of home.

'You were knocked out. That's something. You have to take it easy. Why didn't you call for help? Fat Vik and *nagy* Laci and *kis* Laci were nearby.' He gestured across the courtyard. *Nagy* Laci and *kis* Laci were Big Laci and Little Laci, two dark-skinned, burly men in their early twenties who stood smoking nearby, keeping a wary eye on the long queue of people standing waiting. The two Lacis were cousins, distant relatives of Balthazar and Gaspar. The cousins had grown up in a children's home, joining Gaspar as soon as they turned eighteen. They caught Balthazar's eye and nodded.

Balthazar nodded back. The two Lacis had started out as runners and lookouts. After a while, they had progressed to distributing bribes to the local cops to turn a blind eye to Gaspar's streetwalkers. They now worked as Gaspar's bodyguards and enforcers. Both spent several hours in the gym every day and certainly would have changed the odds in Balthazar's favour.

'Thanks,' said Balthazar. 'But there was no time.'

Gaspar looked him up and down. '*Batyam*. If you don't want a couple of girls to look after you, I'll send the Lacis to stay with you for a few days. I think you need them more than me.'

Balthazar laughed, the movement sending fresh bolts of pain across his ribs. They both knew that Balthazar could not be seen in public, let alone go to work at the Budapest police headquarters, accompanied by two known associates of the most powerful pimp and brothel owner in the city.

Gaspar continued talking. 'Five against one. These *gadje*,' he said, turning to the side, making to spit on the floor. 'Come, sit down. We'll talk soon.'

Balthazar shook his head. 'I'll come back tomorrow. I forgot what day it is.'

'See, I told you you need to rest. You are here now, where you should be. And you are not going anywhere, except over there.' He pointed at a white leather armchair, next to the sofa.

Balthazar sat down and watched the supplicants line up in front of Gaspar. His visit to the moneychangers' on Rakoczi Way to look for Maryam had not been successful. The father, who ran the business, somehow sensed, perhaps because of Balthazar's battered appearance, that this was not official police business. He had denied any knowledge of Maryam or any refugees and told him to come back with a search warrant if he wanted to look inside. The vehemence of his denials confirmed to Balthazar that Maryam was inside. But legally the father was correct and there was no chance of obtaining a warrant at this time on a Friday night.

While Balthazar had thick black hair, Gaspar kept his head shaved. The evening was still hot and sticky, and little air flowed in the crowded courtyard, but Gaspar wore an over-size black silk shirt, open halfway to his midriff to display a thick gold chain with oversized links, and a pair of baggy, shiny trackpants. On his surprisingly dainty feet, he wore handmade black patent loafers, each with a diamond-studded brooch. Heavy jowls hung from either side of his face and his brown eyes were set deep in a doughy face. Obesity, like lavish hospitality, was a sign of prosperity in Gypsy culture. Even without the pile of envelopes stuffed with cash, there was no danger of anyone believing Gaspar to be poor. There were three heavy rings on the fingers of each hand, bright gold, inset with a heavy stone, either a ruby or emerald.

There was no shame in Gypsy culture in conspicuous displays of wealth. Rather, the opposite was the case. Good fortune – however acquired – was meant to be a public affair. Weddings, christenings and funerals were lavish affairs, awash with food and drink. District VIII was home to numerous 'businessmen' who operated on the edge of, or far beyond, legality, but Gaspar was one of the best known. Keeping a low profile, not being ostentatious, would have been met with suspicion. But with wealth came responsibilities, and an obligation to help others, bound by kinship, friendship or just neighbourliness.

Outsiders often believed Gypsy society to be wild and anarchic. In fact, it was governed by strict social codes, the breaking of which could lead to severe consequences, such as ostracism. The first, and most important principle, was loyalty to the family. Family came first, beyond anything else. When the Nazis deported Gypsies to the concentration camps, they refused to be separated from their children. They resisted so ferociously that the Germans decided to let Gypsies live together in Auschwitz, in what was known as the 'family camp', although its residents too were eventually gassed. After family, came friends and neighbours.

There were about twenty people milling around the courtyard in a sort of queue. An elderly man, his gaunt face covered in white stubble, stood at the front of the group. He wore scuffed black plastic shoes and brown trousers held up by an oversized belt and a look of vague shame on his face. The man seemed familiar, and Balthazar realised that he knew him: it was Zoli *bacsi*, Uncle Zoli, his former mathematics teacher at Fazekas school. Balthazar knew that Zoli *bacsi*'s wife, Boglarka, was bedbound. Between them, they existed on a pension of 150,000 forints, about five hundred euros, a month. Zoli *bacsi* caught Balthazar's eye and gave him a wan smile.

Behind Zoli *bacsi* stood a woman in her early thirties, pale, overweight, with dyed blonde hair and dark roots. She wore a pink shell suit, and carried a sleeping baby in one arm while holding a toddler's hand in another. Judit, one of Gaspar's working girls, walked up and down the line, carrying a tray loaded with bottles of cola and mineral water and a bowl of sweets. Balthazar watched her crouch down and offer drinks and sweets to the toddler. Judit wore a miniskirt and a black spaghetti-strap top. She was a plump brunette from Budaors, a small town just outside the capital. A law student at Budapest University, Judit mostly worked as an escort and only occasionally slept with her clients.

The first Friday evening of every month was known as *boritek este*, envelope evening. Friends, relatives, anyone local in need, with some kind of connection to the Kovacs clan, could attend and make their case. It was very rare for a supplicant to be refused. There were three piles of envelopes on the low coffee table in front of the sofa. The first contained a 10,000-forint note, the equivalent of around thirty euros, the second, a 20,000-forint note, and the third,

30,000 forints. Everyone received an envelope and only rarely did Gaspar consult with his *consigliere* about which to hand out. Alongside the envelopes was a large crystal bowl filled with wrapped sweets, a silver tray, where rows of individual cigarettes were laid out, and a second bowl piled high with nuts and dried fruits.

Each month the queue grew longer. Pal Dezeffy, the prime minister, had won the election by promising to redistribute the country's wealth. He had kept his promise. Hungary's wealth had indeed been redistributed – to Dezeffy's straw men, his associates, his and their families. Most nights, when Balthazar went home he found homeless people rummaging through the dustbins, looking not just for something they could sell, but for something to eat. Sometimes Eva *neni* left packets of sandwiches inside a plastic bag on top of the bins.

Balthazar checked his watch. Dusk was slowly falling, the fading light and long shadows softening the edges of the tenement building. As Zoli *bacsi* stepped forward, Gaspar pointed at the third pile. Fat Vik handed over the envelope. Gaspar stood up, his giant bulk wobbling, and the two men shook hands.

Despite the heat, as a mark of respect, nobody in the court-yard wore shorts. The central law of the Romani social code is the distinction between 'honour' and 'shame', which can also be understood as 'clean' and 'defiled', or *mahrime* in the Romani language. The distinction starts at the human body. The upper part is considered clean and may be exposed without shame or disrespect. Roma men may invoke *gadjes'* distaste by not wearing shirts, but there is no shame in being bare-chested, or Gaspar having a shirt open down to his midriff. Gypsy women may go braless in scanty tops, breast-feed their children in public, but the popular stereotype of the

Romani seductress is erroneous – and Gypsy society also has very strict sexual codes that do not allow even the discussion of sexual acts in front of women.

The lower body, however, is unclean and must not be displayed. Like Orthodox Jews, Gypsies believe that menstrual blood is a pollutant. Orthodox Jewish women sleep separately from their husbands for seven days before and after their period. Romani women are not banished from the marital bed but their skirts must never come into contact with anything to do with food, such as pans or cutlery. If a woman wished to humiliate a man, make him *mahrime*, she only needed to wave her skirts over his body.

Sitting in the courtyard, waiting for his brother, triggered a rush of memories. By the standards of Budapest's inner city, the building was comparatively small. There were four flats on each floor, two on either side, and a central staircase that stood in the middle. The courtyard was about eight yards wide and ten deep. The front doors of the ground-floor flats opened straight onto the courtyards. An inner balcony snaked around the first and second floors, held in place by ornamental buttresses underneath, each with a metal fence topped with a wooden handrail. The building had been ramshackle and dilapidated while Balthazar was growing up, the stucco peeling, the courtyard tiles cracked and broken, cables dangling, the metal fence so loose in places that it seemed about to fall off. A century before, the building had stained-glass windows looking out from the central staircase, but they had long been broken, replaced by plain glass and ugly aluminium frames.

Balthazar had grown up here, one of five children, three boys and two girls. His earliest memories were of living in a cramped three-room flat on the third floor, with a toilet in the courtyard. Laszlo, his father, had run a handful of local streetwalkers. Marta, his mother, kept the family home. With his profits, Laszlo had bought a nightclub, with an attached strip club and row of private cubicles. The private cubicles, he soon realised, were the biggest money-makers and he branched out into brothels.

As Laszlo's business grew, the family expanded their living space, buying neighbouring flats, removing walls or installing doors. The change of system in 1990, and the arrival of *vadkapitalizmus*, wild capitalism, brought lucrative new opportunities. The state had owned vast amounts of property, but when the state no longer existed it was easily acquired. Balthazar's father had followed a well-honed path: he set up a company to buy the flats from the municipality. The company received a loan from the bank. After a couple of months, the company sold the flats to Laszlo's relatives at a knock-down price. The company went bust and the bank loan was written off. Any 'difficulties' were smoothed out by well-stuffed envelopes. Laszlo bought up several dozen flats across Districts VI, VII and VIII. Some of them he sold on, but he had retained almost twenty. Most were rented out, but three or four were used by his working girls. By the mid-1990s, the family had taken over all of number 15 Jozsef Street. Balthazar and all his brothers and sisters had their own rooms, for most children in Jozseftown an unimaginable luxury. The apartments were now all occupied by Balthazar's siblings and their children and his parents. Fat Vik and the Lacis also had their own places. Now the paintwork was fresh and even, the cracked brickwork repaired. Even the stained glass had been replaced.

Balthazar's older brother, Melchior, had become a musician, spent much of his time travelling with his group, Roma Drom, Roma Way, on the international festival circuit.

Balthazar's two sisters were both younger than him. Ildiko had married one of the family's many cousins. She kept the books – one set for the authorities and another that showed the actual money movements – and still lived in the family building, on the top floor with her husband and three children. Flora, the youngest, ran a hipster art gallery on Brody Sandor Street, in the heart of the Palace Quarter in District VIII. To the shock and dismay of her parents, she lived alone in her own flat, not far from Balthazar, on Wesselenyi Street in District VII. Flora was away with Marta this weekend, visiting relatives in the countryside.

Balthazar glimpsed movement by a window on the top floor. A male profile, bulky, familiar. His father stood there, looking down, but gave no sign of recognition. Balthazar closed his eyes for a moment, trying and failing to ignore the stew of feelings that the sight of his father triggered.

Gaspar, he told himself. He was here because of Gaspar. As if sensing his thoughts, he felt Gaspar's gaze on him. A look passed between the two brothers, layered with affection, love, mutual exasperation and more.

Finally, the line of supplicants ended. Fat Vik picked up the last few envelopes and sat down next to Gaspar. Gaspar gestured to his brother to sit next to him on the sofa.

'*Mond*, tell me,' said Gaspar.

Balthazar took out his notepad and read out the phone number that Maryam had told Eniko. 'Mean anything to you?' he asked his brother. Gaspar shook his head, turned to his *consigliere*. 'Nope,' said Fat Vik. 'Whose number is it?'

'That's what I'd like to know,' said Balthazar. He took out his telephone and called up the photograph of Simon Nazir. 'What about him? Familiar?' he asked, as he passed the handset to his brother.

Gaspar grimaced as he looked at the picture of the dead man. 'Not to me.' He gave the telephone to Fat Vik. 'Do we know him?'

Fat Vik stared at Nazir's body for several seconds. 'We did.'

NINE

Eniko Szalay was not sure which was making her more uncomfortable: the whisky fumes that Roland Horvath was breathing over her, or the fact that he was sitting so close to her that she had no choice but to inhale them. 'Kriszta was waiting for you in her office at two o'clock. So was I,' he said.

Eniko closed her eyes for a second. *Shit.* She had completely forgotten that she was due to meet with the news editor that afternoon. But there had been no mention of Roland. Why had he been there as well? He continued talking, 'And you didn't call or message her. She tried to call you but could not get through.'

Contrition, Eniko decided. Contrition, and mild – very mild – flirtation if absolutely necessary. Lately, Horvath had been coming on quite strongly to Eniko, with clumsy attempts at gallantry. Hungary was an old-fashioned society where working women had to contend with a much higher level of sexism than their western counterparts. Middle-aged men, especially, still seemed to think that a stream of compliments and comments on a female colleague's appearance were a likely path to seduction. Thankfully, apart from being over-attentive, Horvath was still behaving himself in the office. His hands did not wander. But now they were having

140

an after-work drink, at his insistence, and she was scared they soon would. Eniko could have thought up an excuse, she supposed, but on balance had decided it was better to get the encounter over and done with.

Horvath reminding Eniko of her missed meeting was a way to get her on the back foot. Horvath was trying to show her who was in control, even outside the office. But she also had some weapons in her armoury. The editor of 555.hu was a lonely divorcee, she knew. His former wife, Julia, was now the government's spokeswoman. Julia was married to the mayor of District VIII. Horvath had a teenage daughter called Wanda he adored but rarely saw. Eniko had several times seen him browsing Wanda's Facebook feed on his office computer.

Eniko turned to Horvath, leaning in closer. 'Roland, I am so sorry. My phone was stolen. But of course I could have got a message to her. It's completely inexcusable, especially as I also wasted your time. Not too much, I hope. Let me get you another whisky,' she said, resting her hand on his arm.

Horvath glanced down at her hand, turned pink. 'No, I'm fine. Thanks.' He kept looking down at his arm. She lifted her hand up, picked up her mineral water and sipped it, feeling guilty and uncomfortable. Was that all it took?

They were sitting on an old school bench on the top floor of Retro-kert, the oldest, largest and best known of the ruin pubs in District VII, on Kazinczy Street, a couple of minutes' walk from Balthazar's flat on Dob Street. Retro-kert took up the whole building. The walls were raw brick, covered with spray-painted graffiti, torn flyers and hand-written notes. The floor was bare concrete, the furniture a shambolic array of old-school furniture and cheap office chairs. Three Trabants stood in the centre of the courtyard, each with its roof removed. A decade ago, Retro-kert had been edgy, an outlier crowded with Budapest's bohemians. It was now in every guide book. Eniko had not been back for years.

Loud shouts in English and cheers carried up from the ground floor. She glanced down, grimacing as she watched a pale man in a vest and Union flag shorts carry a tray of beers to his friends. A woman, slim, in her thirties, her dark-blonde hair tied back in a ponytail, walked in. She was not exactly pretty, but she had strong features that made you look twice. The blonde woman passed the stag party, smiled in an amused way at their invitations to sit down, and walked over to the far corner of the ground-floor bar area. She looked familiar. Where had she seen her?

Roland watched Eniko looking at the scene on the ground floor. 'What is it?'

Eniko smiled. 'Nothing. Just another stag party.'

Eniko watched him look down at the boisterous group. He was about to turn back to her when his eye caught something. He was staring hard at the far corner of the bar, where the blonde woman had sat down, she noticed. He turned back to her, picked up his whisky and took a large swallow. Then Eniko remembered. At Keleti Station. The blonde woman was a taxi driver, always hanging around outside. What was she doing here? Why was a taxi driver making Roland nervous? Or maybe she was just over-thinking things.

'Really, Roland,' said Eniko, pointing at his drink. 'Let me get you another one.'

Roland shook his head. 'No, no, don't worry. One is enough. I'm sorry about your phone.' His voice turned serious. 'But where were you?'

Sitting on my ex-boyfriend's bed, wondering if I had made

a huge mistake, after he was beaten unconscious by the Gendarmes, then doing something so appalling for a story that I don't even want to think about it, she wanted to say.

'With a contact. Working on the refugee story.' That was more or less true, she thought to herself. Or at least a version of the truth, which was good enough. 'There's so much material. And the refugees keep coming in. It's amazing that there has not been a riot at Keleti.'

Horvath frowned. 'They are not all refugees. We need to talk about our house style. Half of them – more probably – are economic migrants. I see a lot of fit, healthy, young men in their twenties. Not so many women and children. Wasn't there a mini-riot today? Someone was attacked. A cop, I heard.'

Eniko was about to answer when Horvath's iPhone beeped. Eniko sneaked a glance as he checked his screen. A text message, she saw. Just a time: 9.00 p.m. No name or initial or number showing. That was curious. She glanced at her boss. Worry, even anxiety, flickered across his face. Who was he meeting? But at least she could escape in twenty minutes at the most, perhaps less. 'Anything important? Do you have to go?' she asked, making sure to keep the hope from her voice.

He glanced quickly downstairs, Eniko noticed. 'No. I'm meeting someone here later.'

He put his phone down, turned to Eniko, fixed her with his pale-blue eyes.

'What do you know about the attack at Keleti today?'

'Not much. Only what I saw on YouTube.'

Horvath frowned. 'You've spent days there. You must have some contacts. A policeman was beaten up.' He thought for a moment. 'Where you there?'

Eniko nodded. 'At Keleti. Yes.'

'Then why didn't you file something? An eyewitness account, some colour, anything? We could have had it up on the website immediately.'

Eniko thought quickly. That was a good question. But not one she would answer truthfully. 'I was on the other side of the Transit Zone, interviewing a family from Afghanistan. By the time I walked over to see what was happening, it was all over.' She looked at him, gave him her brightest smile. 'Sorry, Roland. It seemed quite a minor thing, compared to everything else going on.'

Eniko had planned to go back to the moneychangers on Rakoczi Way to check up on Maryam after she left Balthazar's flat. But Roland had called, insisting that they get together so she could bring him up to date on her progress. And she'd been ready to leave Balthazar's flat. Horvath's whisky breath was at least a distraction from the powerful sense of guilt that she felt. She had several times forced herself to ignore the overriding urge to touch the right-hand pocket of her jeans, and check that the SIM was still there.

'It's not minor. It's major,' said Horvath, his voice focused now. 'The guy who was attacked was a cop. Balthazar Kovacs. A detective. You know him, I believe.'

Eniko thought quickly. Roland was a recent arrival. Her relationship with Balthazar had ended six months ago. Her editor was sharper, or better informed, than she had realised. 'I know lots of people,' she said, wary now. 'That's my job.'

'Not like you know him.'

Eniko sat very still. Had he really said that? 'I don't think my personal life is any of your business, Roland.' Her voice was cold.

Roland flushed again, took a sip of his whisky to cover his embarrassment. He had stepped over a line and knew it.

'No. And I apologise for that remark. But, you were at Keleti when a policeman was attacked. You didn't file anything. The policeman is a Gypsy, who you... have some knowledge of. You yourself wrote that "two well-known Roma figures in the Budapest underworld" are rumoured to be connected to a people-smuggling operation. Are they linked to the detective who got attacked? It's your job to make the connections. You are absolutely right about your personal life. It's nothing to do with your job. Let's keep them separate. But a reporter files reports. Do your job, please.'

Eniko nodded. She had been outmanoeuvred. 'Yes. I will. Sorry.'

Horvath continued talking. 'OK. Who are the "two well-known Roma figures in the Budapest underworld"?'

My former boyfriend's brother and his *consigliere*, Eniko thought, but did not say. 'I'm trying to get some more details, but I don't have enough to get it past the lawyers yet.'

'I am the editor. I take the lawyer's advice. But I decide what runs. So you can tell me. Who are they?'

For a moment she was back on Balthazar's bed, watching him while he was asleep, breathing slowly, his battered face restful. Balthazar's connection to his brother was common knowledge among the police and Gaspar's 'associates' but was not in the public domain. The two-way channel was useful for both sides to exchange information. And Eniko still felt a kind of loyalty to Gaspar, who had once stepped in when her family needed him.

Eniko's father, once a high-ranking Communist Party official, had walked out in the late 1980s, defecting while on a trade mission to Vienna, where he had been having an affair with an Austrian civil servant. Eniko's mother had raised her and her brother alone at a time when single parents were rare and unsupported, battling an indifferent bureaucracy, a very conservative society and hostile in-laws. Eniko's mother was an attractive woman, had remarried and had borne another child. David was seventeen, a gangly teenager, and also went to Fazekas school. The middle-class children were no match for the gangs of street toughs who occasionally waylaid them on their way home in the backstreets of District VIII. After David had his iPhone stolen, Gaspar made some enquiries. The iPhone was returned two hours later. David was not bothered again.

So she did not feel like giving Gaspar up. In any case, what was this about? Horvath had never shown so much interest in one of her stories before. Play for time, she decided. 'Umm... I don't have my notes with me, Roland. It's been a very long day.'

Eniko glanced around. A window was pulled shut nearby. There was no smoking in the bar but the room was hot and airless. Her boss had mild but intrusive body odour, smelling of sweat. She smiled at him, pointed at the window. 'Would you mind if I opened that?' she asked. Horvath nodded, and after a second or two realised that he needed to move away from her and let her through. She opened the window and sat back down, this time a good yard away. He noticed the movement and would, Eniko thought, doubtless exert his power by asking again for the names of the 'two well-known Roma figures'.

She needed to pre-empt that, for there was no real reason why a reporter would not share such information with her editor, especially when operating in legally murky waters. There was only thing she could think of. She turned to him and smiled, 'How's Wanda? How old is she now? Thirteen? You must very proud of her.'

Horvath's face softened. 'Almost fourteen. They grow up so fast.'

'You must have some photographs. I'd love to see them,' said Eniko, feeling vaguely ashamed of herself for dragging Horvath's daughter into the conversation.

Her boss did not seem to mind. He quickly took out his iPhone and called up the photographs. A tall, pretty girl with large brown eyes stared out from the screen. Eniko smiled and nodded, made encouraging noises as Horvath scrolled through several photographs, talking Eniko through Wanda's school exams, her love of horse riding, how he wished he could spend more time with her. 'I only get to see her every other weekend. I am supposed to get one evening twice a month as well, but she's so busy with her schoolwork and horse riding...' he said, swallowing hard, and picking up his whisky.

Eniko felt a curious pang, a kind of longing mixed in with her sense of shame. Shame at exploiting Horvath's loneliness and love for his daughter. And longing for a father who wanted to see his daughter as much as Horvath did. Her father was a shadowy figure in her memories, occasionally appearing for birthday or name day celebrations or sending gifts, but never present in any meaningful way. Lately, after Eniko's increasing success and fame as a reporter, he had been reaching out to her. She sometimes returned his calls.

Horvath was still for a moment, a wistful look on his face, then he put his phone away. He sat up straight, his demeanour businesslike now. 'So, Eniko. I'd like a memo from you, outlining what you know about the Roma connection to the people-smuggling operation, how we can cover it and where the story might go. We need to make the running on this. We need to move on from Keleti and take the story forward.'

'OK. When?'

Horvath thought for a moment. 'Tomorrow.'

'Tomorrow is Saturday,' replied Eniko, aware how feeble she sounded.

Horvath raised his eyebrows. 'It is. But if you want a nine-to-five job, there are some openings in the administrative department.' He paused. 'Monday morning. First thing. I expect something clear and detailed.'

Eniko nodded. 'I'm on it.'

'Good. Because we have something else to talk about.' He sipped his drink. 'An exciting potential opportunity for you.'

Eniko's internal radar started pinging rapidly. She knew her editor well enough to know that what he considered exciting was likely to be less appealing to her. 'I'm listening.'

'Mr Kaplan is increasing his investment. We are going to expand. We will be hiring new recruits, covering new areas. And you can be a key part of that. In a new executive role.'

The news, not completely unexpected, triggered mixed emotions. Eniko loved being on the trail of a story, digging deep for the key nuggets of information, persuading contacts to talk, putting it all together. It was still a thrill to see her work on the website with her name underneath the headline. But as 555.hu's most experienced reporter, she had also watched many of her junior colleagues make novice mistakes: approaching a story from an obscure angle, speaking to the wrong people, or asking the wrong questions when they found the right people. Increasingly, they asked Eniko for help and guidance, rather than Kriszta, the news editor. There was even talk of a reporters' delegation making an official approach to management to replace Kriszta with Eniko. Eniko knew she could contribute more as news editor, guiding her colleagues, than as a reporter. She had even considered opening a conversation with Roland about taking on a wider role in the newsroom. But the refugee crisis was the biggest news story she had ever worked on, so she wanted to stay on the beat for at least a while. Now, however, it seemed management had realised of its own accord that she was editor material.

Eniko swirled the remnants of a melting ice cube in her mineral water, then looked at Horvath. 'Thanks, Roland. I think Kriszta can still bring a lot to 555, but you are right, her skill set isn't quite right for the newsroom. I am definitely interested, but could we hold off, at least until the migrant crisis has eased?'

Horvath frowned. 'I am not sure what you are talking about, Eniko. Kriszta will remain as news editor. In fact she will have increased day-to-day responsibilities, overseeing the news diary and the reporters' assignments.'

A weight appeared in Eniko's stomach. 'She's staying?'

'Absolutely. In fact, we are bringing in her deputy from the state news agency as well. There will be much tighter manage-ment of the whole newsroom operation. I will be overseeing both of them, of course,' Horvath added quickly.

The weight turned heavier. This was a disaster. 'Then what would I be doing?'

'It's a new challenge for you and a great opportunity. But I am absolutely confident that you can rise to the occasion.' Horvath took out his wallet and fished inside. It was sleek black leather, with a white-gold clasp, Eniko saw, its three compartments filled with 5,000-, 10,000- and 20,000-forint notes. As far as she knew, he earned around 300,000 forints a month, had a mortgage and was expected to contribute to Wanda's fees at the American school. Where did all that money come from? 'The drinks are on me,' Horvath said.

'Can you please tell me what?' asked Eniko, barely able to keep the exasperation from her voice.

'Sandor Kaplan has purchased Szilky.hu. The site will keep its name but will be absorbed into the 555 brand. Mr Kaplan thinks – and Kriszta and I agree – that Szilky needs a new editor.' He turned to her, raised his glass. 'Congratulations.'

Royal salon, Buda Castle, 9.00 p.m.

The Qatari businessman stared down at Reka Bardossy's breasts as he asked, 'And who do you work for, my dear?'

They work for me, because they are attached to me, Reka felt like replying. Instead, she smiled sweetly, glanced again at the name tag on the pocket of his dark-blue Brioni suit: Abdullah al-Nuri, business development director and executive vice-president, before she answered. 'I work for the prime minister, Mr Al-Nuri.'

So far, this had proved easy but dull. Al-Nuri was in his early sixties, short, paunchy and balding with straggly black hair that was too dark to be natural. He had talked about himself for five minutes without a break before asking this, his first question. She had merely smiled and nodded every now and then, which seemed to be all he expected. She wore a black, long-sleeved Donna Karan cocktail dress, a grey silk-and-cashmere pashmina over her shoulders for modesty's sake, and white Christian Louboutins with hundred-millimetre heels. Her outfit, elegant but restrained, had turned the head of every male in the room, and drawn barbed looks from many of the women present. So far everything had gone to plan, apart from the growing ache in her calf muscles and balls of her feet. The hundred-millimetre heels, she realised, would be OK for a dinner or a theatre outing, but were a mistake for a standing reception.

Al-Nuri, one of the most important guests at the Hungarian government reception, was to be humoured and entertained, she had been instructed. She was to laugh at his jokes, flirt if necessary, make him feel as though he was the centre of her world. That was all, thankfully. Anything more would be supplied by the city's most upmarket madame who had been paid to keep all her *oromlanyok*, joy girls, free for the evening and ready to work at a moment's notice, once the reception was over.

The business development director was in charge of a planned ten-billion-dollar investment. If the development went ahead, Hungary would be catapulted out of its post-Communist torpor. New cities would be built in the impoverished east. Cracked and pitted two-lane roads would be turned into smooth motorways. A high-speed rail link would reach to Vienna, and on to Frankfurt. The country would be blanketed in super-fast broadband. A state-of-the-art medical centre would be built in Budapest to attract patients from across the Arab world. And while the government and state media railed against the migrants and refugees at Keleti, other, richer immigrants were more welcome. An investment of €500,000 in Hungarian government bonds would bring immediate permanent residence for the bondholder, his parents and children, with a fast, smooth path promised to citizenship and a Hungarian passport, which meant the right to live anywhere in the European Union. Mr Al-Nuri, and several of his colleagues, had already been offered such benefits as a 'goodwill gesture', without having to invest a single euro.

Reka glanced across the room. Pal Dezeffy was in the corner, nodding enthusiastically as the Qatari ambassador spoke to him. The reception was taking place in the grandest salon of the Buda Castle. Dezeffy had recently spent hundreds of millions of forints refurbishing a palatial suite of offices overlooking the city. The building work on the outside was still going on. The rooms had barely been used. After a couple of weeks overlooking the Danube, Dezeffy tired of the view and realised that he preferred to be at the epicentre of political intrigue, rather than overlooking it.

The government protocol department had gone all-out. Attractive young male and female waiters circulated with silver trays of mineral water, fruit juices, several types of colas, and canapés. There was no pork or alcohol served. The parquet floor had been polished so that it shone, the walls were lined with specially selected masterpieces of Hungarian art – none with any human forms, out of deference to their Muslim guests – and the view over the Danube and the city was spectacular.

Al-Nuri smiled, drawing back two purple, fleshy lips over some expensive cosmetic dentistry. 'How nice. Are you one of his secretaries or personal assistants?'

Reka smiled sweetly, took a sip of her mineral water. 'No. I am his minister of justice.'

Al-Nuri flushed a satisfying shade of red and looked at her chest again, but higher up this time, where her name badge was pinned. 'Ah. Ms Bardossy. Of course. You are related to Peter Bardossy?'

'My husband.'

Al-Nuri sipped his orange juice. 'I saw Peter last week in Dubai. Such a charming, clever man. Peter is doing a wonderful job, for his country and for our two countries' growing friendship.'

Peter Bardossy was one of the richest men in the country, and ran an opaque business empire through a web of local and offshore companies. He was an old friend of Pal Dezeffy. Like Dezeffy, he was a scion of a former Communist dynasty. His father, several uncles and a grandfather had all served as ministers under the old regime, including during the worst times of Stalinist repression. The two men had shared a room while they were history students at Budapest University. During the 1990s Peter Bardossy had worked in the Ministry of Finance, overseeing tenders for privatisation of state-owned factories, land and holiday resorts, while Pal Dezeffy served as minister of finance in several coalition governments. A large number of these tenders had been won by companies ultimately owned or controlled by allies or relatives of Pal Dezeffy. Several had then been passed back to Bardossy through a complicated web of offshore holding companies. Reka and Peter had not discussed the passport operation. He operated at a much higher level, diverting EU subsidies and foreign investment to companies favourable to government – and Dezeffy. Lately, he had been spending more and more time in the Gulf on business, working on the massive investment plan.

Reka was about to reply, when her mobile phone trilled twice in her Prada bag. It was the sound made when a new Snapchat message arrived. Snapchat was a messenger service that automatically deleted messages once they had been viewed. Reka only used Snapchat to communicate with one other person: Pal Dezeffy, to arrange their assignations.

She gave the Qatari her sweetest smile. 'Would you mind terribly, Mr Al-Nuri? I really have to take this.'

He shook his head, jowls wobbling, more than happy to have a reason to escape. 'Please, I leave you to it,' he said, scuttling off.

Reka walked over to a corner of the room. She took out her iPhone and stared at the screen. A document was attached to the message. The document showed two columns: the first was a list of two letters and seven numbers. Some of the letter combinations were random, but the top half-dozen all started with 'HM'. The second column showed a list of numbers, usually between 30,000 and 40,000. She realised immediately what she had been sent and took a screenshot of the message before it disappeared. Who had sent this? Whoever it was, it was not Pal Dezeffy. She thought rapidly. There was only other person who had this information. He was supposed to have been taken care of, neutralised.

But it seemed he was still at large. What did he want? She left the room without saying goodbye and headed to the ladies' toilets. On the way there, her phone trilled again. The message showed a photograph: the old castle wall, a corner spot at the far end. A shiver of fear rippled through her. She was being blackmailed and lured somewhere remote, at night. On the other hand, she was not afraid of Akos Feher.

She stepped away from the toilets and walked outside, along the side of the castle wall. The medieval ramparts were just higher than her shoulder, blocks of large grey stone a couple of yards wide, with two-foot gaps between them. Each had an indent for bowmen to fire down on besieging troops. Several now housed powerful lamps, which shone on the side of the building, bathing the edge of the castle complex in a reassuring yellow light. The path was several yards wide, made of small grey cobblestones. The side nearest the castle wall was still filled with construction equipment, piles of old stones and debris. She peered down between two of the ramparts. The wall fell sharply away, an almost-vertical dark slope of greenery that reached a hundred feet or so down onto the Buda embankment where the number 19 tram snaked along the waterfront.

Reka had grown up a few blocks from here, in an eight-room villa with an attached servants' flat, an only child of privilege under Communism. Her father, who had served as minister of justice during the old regime, had purchased the family home after the change of system for perhaps ten per cent of its value. He had died in 2002 and bequeathed the house to Reka in his will. It was a beautiful property, now worth more than a million euros. Reka had added a gym and steam room, private cinema and a covered swimming pool in the garden. She tried not to think about the metal box filled with Hebrew prayer books, wrapped in a silk prayer shawl, and women's jewellery, that she had found there while playing as a child, and had kept hidden in secret for years.

Reka took a step away from the rampart, but her right leg could not move. She glanced down and around, her adrenalin levels rising, her eyes wider in the gloom. There was no one else around, at least that she could see. She pulled her right leg again. It still did not move. She turned her right foot left and right. A tearing noise sounded. She looked down. Her heel had caught in the gap between two cobblestones. She really had chosen the most impractical footwear – but then she had not anticipated a night-time walk on a medieval cobbled street. She stepped out of her shoes, knelt down and pulled the stuck heel out of the road. It was still in place, but definitely looser. Now what? Barefoot or Louboutins? No contest. She was not going to this... encounter... whatever it was, at a psychological disadvantage. She put her shoes back on, carried on walking to the end of the path, making sure not to place all her weight on her right foot.

Reka walked under a low arch topped by a small gatehouse, and on to the end of the path. Her unease grew. Here too there were small lights set in the archers' recess. But none worked. The view was as beautiful as ever: the river shimmered black and silver, the Pest side shimmering, reflecting the five-star hotels along the riverbank. The Chain Bridge spilled golden light onto the water. A mile downriver, the Elizabeth Bridge, a graceful four-lane arch, swept traffic back and forth between Buda and Pest. A cool breeze blew in across the river. She watched a flotilla of tourist cruise boats slide by, faint noises of revelry carrying over the water. Part of her – a small but significant part – wished she was on one of the boats, gliding downriver towards the border, into Serbia, Romania and the Black Sea. She was, she knew, in way too deep for that. The Louboutins had come at a price, and she had chosen to pay it. And she would fight as hard as she could to keep what she had. Reka looked around until she saw what she wanted. She bent down and gathered a handful of the stones.

'Madame Minister, Ms Bardossy, over here,' called a male voice, and not one she recognised.

TEN

Balthazar sat back in the front passenger seat of Gaspar's black 7-series BMW, clipped the seatbelt buckle in place, and firmly grasped the armrest as Fat Vik took the wheel. He knew what was coming. The car had a long, curved dashboard with a console that displayed more lights, buttons and controls than a small aeroplane. Fat Vik fiddled with one until he found the music that he wanted: Gangsta Zoli, Hungarian rap. He opened the windows all the way down, turned up the volume, tugged on Balthazar's seatbelt and released it, laughing as it slapped against his chest, then pressed the ignition button with childish glee. The engine fired up. He revved the accelerator and took the wheel in his right hand, his left tapping on the window ledge in time with the music. His own seatbelt remained coiled in its holder.

The car screeched backwards down a one-way street, turned onto Rakoczi Way, roared down the bus lane, speeding past the dense night-time traffic as it headed towards Blaha Lujza Square and Elizabeth Bridge. A blue handicapped driver's pass was prominently displayed on top of the BMW's dashboard. Even with that, it was illegal to drive in the bus lane. The road was monitored by cameras, which recorded car number plates. Those caught faced a substantial fine but

Balthazar knew that Fat Vik had nothing to worry about, as long a helpful clerk in the municipal bureaucracy received one of Gaspar's envelopes each month.

The handicapped driver's pass, however, was new. Balthazar pointed at it. 'How did you get that?'

Fat Vik smiled, prodded his chest, wheezed unconvincingly. 'Heart condition, brother. Same as Gaspar.' He glanced at Balthazar, smiled. 'It probably runs in the family. Want one? You wouldn't even need a medical. You only need to pay the processing fee.'

'How much is that?'

'Fifty thousand and ten forints.'

'Ten?'

'Envelope.'

'That's tax-deductible, though,' said Balthazar. Both men laughed, the movement sending waves of discomfort through his back and shoulders. Balthazar sat back against the plush leather seat, very glad of the ride, but unable to get settled. Despite the merriment, he felt completely exhausted. His fruitless talk with Gaspar had used up the very last of his reserves. His brother, like so many Hungarians, indeed every nationality that had grown up under Communism, was too focused on the short term. Decades under an intrusive one-party regime had fostered a strong folk memory of seizing not just the day, but the moment, for potential profit and advantage. Playing the system was everything. As far as Gaspar was concerned, there was excellent money to be made smuggling migrants across the border and no reason to stop, as long the opportunity was there.

Balthazar had at least learned more about how the smuggling operation worked. There were two channels. The VIP channel provided customers with actual Hungarian passports. Gaspar said he was not involved in that. Balthazar believed him, especially when Gaspar said who was running that operation – one of the most violent and dangerous organised crime bosses not just in Budapest, but the whole region. Gaspar's operation took the refugees across the border to Vienna dressed as Gypsies, as Eniko had reported. Gaspar even provided the clothes. He worked with Goran Draganovic, a Serbian people-smuggler who had set up shop in Budapest, operating out of the Tito Grill, a Balkan restaurant on Rakoczi Square. Gaspar's roof was Reka Bardossy, who took twenty per cent. With Bardossy covering them there was nothing to worry about, Gaspar had explained, waving away Balthazar's concern. Bardossy was a rising star. She and Pal Dezeffy were lovers. The operation was rock solid. Everything was covered, Gaspar insisted.

But lovers fell out. Rising stars plummeted back to earth, Balthazar had explained. The man running the passport operation was utterly ruthless and would soon demand a piece of Gaspar's operation. Then another, and another, each time larger and larger. And today's events were a game-changer. A dead Syrian, whose body had since disappeared. The man they called the Gardener on the loose in Budapest. The beating at Keleti this morning. Gaspar needed to understand that he was putting his family in danger. There was no way for him to check the real identity of the people he was taking across the border. And no amount of money could compensate for the consequences if he turned out to be smuggling Muslim terrorists.

But Balthazar could see that his brother did not grasp what was happening. Gaspar was unconvinced. Who knew what Nazir had been mixed up with? And who was this Gardener? Thousands of people were pouring across the border every day. In any case, while it was a shame that Nazir was dead, there was still business to be done. Fat Vik had sat in on the discussion and thankfully had taken Balthazar's side. Eventually, Gaspar had agreed to postpone the next group, but Balthazar was not sure how long it could be put off.

After an hour or so of talking, Balthazar had started fading. He had planned one more stop in the evening, to see Goran Draganovic at his restaurant, but he was utterly exhausted and knew he was not going to make it there tonight. His jaw was throbbing, his upper body aching, and the iron bar in his head had returned and grown. All he wanted to do was take some more painkillers and sleep. But Gaspar was not the only dilemma.

Eniko, he realised, must have taken the missing SIM card while he was asleep. That knowledge made him feel confused and angry. Had she really taken him home and looked after him to get the SIM card? Rule one of police work when identifying suspects: who had the motive and who had the opportunity? She certainly had both. Part of him actually hoped she had planned it all along. It would make life much easier, clarify their relationship. She saw him as a source, one with access to inside information she needed for her reporting. There was nothing to think about, to hope for.

But Eniko could not have known about the SIM card when she had brought him home. So her motives, at least, had been altruistic. She just... made the most of her opportunities. For a moment he was back on his bed, lying next to her while she tapped away on her computer keyboard, smiling shyly when she caught him looking at her. But if she hadn't known about the phone, then how had she found it? That meant she had gone through his clothes while he was asleep, looking for something useful. He exhaled loudly. Was that better or worse? Worse, he decided. What were his options? He could threaten her with arrest for stealing evidence, obstructing the course of justice, even arrest her. But it would be almost impossible to prove that Eniko had taken the SIM card. And that would set the whole police bureaucracy in motion, which was not an option when he was working off the books. He needed her to confess. Most of all, he needed the SIM card back.

The SIM card was a vital piece of evidence. In fact, it was the only one. There was no body, and no proof that a body had even been there, especially after the Gendarmes' visit. Attila Ungar would be sure to remove any sign of the dead man. The Gendarmes reported to Pal Dezeffy, the prime minister. There was a government connection here, Balthazar knew. But what?

Fat Vik slowed down Rakoczi Way to turn right onto Akacfa Street, triggering an angry honking from the bus driver behind them. It was a narrow thoroughfare, barely wide enough for two cars to pass each other. 'This passport operation...' said Balthazar.

Fat Vik immediately interrupted him. 'Don't go there, brother, please.'

Balthazar pressed his point. 'Are you sure that Gaspar is not involved?'

'Totally. We have enough to deal with without a turf war.'

'And the antiques business?'

'I miss it. We pay better than BAV and it's all cash in hand. I like buying and selling things, paintings, furniture. I don't like buying and selling people.' He turned briefly to Balthazar. 'They are families. Dark-skinned people, like us. Sometimes children, travelling without their parents. It's awful. They try to be tough, then they cry when they think nobody's looking. How can someone send their kid on a journey like that, knowing they might be killed, or even worse?' He shook his head in wonder. 'It's beyond me.'

'Me too. But what's the alternative once they are here? They cannot go back. They cannot stay here. At least in western Europe they have a chance of a new life.'

'True. And we don't charge kids. Sometimes we even give them money. That's something, I guess.'

Balthazar squeezed Fat Vik's fleshy leg. 'It is.' He watched a Hasidic Jewish man and his wife walk towards Klauzal Square. The man wore a white shirt and long black frock coat, the wife a blue summer dress that covered her arms. She pushed a double pushchair in front of her, with two sleeping toddlers.

Vik glanced at the family as he drove past. 'Twins. Double trouble. You got any more planned, Tazi?'

Balthazar laughed. 'I need another wife first. And I'm in no hurry.'

Vik kept his eyes on the road as he spoke. 'Can I ask you something, Tazi?'

'Of course.'

'Why do you live here, all on your own? Why don't you come home?'

It was a good question, and one that lately Balthazar had been asking himself. He knew all the ready answers: he had a comfortable flat in an up-and-coming area; District VII had everything he needed, late-night shops, good public transport, bohemian nightlife, Eva *neni*. But the bohemians, the gentrifiers, the tourists who thronged the quarter every night, the liberal activists, the academics from Central European University – perhaps especially those – were not his people. Even the hipsters did a double take, gave him the Look, when he appeared in one of the artisan coffee bars or bought lunch from a street food truck. He was a cop and a Gypsy: a double outsider. His people were across the main boulevard: in the narrow streets behind Rakoczi Square, in the tenement court-yards, the cheap restaurants, grimy *borozos*, wine bars, the dilapidated grand palaces hidden away on tree-lined squares. In District VIII. But there too, he was partly a stranger now.

For a second, Balthazar was back in the courtyard at Jozsef Street as his father passed in front of a window. 'I can't come back to Jozsef Street, you know that, Vik. I lost that when I joined the police.'

'Your dad would come around eventually. You are his son. You know what that means for us.'

'Maybe. But I'm a cop. I can't live with Gaspar.'

Vik laughed. 'I know. I'm not saying move in. Just relo-cate somewhere nearer. You could come round more often. How can you bear it, eating on your own, every morning and every night?'

Sometimes I almost can't, Balthazar nearly replied. 'I'll think about it.'

'Good. How's your son?'

'Great. We're meeting tomorrow afternoon.'

'You're lucky to have each other. A kid needs a father.'

Balthazar and Gaspar had grown up with Fat Vik. He had lived in the next-door tenement in a tiny one-room flat with his mother. She was a drug addict and a prostitute and had no idea who her son's father was. One summer's evening, when Vik was six years old, he had hammered on their front door, shouting that *anyu* was asleep and he couldn't wake her. She had overdosed, but an ambulance came in time and she lived.

Balthazar's parents had taken in Vik for a while. There was not much to eat, but he was happy, and more settled than he had ever been. Then he had been caught stealing a bar of chocolate from the corner shop and moved to a children's home. His mother went clean for several years, found a job as a supermarket cashier, even came to visit him sometimes. Then she lapsed back into her old ways. Vik left the home when he was sixteen, found his mother, tried to help her. She was still a drug addict, working as a prostitute. Any money that he gave her went either to her pimp or on heroin. One day, he had gone to visit her in the squalid room where she lived near Rakoczi Square and found her beaten unconscious by her pimp. Vik dragged him out of the bar where he had been drinking. He did not survive the encounter. Vik served five years for manslaughter.

Roma men married young. Vik was in his early thirties, unmarried. For a woman, that would be a scandalous situation. But a man could still find a bride.

Balthazar asked, 'How about you? Any pretty *chaisis* caught your eye?'

Vik shook his head, laughed, his jowls wobbling. 'Not now. I'm too busy, with your brother. No time for women. Maybe later, once things have calmed down,' he said, but Balthazar could hear the depth of longing in his voice.

Balthazar glanced behind him as the car pulled into Klauzal Square, on the opposite end to his flat. There were no other vehicles in sight, but he wanted to make sure. 'Thanks for the lift. I'll get out here.'

'Tazi, no worries, I'll take you to the door.'

'No. I'm fine. I'll walk. I need to stretch a bit.'

Fat Vik pulled in to the kerb, in front of the denture-repair shop. 'I'll wait until you get in the front door. Then you call me once you are home. OK?'

Balthazar squeezed Fat Vik's shoulder. 'Thanks. Keep working on Gaspar.'

Balthazar walked down the side of Klauzal Square's park. The gates were locked and bolted, the playground deserted now. The party was in full swing outside Csaba Kiss's ABC, half a dozen men and women in their fifties and sixties drinking beer from bottles and smoking. A neat row of small, two-shot bottles of chemically flavoured alcohol masquerading as palinka, fruit brandy, was lined up along the window ledge. Shouts, raucous laughter, a cimbalom and violin echoed across Klauzal Square. On the corner of Dob Street, Balthazar saw a woman sitting on a green municipal bicycle. She seemed to be watching him. Early thirties, athletic build, dark-blond hair, ponytail. He did a double take. It was her. Definitely. Had she been sitting here waiting for him? Who was she? Was this a threat? He stared at her. She held his gaze, smiled, turned the bicycle around and glided away.

His options were limited. Under normal conditions he could give chase. But that was not going to happen tonight. He could call Vik, he supposed, but the huge BMW would be no match for a bicycle on the narrow streets and alleys. And his sixth sense, his street instinct, told him that she was not hostile. Whoever she was, and whatever she wanted, could wait until tomorrow. He walked to the door of his apartment building and tapped out the entry code.

Just as he stepped inside, Eva *neni* came out of her flat, holding something in her hand. She stared at him. 'Tazi. Go to bed. You need to sleep.'

He smiled, nodded. There was nothing to argue about. 'A young lady left this for you,' said Eva. 'She made me promise I would deliver to you myself, by hand. So here it is,' she said, passing it to Balthazar.

Balthazar took the A5 envelope in his hand, turned it over.

There were papers inside, he could feel, but otherwise nothing out of the ordinary. 'Did she say who she was?'

Eva shook her head.

'Did she leave anything? A business card?'

'Nothing.'

'What did she look like?'

Eva glanced upwards for a few seconds, ordering her memories. 'Quite tall, slim but not skinny, brown eyes, blonde hair in a ponytail – dark blonde but natural – not especially pretty but still attractive. An engaging, persuasive manner. Nice teeth. Spoke very well, no slang. Quite classy, I would say.'

The woman on the bicycle, Balthazar was sure. He smiled at Eva. 'How do you remember all that?'

Eva shot him a look. 'How do you think I lasted this long?' She tilted her head to one side. 'You could do a lot worse. She'll be back.'

Balthazar thanked Eva, kissed her on the top of her head, and walked up the stairs. The entrance foyer, with its curved banisters, black-and-white entrance foyer and original period lights, had recently featured in an architectural magazine. One day, he had come home to find a movie crew there shooting a detective film set in the 1930s. He watched for a while, noting that the storyline had several procedural errors. He had tried to find someone to talk to, was eventually passed to an earnest young woman with two mobile phones and a clipboard. She given him the Look, had taken a call as he had tried to explain how he could help, and spoken so long that eventually he walked away. No one had tried to stop him.

He took the lift up to the fifth floor, put the envelope on his bedside table, took two more paracetamols, brushed his teeth and went to bed. He lay back for a few moments, summoning the strength to open the envelope, but immediately fell into a deep sleep.

Tito Grill, Rakoczi Square, 9.10 p.m.

Across the Grand Boulevard, the party was roaring at the Tito Grill. The tuba and trumpets of the Boban Markovic Orchestra blared out, the air was thick with *rakija* fumes, the smell of grilled meat and the sound of laughter. The walls were a dirty off-white, the floor lined with faded yellow linoleum. The tables were covered in cloths chequered in red and white. A red, white and blue Yugoslav flag with a red star in the middle, dating back to the partisan era, was framed over the bar. Faded posters of London, Paris, Berlin, Vienna and other European capitals decorated the walls. There was no menu, only three options: one, five and ten. One was *pleskavica*, a hamburger made of minced beef and pork. Five or ten were *cevapcici*, small grilled kebabs from the same combination. All were served with *ajvar*, spicy pepper sauce, chips, onions and salad.

Goran Draganovic surveyed the scene with satisfaction. He sipped his *rakija*, savouring its fresh, clean taste, and the way it warmed first the back of his throat, then his stomach, suffusing his whole body with a pleasant glow, with no afterburn. The fact that his uncle's home brew was smuggled across the border in hundred-litre barrels, its passage aided by several hundred-euro notes, only enhanced his enjoyment of the drink. Business was good. He was safe here. Budapest wasn't home, for sure, but now nowhere was. But this was the nearest he could find, and for now, it would more than suffice. The old Yugoslavia had gone forever, vanished in the lunacy of the wars that had convulsed and destroyed his former homeland. He glanced at the flag. The memories pushed themselves back into his mind, as insistent as ever.

He took a longer slug of *rakija*, but this time it burned as it went down. The past is the past, he told himself. Like his homeland, the past had gone forever. Until the door opened, and he saw the man who stepped inside.

Buda Castle walls, 9.15 p.m.

Reka turned to see a tall, broad-shouldered man approach her with long, swift strides. His face was hidden in the shadows and he did not speak again. There was no point asking who he was or what he wanted. There was nobody else around and no help coming. She felt the acid flush of fear in her stomach, instinctively looked behind her, down the dark slope that led to the riverbank, immediately understanding the man's plan. All he had to do was tip her over the rampart and she would fall to her death, bouncing down the wall, smashing into the trees, breaking her limbs on the way, before she slammed onto the pavement below and likely rolled into the oncoming traffic. The Snapchat message would vanish. So would she, from Budapest's political life. Except that was not going to happen.

Reka no longer fenced. The sport demanded too much time to stay at her level, especially after she turned thirty. She had no intention of sliding down the rankings, so had stepped down at her peak. But she trained every day in the gym, and had substituted fencing for Krav Maga, the Israeli self-defence system. Krav Maga had been invented by a Hungarian Jewish policeman in the 1930s. It combined boxing, martial arts and dirty street fighting. It was fast and effective, and most of all taught its adherents to control their fear and think on their feet.

She dropped down and grabbed a handful of dirt and stones. By the time she stood back up he was almost upon her. The breeze carried his smell towards her: a rank mix of sweat and sour milk. He stepped out of the shadows and she saw a knife-scar beneath his right eyebrow. For a second she was back on the piste at the London Olympics, in the final, two points behind, fifteen seconds to go, the difference between silver and gold.

She felt the weight of the stones and sand in her palm, heavy, cool, reassuring. Her heart thumped, the adrenalin coursed through her. She stepped away, turned her hands inwards, towards herself, raised her arms as if surrendering.

'Who are you? What do you want?' she asked, allowing her fear to infect her voice. If her plan was to work the attacker would need to believe she was scared and enfeebled.

The attacker kept walking towards her, a grin on his beefy face. Reka waited until he was two yards away. She spun on her left heel to gain momentum, twisted her body at the hip, swung out with a slashing motion, with all the speed, momentum and precision that had won her three points in nine seconds, and the gold medal. The stones and the rocks hit the man full in his upper face. He shouted in pain, stumbled backwards, scrabbling at his eyes. Reka dropped her bag, skipped forward, fired a jumping front kick at his groin. Her plan was simple: she could not win in a straight fight, but if she could disable him for a few minutes, she could sprint back to the reception and raise the alarm.

Just as she launched herself, her damaged shoe came off. The kick never connected. Instead, she stumbled forward, against the attacker. He instantly grabbed her, clamped one hand over her mouth, spun her around and started pushing her towards the rampart.

She tried to get traction on the ground, but he was far too powerful and it was impossible with one foot bare and the other still wearing the Louboutin. Her feet scraped along the cobbles as he dragged her forward. The ramparts drew nearer and nearer. She hooked her right hand over the edge of his palm, managed to slide her finger through the gap between his hand and her face and pulled down as hard as she could. The man's hand moved a fraction of an inch. She yanked down again, even harder, knowing that she was now fighting for her life. His hand slipped further.

She grabbed his palm, dropped her face to the flat edge and bit down as hard as she could, feeling her teeth pierce his skin. He yelped in pain, released her and stepped backwards. She spun around and limped forward, kicked up with her right foot between his legs. This time her foot connected, its front slamming into his groin. He grunted. She leaned back and kicked again and again, using her whole body weight. He staggered back. She turned to run and the heel of her left shoe broke off, sending her stumbling.

That second delay was all that he needed. He grabbed her leg and she went down hard, her head sliding against the cobblestone path. He lumbered over towards Reka. She was on her back now, winded and dizzy.

He sat over her torso with his hands around her throat. She scrabbled at his right hand and gained purchase, but his palm was slippery with blood where she had bitten him. She slid one leg between herself and the attacker, tried to lever him off her, but he was too heavy. His grip tightened around her throat. She had a few seconds at the most, tried to remember what she had learned and the different defences: against an attacker choking her from the side, kneeling between her legs, sitting on top of her stomach as he was now, but the moves all blurred into one as the fear turned to panic and she flailed helplessly. His face was curiously calm as he worked, she saw. Her instructor's voice sounded in her ears: 'eyes, groin, eyes'. She reached upwards, tried to force her thumbs against his eyeballs. He batted her hands away with ease, but the moment gave her a second's reprise. She coughed, spluttered, as her lungs filled with air again and scrabbled on both sides of her.

Her fingers slid across the dirt until her right hand found something, a sleek shaft a few inches long, with a pointed, square end: the broken Louboutin heel. Now his face was set with determination, his rank breath catching in her throat. Her vision began to turn grey, her strength faded. His hand slid between her legs, tearing at her dress. It was all the opening she needed.

Her right hand flew upwards, slammed as hard as she could into the side of his neck; she felt the skin resist for a second, yield then tear as the heel slid in.

He roared in pain, lurched upwards. Blood fountained out as he grabbed and scrabbled at the shank sticking out of the side of his neck. She swung her arm out and hammered her right palm into his hand, forcing the edge of the heel deeper into his neck. His arms flailed for several seconds as he tried to pull the heel free. He coughed, retched, convulsed. Panic filled his eyes for several long seconds. They rolled back in their sockets and he toppled over.

Reka pushed him off her. She lay on her back for several seconds, staring at the sky, panting. She sat up, slowly got to her feet, her legs shaking underneath her. She sensed movement in the shadows, stood up, looked around for another weapon.

Akos Feher stepped towards her, glanced at the dead man, an iron bar in his right hand. Blood was seeping out of the

171

hole at the side of the dead man's neck, pooling black under the dim light. Bardossy stood still, breathing hard, her dress torn and filthy, her hair in disarray. Her shoulders were locked solid, her eyes still wild as the adrenalin coursed through her. She looked down at her right hand with a kind of wonder, watching the crimson blood seep between her fingers.

Feher put the bar down and looked around at the pile of builders' debris. A thin plastic bag, the type used by green-grocers to pack fruit, lay under half a brick. He picked the bag up, put his hand inside as though it were a glove, and pulled the heel from the dead man's neck.

Reka watched, shaking, as he wrapped the bag around the spike, and slipped it into his jacket pocket. Part of her wondered what he was doing, and another began to under-stand. But she was too shaken to stop him. She looked at the dead man, back at Feher. He nodded reassuringly. He was no threat, she realised. Reka forced herself to calm down, to *think*, took several long, deep breaths. She walked over to her bag, picked it up and reached inside for her phone. There was only one person she knew who could clear up this mess.

ELEVEN

Balthazar's flat, Saturday, 5 September, 10.00 a.m.

HUNGARIAN STATE SECURITY SERVICE
SECRET

From: XXXXXXXXXXXX
To: XXXXXXXXXXXXX

Operational report KN3/9/5

At 6.00 a.m. on 4 September 2016 I took over from GS1 at Keleti Station at vantage point 2 (the taxi rank at the side of the station on Thokoly Way). We estimate that there are now approximately 5,000 people sleeping out at Keleti. Numbers are rising continually after the government cancelled all trains to western Europe, but the southern frontiers remain open. There are increasing scenes of squalor but tensions remain under control, in part due to the pact agreed by different Syrian opposition groups (excluding the Islamists).

At 6.06 a.m. MAHMOUD HEJAZI appeared, having walked to Keleti from the nearby Hotel Continental on Baross Square. He then made contact with two other males, both men of Arab appearance in their early thirties. These two had slept at Keleti, in the station forecourt, away from the other Syrian refugees. These two are hitherto unidentified. Considering HEJAZI's prominent standing in the Islamist opposition we believe the two to be Islamist cadres and expect some form of identification later today from the station CCTV.

To recap what we know so far: HEJAZI is a high-ranking Islamist operative from Aleppo and a person of interest to all western intelligence agencies. HEJAZI is on an inter-agency watchlist and has been tracked since he left Syria three weeks ago. He arrived in Hungary yesterday at 3.06 p.m. The British MI6 and United States embassy CIA stations have liaised continuously with us. HEJAZI crossed the Serbian border illegally at Kelebia with several dozen others, then left the group to take a taxi to Budapest.

The Kelebia taxi driver, DEMETER CSONGRADI, is a part-time asset of the ABS and one of several Kelebia drivers we keep on a retainer. CSONGRADI has supplied me with a detailed account of HEJAZI's arrival in Hungary and the journey he took to Budapest in CSONGRADI's car. CSON-GRADI had been supplied with several photographs of HEJAZI and told to look out for him. The top of HEJAZI's right ear is gnarled and misshapen, the result of a burn from an incendiary bomb.

CSONGRADI observed other anomalies. (CSONGRADI's mother was born in Syria and studied medicine in nearby Szeged, where she now works as a GP. CSONGRADI speaks fluent Arabic.) His suspicions were aroused for mul-tiple reasons. While chatting in English with CSONGRADI, HEJAZI claimed to be from Basra, in southern Iraq, but spoke Arabic with a Damascene accent.

HEJAZI spoke at length in Arabic on his mobile phone about deliveries, arrival times and a birthday party. He asked several times for confirmation that the deliveries and the birthday party were guaranteed to take place on time. It is inconceivable that a newly arrived Iraqi migrant would be organising a birthday party in Budapest while speaking in Arabic. After this conversation, HEJAZI removed a blue-and-white SIM card from his phone and changed it. CSONGRADI observed that HEJAZI seemed to be about to place the first SIM card in some kind of box when his telephone rang. He took the call and quickly placed the blue-and-white SIM card in his shirt pocket as if to put it somewhere secure for the moment. He did not touch it again during the journey.

Like many migrants, HEJAZI carried only a small backpack, but he also had a very thick money belt under his shirt. HEJAZI paid the €500 fare in cash from a thick wad of €100 notes. The receptionist at the hotel passed us a copy of HEJAZI's fake Iraqi passport. Although the photograph was taken before HEJAZI suffered his injury, we were able to positively identify him from the photograph.

To summarise, after some discussion with our partner agencies, it was decided to follow HEJAZI and try and unravel his network of local contacts rather than arrest him. At around 6.10 a.m. HEJAZI and his two colleagues gathered their rucksacks. At this point SIMON NAZIR got up and followed them. NAZIR is here with his wife MARYAM. They are both Christians from Aleppo. I have been developing NAZIR as a source over the last ten days. He is a well-informed observer. NAZIR stayed behind HIJAZI and the two unidentified men as they walked down Rakoczi Way. I followed NAZIR at a distance until my path was blocked on the corner of Luther Street by ATTILA UNGAR and three others. However, I could see NAZIR lying face-down on the site of the former Party headquarters and assume that he is dead as he has not returned to Keleti.

Balthazar put the document down. The rest of the account related how the author had shown a state security ID card to Ungar and demanded to pass. Ungar had laughed, refused to move. The author had insisted. Ungar then threatened violence and sexual assault. The report also detailed how MI6 had informed its Hungarian counterparts that several known Islamic radicals had been apprehended at British airports while travelling on Hungarian passports.

These were the papers in the envelope Eva *neni* had handed him last night: an internal report from the *Allami Biztonsagi Szolgalat*, the domestic state security service.

Balthazar digested what he had read. The report seemed to suggest that Attila Ungar was running some kind of clean-up squad and had disposed of Simon Nazir's body. The Gendarmes did not want anyone poking around the square, especially from another government agency. Presumably the site was under some kind of surveillance by the Gendarmes, which is how Ungar knew that Balthazar had arrived. Ungar's threat of sexual violence made it likely that the agent was female, although that was not guaranteed. But why, and what were the Gendarmes guarding so fervently?

And could Balthazar work with state security? Relations between the police and the ABS were guarded at best. Both forces came under the purview of the Ministry of the Interior. While the police needed to persuade a judge to intercept a suspect's communications, the ABS had carte blanche to tap telephones, hack computers, plant bugs, and break into apartments at will. The ABS also had an annoying habit of letting the police do all the heavy lifting on the most interesting murder cases, then walking in and taking them over on the grounds of 'national security' – as had happened to him last summer, just as his investigation into the murdered Iranian property developer at Keleti was getting somewhere.

But Pal Dezeffy's private police force, the Gendarmerie, had upended the old power relations. Balthazar's encounter with Attila Ungar at Republic Square, and his beating at Keleti, had shown that the Gendarmes held the police in contempt – and felt confident enough to show it. It seemed from the ABS report that the Gendarmes had declared war on the ABS as well. It was surely no coincidence that all this was happening after Bela Lidaki, the minister of the interior, had resigned, brought down in a corruption scandal exposed by Eniko.

Which reminded him. The SIM card. He tapped out an SMS on the Nokia burner that Sandor Takacs had given him: 'One/12'. Balthazar had shared the telephone number with Eniko the previous evening. He and Eniko were also using a code: the first number referred to one of three different meeting places, the second, the time, plus two hours. It was crude, but should be effective enough, Balthazar believed. And after his beating and the report he was reading, clearly necessary.

Balthazar carried on reading. The report further detailed how the author had tried three different routes to follow Nazir. Each had been blocked by the Gendarmes. Which was why, presumably, these papers had been delivered to him. For now, at least, the police and the ABS were allies. Contact, he expected, would soon follow. As if on cue, there was a knock on the door. He opened it to see Eva *neni* standing there, holding an aluminium tray. A small, brown padded envelope lay next to a white china plate with another plate on top.

'Do I look like a post office?' she demanded.

Balthazar laughed, shook his head. 'Good morning, Eva *neni*. No you don't. You are much prettier, for starters.'

She huffed with mock indignation, stepped towards him, lifted the envelope and handed it to him. 'Then why do people keep giving me things to deliver to you?'

Balthazar took the envelope. It was heavy in his hand, a weight inside. 'I don't know. But thank you. Who brought it?'

'A motorbike courier this time. He kept his helmet on. He didn't tell me his name.' She softened her voice. 'Are you OK? Sleep OK?'

He nodded. 'Yes and not bad. The storm woke me. But I went back to sleep.'

She looked him up and down. 'Me too. Get that girl-friend of yours to put some more Betadine on those cuts and scratches.' Betadine was iodine solution. Hungarians coated every abrasion with the black liquid, believing it far more effective than modern antiseptic creams.

'She's not my girlfriend. She's my ex-girlfriend. I think she has a boyfriend, Tamas Nemeth, the actor.'

Eva *neni*, Balthazar knew, was a voracious reader of the gossip press. Her daughter had bought her an iPad on her last visit, so she could read Szilky.hu. She snorted with derision. 'Don't be ridiculous. She's not interested in Tamas Nemeth. He can't string a sentence together without a director whispering in his ear. She's probably only meeting him to make you jealous. Any woman who brings you home in that state and looks after you is either your girlfriend or your wife, or wants to be.'

Balthazar smiled. 'Thanks, Evike. I'll tell her next time we meet.'

Eva nodded. 'Do that.' She handed him the tray. 'Mean-while, breakfast.'

Balthazar took the tray, lifted the first plate up. Four pancakes lay in a row, each oozing soft white cheese, topped with grated lemon zest and a dusting of icing sugar. His favourite. 'Thank you.'

Eva smiled. '*Turos palacsinta*. Easy to chew.' She wagged her finger at him, mock-stern. 'Betadine, Tazi. Don't forget.'

He stepped back inside, suddenly ravenously hungry, put the tray down on the coffee table and picked up the envelope, still smiling. His name was written on the front. He turned it over. No sender's name or address, but there was a green-and-white sticker advertising Bubi bikes. He opened the envelope. Inside was a mobile phone, another old-fashioned Nokia candy bar model, this time grey.

He walked over to the small balcony, phone in his hand and looked out over Klauzal Square. Each movement, no matter how small, was stiff, almost painful. His back and shoulders ached and throbbed. He touched his jaw. It felt bruised and tender as he squinted against the bright morning sun. The square was almost empty, although he could see a few children romping around the playground, while their mothers stood at the edge, watching their charges and gossiping. For once, the morning was cool and fresh, but it was a temporary respite. The summer heat in Budapest built and built, the air becoming heavier and stickier, until every ten days or so it broke. The skies opened, the rain poured down, sometimes just for a few minutes, the temperature dropped, then the cycle started again.

There were no blondes lurking nearby and smiling enigmatically. But it was clear enough who had sent him the report. The question was, why? He stepped back inside, found some cutlery, and started to eat his breakfast. The pancakes were delicious, thin but sturdy enough to hold the filling and every mouthful was a pleasure, not least because someone cared enough about him to cook for him. Turo was Hungary's version of cottage cheese, but thicker and heavier, its sweetness perfectly set off by the sharpness of the lemon zest. He ate slowly and carefully, wary of his bruised jaw. Three was all he could manage. He stood up, picked up the grey Nokia, walked back out to the balcony, sat on the rickety office chair and waited. A minute later the phone rang.

Bardossy home, Remetehegyi Way, 10.00 a.m.

Reka stared at herself in the bathroom mirror, her hands resting on the edge of the black granite twin sink. Her face was pale, her blue eyes surrounded by dark shadows. Her blonde hair hung in lank tendrils down the sides of her face. She had stripped off her dress and fallen asleep on the bed without showering, waking up an hour later to find a T-shirt and crawl under the cover. She had slept badly, her recurring nightmare especially vivid last night: she was trapped in a luxurious hotel suite. The door handles were solid gold, but the rooms had no windows and no doors. She ran from room to room, banged and banged on the walls, shouted as loudly as she could, but nobody came. Still, while she looked awful – there was no other word – her face had more or less escaped. She did not have a black eye or split lip. She was alive. Even though someone had wanted her dead. She had fought and she had won.

She glanced down at her hands. She smiled for a moment as she imagined her manicurist's expression if she saw them. Every nail was scratched, chipped and filthy, the clear varnish scraped away in patches. At least three were broken or torn. Her fingertips were covered with mud and dirt. Her palms

180

were grazed, marked with swipe marks as she had skidded along the ground. Her arms were bruised and her back and shoulders throbbed. Her neck was sore and stiff. Her hands she could patch up; she could claim that she had fallen over and scraped them. Then she remembered what she had done with her hands last night. She stared at her right palm for several seconds, felt it slam into her attacker's neck. She began to shake, dropped her head down, drew several deep breaths to steady herself.

She looked back into the mirror, traced the vivid red line around the base of her neck with a trembling index finger. That would be harder to explain away. She glanced at the row of men's toiletries by the second sink. Several had not been opened. The sink was dry and unused, polished to a sheen. Peter was rarely here now, spending more and more time in Gulf or Russia or China, courting investors. Generally, that suited Reka. They had grown – were growing further – apart. She was fairly sure that Peter was having an affair with his executive assistant, Zita, a slender brunette in her mid-twenties, who accompanied him everywhere. But on days like this, she wished her husband was at home.

Reka had two problems, she realised. Both were pressing. The first was that someone had tried to kill her. She had been lured out of the reception by someone who knew that she was there – which was a lot of people – and also knew that the Snapchat messages, detailing the passport operation, would leave her no choice but to show up. That could be one of three people: Akos Feher, the man they called Black George, and Pal Dezeffy. Akos Feher had been there while she was attacked, and had not tried to save her. But why would he? Her death would solve a number of problems for him. She had tried to destroy his life.

Had Feher really hired a hit man? Anything was possible, she supposed, but then why hadn't he finished the job? She had been half out of her mind after killing the attacker with the heel of her shoe. It would have been simple for Feher to push her over the castle rampart. But he hadn't. Perhaps it had been a mistake to try and make him the fall guy for the passport operation, and so brutally, especially when he had so much information. And now he was a witness to murder, one in possession of the murder weapons. The Louboutin heel had her fingerprints all over it. She needed that back. Akos Feher was a smarter operator than she had imagined. And that meant that he would do a deal, she was confident.

Reka turned on the water, put her hands into the warm stream, wincing as it found its way into the cuts and grazes. And Black George? She had met him once, by chance, at the Japanese restaurant downtown, where he was holding court, surrounded by beautiful young women and his female bodyguards. Reka was not easily frightened, but Black George scared her. He was of medium height, wiry, with dark-brown skin and piercingly intelligent black eyes. It was instantly clear that he was capable of extreme violence. Her dealings with him were handled by a series of intermediaries. There was no reason for Black George to kill her, as far as she could figure out. The operation was making plenty of money for everybody. Black George would not care about diplomatic difficulties and complaints from MI6. But Pal Dezeffy certainly would. Enough to kill her?

She let her silk bathrobe slide off and stepped across the room into the rainforest shower. The bathroom was the size of a studio apartment and seemed even larger, thanks to the efforts of the Swedish interior designer Reka had flown in when she had inherited the house from her father. Three walls were white, covered to chest height with tiny tiles, the third a floor-to-ceiling mirror. The floor was black Italian marble, while a crystal chandelier hung from the ceiling. A Bose sound system was built into the room, while a touch-screen next to the shower cubicle was linked to the internet and her telephone by Bluetooth.

She turned on the music system. The voice of Marta Sebestyen, once of Hungary's best-known singers, filled the room as violins surged in the background. Reka stepped into the shower cubicle, turned on the water as hot as she could stand it, and leaned back against the wall.

She looked down again at her hands, started to scrub and scrub until they were raw. She slid down the wall until she was sitting on the floor, the water pouring on her, running down her back and neck, her head resting on her knees. The sobs were small at first, then grew until she was crying hard, her breath coming in jagged bursts as her tears mixed in with the shower water, flowing brown and red down the plughole.

Kadar restaurant, Klauzal Square, 11.00 a.m.

'I was thinking of inviting you to go for a bike ride,' said the blonde woman Balthazar had seen on the Bubi bike in Klauzal Square, a glimmer of a smile on her face.

'I'd fall off. Walking is enough at the moment.'

'I guessed as much. That's why I suggested we meet here.'

They were sitting at a table in the back room of the Kadar restaurant. The eatery, on the square, fifty yards from Balthazar's apartment, was a venerable Budapest institution. It served traditional Jewish food and was renowned for its *cholent*, a heavy stew of beans and meat, traditionally cooked overnight for the Sabbath lunch. The tables were covered with blue-and-white plastic cloths, the walls bedecked with signed photographs of celebrities, local and international. The owner, a jolly, bearded man in his sixties, sat by the door, nursing a murky coffee served in a stubby brown glass, calculating yesterday's takings in a school exercise book.

Balthazar picked up the old-fashioned heavy-glass soda siphon and filled both their beakers. 'I still don't know who you are. Other than someone who sends me documents and phones.' He took a sip of the drink. It was cold and refreshing. 'And instructions to meet in restaurant back rooms.'

She reached into her trouser pocket, took a small leather folder and handed it to Balthazar. He opened it. Her photograph stared out from a laminated ID card, with her name, Ferenczy Anastasia, underneath the words *Allami Biztonsagi Szolgalat*. Dark-blonde hair pulled back, a long face with a straight nose, large green eyes that looked at you questioningly, a determined set to her chin. Someone you could rely on. Not pretty, exactly, but a face that drew you in. A face to confide in.

'Thank you.' Balthazar handed the ID back. 'Are you one of the...'

'Famous Ferenczys,' she said, interrupting him. 'Yes.'

The Ferenczys were one of the best-known aristocratic dynasties in Hungary. Every schoolchild knew the family history. During the nineteenth century the family castle in Transylvania was the centre of one of the largest estates in the Austro-Hungarian empire. The Ferenczys had played a pivotal role in the failed 1848 revolution, when Hungary fought for independence against Vienna, for which several of their menfolk were later executed. After the Treaty of Trianon in 1920, Transylvania was handed to Romania. The Ferenczys, like most of the Hungarian aristocracy, lost their land and their family seat. They moved to Budapest, where they tried, with some success, to rein in the anti-Semitic excesses of Admiral Horthy, the country's ruler from 1919 to 1944, when the Nazis invaded. The family went into hiding and helped organise Hungary's meagre resistance. When the Russians arrived, they emerged, hoping to build a new, democratic Hungary. The men were promptly deported to Siberia and the Gulag, the women forced to work as maids and cleaners. Some of the men returned after Stalin's death in 1953 and took part in the 1956 revolution, for which they were again arrested, before being released in an amnesty in the 1960s. The family's tumultuous history symbolised the country's.

For a moment Balthazar was a schoolboy again, devouring his history book. He was having coffee with an actual Ferenczy. 'Do you have a title?'

'Sure.'

'*Grofno*? Countess?'

'Senior officer, counter-intelligence.'

'Almost as good. You made an interesting career choice.'

The ABS was the successor to the Communist secret police, which had arrested many of Anastasia's relatives. Even now, twenty-five years after the change of system, the state security service was one of the last bastions of the power networks from the Communist era. Some senior officials, who had trained in Moscow, were still in place, although a new young guard was advancing. Time, if nothing else, would eventually hand them victory.

Anastasia raised her eyebrows. 'I could say the same.'

Balthazar smiled. 'You could. And you would be correct.'

'We are both outsiders, Balthazar. May I call you by your first name?'

He nodded. 'My friends call me Tazi.'

She laughed, her face coming alive. 'So do mine.'

They raised their soda glasses. Anastasia continued talking. 'It's true, my parents were not best pleased when I joined the service. We had many... *spirited*... discussions about that. Perhaps you know what that's like.'

He smiled. 'We are Gypsies. So they were *very* spirited.'

Anastasia continued talking. 'But we are both realists as well. You believe in the law and the police enforce that law. I believe in my country. Every state has a secret service. Here, it's the ABS. Politicians come and go. We remain. We don't live in a perfect world. We have to work with the world as it is and our institutions in Hungary as they are.' She paused, shot him an appraising look. 'Especially at the moment. You have a difficult case. I thought I might be able to help.'

'How do you know?' asked Balthazar, his voice wary.

'Because that's my job. Keleti is a national security issue. You are part of that story now. Do you want my help or not?'

'Sure. We can start with a photo of the Gardener. Do you have one?'

Anastasia nodded, reached into her shoulder bag and passed a printout to Balthazar. Mahmoud Hejazi was in his mid-thirties, tall and lean, with black hair and piercing brown eyes. The burn scar on the top of his right ear was very prominent.

'Thanks,' said Balthazar. Such help, Balthazar knew, always came at a price. But still, it was worth asking Anastasia what she knew. 'Where is Simon Nazir's body?'

'We don't know. Nazir followed Hejazi from Keleti to Republic Square.'

'It's not called that any more.'

Anastasia reached for the photograph of Hejazi and placed it back in her bag. 'You were born in Budapest?'

Balthazar nodded. 'Semmelweis.' The hospital, on the edge of District VIII, was also the city's medical university.

'Me too. At least it's still called Semmelweis. I'll give them back Lenin Boulevard and Karl Marx Square. But not Republic Square.'

'Or Moskva,' said Balthazar. Moskva Square, the main transport interchange on the Buda side, had been renamed for Szell Kalman, a nineteenth-century prime minister. No self-respecting Budapester would ever use the term.

Balthazar raised his drink. 'Here's to proper names.'

Anastasia raised hers. 'And proper squares.'

They raised their glasses again and clinked. Anastasia continued talking. 'Hejazi met the Gendarmes at Republic Square. They will guard him before they move him out of the country. I followed Nazir, then the Gendarmes appeared and stopped me from going any further. When I finally got to Republic Square, Nazir was gone. He did not return to Keleti. I believe he is dead. If he is, the body has gone. Maybe the Gendarmes took it. What a miserable end. He almost made it.'

For a moment Balthazar was back at Republic Square, talking to Jozsi, the Gypsy street kid. *'The men took him away,'* he had said. Balthazar asked, 'Why do the Gendarmes care about Nazir?'

'Dezeffy and Reka Bardossy are selling passports to traffickers. The traffickers are selling them to Islamic radicals, like Mahmoud Hejazi. Hejazi made a mistake and showed his face at Keleti. It was early, everyone was asleep, so he thought he wouldn't be noticed. But he was. Simon Nazir made a bigger mistake – to follow him. Now Dezeffy is running scared. This has gone way beyond the usual corruption. It's about international terrorism. Dezeffy is a thief, quite a good one, but he's way out of his league.'

'Then why don't you hand over your evidence to the police, and we can arrest Dezeffy and Bardossy and shut this whole thing down before anyone else gets killed?'

'Because we need more evidence. Much more. This would – should – bring down the government. We need to show a clear connection between Dezeffy, the traffickers and the Islamists. We can't shoot from the hip, or this will end very badly for all of us. And there are other interested parties. Very interested.'

'Who?'

'Our friends in London and Washington DC. Nobody there wants Hungary to become the Islamists' entry point into western Europe. We are a small country, Balthazar. We need friends. Especially at the moment.'

'How can I help? I'm a policeman, not a spy.'

'Yes, and a very good one. With a network of contacts that most of your colleagues don't have. You can get in where they can't.'

Balthazar smiled wryly. 'You mean because I'm a Gypsy.'

Anastasia held his gaze, her eyes resting on his. 'Yes, Balthazar, that's exactly what I mean.'

'Where did you have in mind?'

'Not so much a place, as a person.'

'Who?'

Her answer chilled him. Black George was the boss of District IX. He was utterly ruthless and the most dangerous, violent crime leader in the city. He had been sending probing missions to District VIII, testing Gaspar's responses, for weeks.

Balthazar asked, 'Why him? He runs hookers, protection rackets. He's not interested in terrorism or terrorists.'

'No, but he is interested in money. He is the point man between Dezeffy and Bardossy and the traffickers.'

That explained the probing missions into District VIII,

thought Balthazar. He would want to take over every people-smuggling operation in the city. 'Let's say I get to him, have a meeting. What am I offering?'

Anastasia glanced around the restaurant before she answered. They were still the only two customers. 'Cooperation.'

'Whose?'

'Ours. The state security service. Occasional tips, useful information. *Kez kezet mos.*'

Balthazar sat back in amazement. 'Are you serious?'

'Absolutely. Black George's network runs deep into the Balkans. He knows all sorts of things. The Islamists are setting up networks in Bosnia, Kosovo, even in Serbia. He has contacts everywhere.' She looked at Balthazar. 'Why are you so surprised? You have informants? Criminals?'

'Of course.'

'You trade? With pimps, burglars, robbers? A quiet word of warning in exchange for useful information?'

'Sometimes.'

'So what's the difference?'

It was a good question and he was not sure that he knew the answer. But another idea was germinating. 'What if he says no, he won't cooperate?'

'Then he won't know what's hit him. Meanwhile, you have something we need.'

'What?'

'The SIM card from Hejazi's telephone. Those numbers will help us unravel his network here.'

'What SIM card?'

'The one you found on the ground at Republic Square.'

There was no point denying it. 'How do you know about the SIM card?'

Anastasia smiled. 'A breakfast at McDonalds and a big bag of cakes for brothers and sisters will get you a lot in District VIII.'

Balthazar sat back. 'Jozsi? The kid who was watching me?'

'Yes. He'd never been to McDonalds. His parents don't have any money. Imagine, he's never had a hamburger. He saved up once for months and tried to go to another burger restaurant, but the security guard would not let him in. I don't know many Gyp... Roma people.' She paused. 'Actually I don't know any. Apart from you. There're none at the ABS. Is that what it's like, always being turned away?'

Balthazar gave her a wry smile. He was starting to like Anastasia. She was a rare professional who had not given him the Look when they first met and asked straightforward questions. 'Pretty much. Especially when you are a kid. Not so much when you are a cop.'

Anastasia laughed. 'I'm glad to hear it.' Her voice changed, became businesslike. 'So, the SIM card. Where is it?'

'Somewhere safe,' he replied, surprised at how easily the lie came.

'We need that card.'

'And what do I get in this trade?'

'Our cooperation. In this case and future cases, Bal-thazar,' she said, tapping her fingers on the table.

Future cases. A helpful contact at the ABS would be extremely valuable. The service had means of gathering information, contacts and networks far beyond the Budapest police. Was she flirting with him? Balthazar wondered. She was a Hungarian woman who wanted something from him. So the answer was obvious. He was even starting to enjoy this encounter. 'Thanks for the report.' He sipped his soda. 'I have another question.'

'Shoot.'

'The Iranian property developer who was murdered at Keleti last summer. The ABS took the case. What happened?'

'We found out that he was connected to a money-laundering operation. The funds went through Budapest to Zurich to Doha. Then we were ordered to close it down. By the prime minister's office.'

'Did you?'

'Officially, yes.'

'And unofficially?'

'We think it was some kind of advance network, in preparation for what happened this summer. Mahmoud Hejazi is a trial run, we think. If the Gulf countries can get him through Hungary and into Europe, they will bring many more. The Gulf monarchies are unstable. The Islamists are organised, dynamic, believe they have God on their side. There are more and more terrorist attacks there. The monarchies are autocratic, repressive. Sooner or later the Islamists will take over.'

'But not if they are blowing people up in Paris and London,' said Balthazar. 'The Gulf states are using Dezeffy's scam as a channel to get rid of their Islamists, to ship them to Europe.'

'Exactly.'

Balthazar asked, 'You've seen the National Security Committee's report?'

'Yes.'

The parliamentary report was classified, above Balthazar's pay grade, but Sandor Takacs had somehow obtained a copy and shown it to him. The report warned that the Qataris would expect more than business opportunities for such a large investment. In other countries, with substantial Muslim minorities, that had meant new mosques and schools run by Islamic hardliners and radicals. The report also warned that there was growing evidence that certain circles in Qatar were funding the Islamic State and its European terror networks. Qatari investments would need to be scrutinised and monitored at the highest level, the report said.

Anastasia said, 'They usually want to influence the local Muslim community. But there's no point spending time or money on that here. There are only a few thousand Muslims here, and a handful of local converts.'

'Are they are funding a network to carry out a terrorist attack here?'

Anastasia shook her head. 'We think that's unlikely. Islamic State and Al-Qaeda like what they call "spectaculars" – 9/11, or 7/7 in London, *Charlie Hebdo*, something that sends shockwaves around the world. It takes a lot of time, energy and organisation to engineer a spectacular. You need local networks, access to explosives and guns, trained people and a high-profile target. Hungary is not high-profile enough. And we keep a very close watch on the Muslims here. There's no chatter, no word of new people preaching Salafism. The terrorists want Hungary to be their *kis kapu,* not their target.'

She sat up, placed a thousand forints on the table and handed him a piece of paper with a telephone number written on it. 'It was a pleasure to meet you, Balthazar. Call this number when you have the SIM card. No need to say anything, just call and hang up.' She looked hard at him. 'And tell your brother to get out of the travel business.'

He watched her walk out, her stride rapid and decisive, then glanced down at the piece of paper. Balthazar smiled as he saw that the last six digits spelled out his birthday.

Neither of them noticed a bald, middle-aged man standing by the window of a second-floor flat on the other side of the square, watching Anastasia as she left the restaurant.

TWELVE

'Where is it?' asked Reka.

Akos Feher sat back on the white leather sofa, making himself comfortable. 'Somewhere safe.'

'Safe for who?'

Feher smiled, enjoying the moment. 'For me, very. For you, that depends.' He stretched out his legs and placed his socked feet on the coffee table. 'May I?'

'I would prefer if you did not. It's delicate.' The Philippe Starck table dated from the 1980s. It was one of her favourite pieces, a thick square of smoked glass with round edges resting on four legs, each topped with a black rubber ball.

'OK. It's your house.' Feher smiled, lifted his legs back off the glass and settled down on the sofa, his point made.

'Would you like some coffee, Akos?' she asked, making sure to keep her voice pleasant and steady. A crystal carafe of mineral water stood in the centre, next to a French coffee press and two bowls, one of fruit and another filled with biscuits. A MacBook laptop stood next to the food and drink, the open browser frozen on a YouTube video. Reka had dealt with plenty of unpleasant people during her legal and political career, but never in her own home. This current mess was, though, nearly entirely of her own making. Feher nodded,

194

almost smirking now. Reka poured him a cup, resisted the urge to throw it in his face, and handed it to him instead. At least she had asked him to take his shoes off when he had come in.

They were sitting in the front lounge of Reka's home on Remetehegyi Way in District III, on the Buda side of the river. The Swedish interior designer had redecorated the large 1940s villas with taste and style, making the most of the curved balcony and picture windows that gave a panoramic view over the Danube and Pest. Bright summer sunlight streamed in. Abstract works of modern art by Hungarian painters hung on the pale cream walls. Reka was perched on a curved 1930s black leather armchair, her legs tucked underneath her. She had made a mistake last night. A major mistake. She should have told Antal to force Feher to hand over the heel. But she had been in shock and it'd been all she could do to focus on getting rid of the body. So now she had another problem to sort out. She definitely needed to talk to Feher, and they could hardly be seen in public together, especially considering the nature of the discussion.

Reka looked him up and down. This was the first time she had seen him out of the office. She never socialised with colleagues, especially those who were involved in her darker operations. Feher was dressed casually in a blue Ralph Lauren polo shirt and navy skinny-cut chinos. His blue boating shoes stood by the front door. He looked fit and well and seemed relaxed. That was one reason why she had chosen him to be the insider for the passport operation. He was presentable, intelligent and calm under pressure. But she sensed his nervousness underneath. They both knew that their fates depended on this meeting. Feher wanted his life back. Reka wanted the heel of her Louboutin. They needed to trust each other. But long before Akos Feher had appeared in her life, Reka had learned the cost of trusting the wrong person.

She sipped her coffee, a mix of Colombian and Ethiopian beans that were hand-blended for her by a small shop in a nearby Buda shopping mall. The caffeine invigorated her. This was her house. Akos Feher worked for her. His fate was in her hands. He would do as she bade. She asked, 'Were you there all the time?'

'Yes.'

'Why didn't you help?'

'I did.'

'You did nothing. You watched in the shadows. You would have let me die.'

'I helped myself. Why would I intervene? You wanted to make me your fall guy. To destroy my life. To send me to prison. Your attacker was solving my problem.' He paused, sipped his drink. 'This is very good coffee. Actually, I was going to. That's why I had the iron bar. I found it nearby. I was going to hit him with it while he was trying to strangle you. I draw the line at murder.' His face turned serious. 'But you don't.'

Reka was indignant. 'It was self-defence. I had no choice.'

'I don't mean him. He deserved it. I mean your thug, Antal, the one that you sent to me. Mr Clean-up. He threatened the life of my child. Is that how you work now, Madame Minister? By threatening kids?'

Reka started with surprise. 'No, of course not. What do you mean?'

For a moment Feher was back on the banks of the Danube, as Antal's hand slid down the child-sized metal shoe at the Holocaust memorial. 'He made it clear when I met him that he spoke for you. Then he made it even clearer that if I did not do what you wanted, he would kill my child.'

Reka's eyes widened. Even in her world there were limits. And this went beyond them. 'Akos, please believe me. I didn't tell him to do that. I didn't know anything about that. I'm sorry. Whatever you… decide, your family will be safe. They are not in danger. I give you my word.'

Feher snorted. 'But you were ready to let me take the fall?'

Reka nodded. 'Yes, I was. We both play hardball when we have to.' She raised her eyebrows. 'Like you are now. And, *kedves Akosom*, my dear Akos, you are hardly the innocent here. You knew the risks. You were happy to take your cut. To enjoy your loft apartment downtown, your BMW and your Porsche, long-weekend and summer breaks at your Balaton-fured apartment. None of which could ever be paid for by your civil servant's salary. If I go down, you come with me.'

'Why? I didn't kill anyone. You did.'

She looked down at her hands, her nails, now clipped as short as possible, her skin stained brown where she had dabbed the cuts and abrasions with Betadine. 'But you were there. You obstructed the course of justice. That's a serious offence.'

Feher was indignant. 'How?'

'One, you witnessed an attempted murder and did not inform the authorities. Two, you witnessed a killing in self-defence and did not inform the authorities. Three, you witnessed a body being illegally removed and the destruction and contamination of a crime scene and did not inform the authorities. More than that, you have in your possession the key piece of evidence.'

'But you killed the man, and organised the clean-up.' Feher paused for a moment. 'So what we have here is mutually assured destruction. Two unusable nuclear options.'

Reka laughed. 'Something like that. So why don't we find a way to disarm and move forward?'

'Who was the dead man, anyway?'

'A Gendarme.'

'How do you know?'

She leaned forward, turned the computer to face Feher, and pressed play. 'I checked the Gendarmerie's personnel files. Watch this. It's the same guy. They don't do anything without Dezeffy's say-so.' The video of Balthazar's fight at Keleti started. Feher watched until the end. 'Balthazar Kovacs. That's quite a pounding he took. Why did it stop so abruptly?'

Reka looked away, suddenly embarrassed. 'That's a Grade One. The victim is to be taken down to the floor, suffer bruises and moderate lacerations but no broken bones or lasting damage. Kovacs was knocked out for a few seconds, but they weren't supposed to do that.'

Akos looked at her as if seeing her for the first time. 'You mean there are...' he asked, his voice incredulous.

Reka exhaled hard. 'Instructions, yes. Quite precise instructions. There are five grades of beatings. Five is terminal. It's all in the Gendarmes' manual, like their interrogation techniques, based on the KGB's methods. It's highly classified.'

'But you knew about this manual?'

'Of course. I am the minister of justice.'

'It's revolting.'

'Yes. It is. But it won't last much longer.'

Feher sat back, thought for a moment. She looked remarkably composed, considering she had fought off a killer last night, killed him instead, then disposed of the body. She wore a loose pair of cream linen trousers and a tight, pink, long-sleeved cotton top. It was too warm for the weather, but doubtless covered up the scrapes and scratches. Her hair was tied back and she wore no make-up on her face, but the foundation cream around the base of her neck did not quite cover the red line. She was right, of course. He had been a willing participant in the passport operation from the start and had enjoyed all the profits that followed. Now that the dead Gendarme had been disposed of – he had no idea how, but had no doubt that Antal and his friends would have taken care of the job – the heel was the only loose end.

But the heel was also his insurance. Celeste Johnson, MI6, and the terrorist connection would not go away just because Reka Bardossy had killed whoever had been sent to kill her. The exchange was obvious. He would hand over the heel. She would make someone else the scapegoat. But what if he handed it over and then she reneged on the terms? And he was the only witness to the killing. For now, he believed Reka when she said that his family was safe. But what if he himself was not? He was sure that she had hidden all the details of the passport operation somewhere safe. Perhaps he needed to do the same, let it be known that if anything happened to him, they would be released. A glimmer of a smile flickered over his face... or sent straight to Celeste Johnson. He needed to think this through. He put his cup down on the table. 'What do I get if I give you the heel? Where do we go from here?'

'That's what I wanted to talk to you about. We're partners now.'

'Really? So we are splitting the profits fifty-fifty?'

Reka laughed. 'I like your chutzpah, Akos. But there won't be any more profits on passports. That operation is done now. I know you met with Celeste Johnson at the British embassy. How much do they know?'

'Almost everything. That the passports come from this ministry. That terrorists are using them. That bribes are being paid. She wanted me to spy on you and whoever else is involved, report to her.'

Reka's feeling of dread deepened. This was worse than she had imagined. 'And you said?'

'I'd think about it.'

'What do you want, Akos?'

For a moment he did not answer. He looked through the picture windows, at Budapest spread out below them. Para-gliders floated in the distance, riding the thermals over the hills. 'A written guarantee of immunity, that anything I did was authorised by you as the minister of justice as part of a law-enforcement operation. Signed by you.'

Reka frowned. She hated signing anything, let alone a con-fession of guilt in criminal activities. She drank some more coffee, thought for a moment. In fact, it might be feasible. She could backdate it, then spin it with the Brits that the ministry had been running a sting operation with the people-smug-glers to catch the Islamists. In fact, it was more than feasible. It could be a rather clever way out, but she would not let Feher know that so quickly. 'I'll think about it. What else?' There would, she knew, be more.

'My Porsche convertible.'

Reka gave him a wry look. Boys and their toys. This was a minor matter. 'Perhaps there is a way of importing it without too much paperwork. Or taxes.'

'Ministry plates?'

Reka laughed. 'Don't push it, Akos.'

'The Balatonfured apartment?'

Also solvable. 'It will be transferred to your child's name at the Land Registry. Nobody can take it from him. Any-thing else?'

'The most important thing. A fall guy. Who is not me.'

Reka smiled. 'Absolutely.'

'You prepare the paperwork. Immunity, the car and the Balatonfured flat. Then you get the heel.'

Reka leaned forward, proffered her hand. 'It's a deal.'

Akos shook her hand. She sat back, poured herself some more coffee. Would he stick to the deal? She thought so. Cars, holiday homes, even immunity were peripheral matters. What mattered was the fall guy. That plan was already part-formed in her head. It was clear, after this conversation, that it was her only option. But in order for it to work, she needed to see two people as soon as possible. The first, she was confident, would not be a problem. But Celeste Johnson would be considerably harder to persuade.

'Who's the lucky guy?' asked Feher.

He laughed when she said a name. It was a high-risk idea, very dangerous and quite beautiful in its simplicity – if she could make it work.

Bajnok bar, Mikzath Kalman Square, 2.00 p.m.

Across the river, in a backstreet in District VIII, somewhere far less salubrious than Reka Bardossy's villa, Balthazar was asking the same opening question.

Eniko leaned back, her arms crossed. 'Where is what? Nice to see you too, Tazi. The afternoon I spent looking after you yesterday – you're very welcome. Yes, I got home fine last night. Of course, I was delighted to get your text, asking me to meet you here with less than an hour's notice. No, I didn't have anything else to do this Saturday afternoon.'

Eniko's feistiness, her refusal to back down, was one of the first things that had attracted him to her. But he was a cop now, not a former boyfriend or even a platonic friend. And he needed to act the part, because they both knew that she had committed a crime. They were sitting in Bajnok, meaning 'champion', a gloomy bar on the corner of Mikzath Kalman Square in District VIII. The square itself had been recently gentrified, with new trees planted in the centre, modern grey-steel park benches, the facades of the nineteenth-century apartment buildings scrubbed and repainted. The side streets, dark, narrow, spattered with graffiti, were fighting a rearguard action with some success.

Nowhere more than Bajnok. There were two rooms, one in the front that looked out onto the street, and a smaller one in the back, where Balthazar and Eniko were sitting. The owner, Csongi, stood behind the bar in the front room, keeping watch. Csongi was a former flyweight boxer, a childhood friend of Gaspar's. The walls, floor and ceiling were varying shades of brown, stained with decades' worth of nicotine. Framed photographs and faded news stories about Csongi's fights provided splashes of colour. An array of cups, each carefully shined, stood on a small shelf above the cash desk. It was, Balthazar thought, as safe a place as any for the conversation he needed to have, and not somewhere that Eniko frequented or where she would feel in control.

Balthazar sipped his coffee. Like that served in Sandor Takacs's office, it was thick and tepid, strong, but not too bitter. The kind of brew he had grown up with and still preferred. 'Thank you for looking after me yesterday, Eniko. It was good of you to give up your afternoon. And I appreciate that. But you still have something of mine. And I need it back.'

He put his cup down, stopped talking, let the silence hang in the air as he kept looking at Eniko. It was an old policeman's trick. Make the accusation, then let the suspect fill the gap. Eniko, he was sure, used the technique as well during interviews with tricky or obstructive sources. But it was irresistible, particularly when the other party had done something wrong. Eniko was looking especially pretty today. She wore a sleeveless white blouse and a pair of cream pedal pushers. Her hair was pulled back in a ponytail and she had very little make-up, except plain lip gloss and a light touch of mascara. Perhaps she was going to have lunch with Tamas Nemeth. He pushed that thought aside.

Eniko caught Balthazar scrutinising her, was about to smile, then thought better of it. She looked around. 'This is a cool place. Why didn't you ever bring me here? It's really authentic.'

'Because then you would come back not with me, but with all your hipster friends. And then it wouldn't be very authentic any more.'

Eniko winced. 'Mee-*ow*. How are your bruises? Are you feeling better or worse than yesterday?'

He stretched his left arm out, palm up, ignoring the flash of pain the movement triggered in his back and shoulders. 'The SIM card?'

'Why did you ask me here if you don't want to talk to me?'

'I do want to talk to you. About the SIM card that you took from my pocket.'

She glanced down at the table for a second. 'I don't know what you are talking about, Tazi.' Her voice was flat.

'I think you do. While I was asleep yesterday you went through my trouser pockets and took out an evidence bag that held a blue-and-white SIM card.'

She kept staring at the table before she looked up and answered. 'Why do you think that? You were in a fight. Anything could have happened. It probably fell out at Keleti.'

'It did not fall out of my trousers.'

'How do you know?'

'Because I jammed it deep inside the ticket pocket. Because I remember checking that it was still there when we were in the taxi going home.' He leaned forward, his voice serious. 'This is not some kind of journalistic adventure, Eniko. A man is dead. This is a murder investigation. And you have the prime piece of evidence. I could, should have you arrested...'

She slid her iPhone across the table. 'The number for the police is 112.'

Balthazar picked up the handset. 'Good idea. I'll need a female officer to search you, before you are taken into custody.'

Eniko's eyes widened. 'You wouldn't...'

Balthazar said nothing, pressed his finger down on the 1 button. Eniko also said nothing. He pressed the 1 button again.

Eniko waved her right hand. 'Wait, wait.'

Balthazar paused, his finger hovering over the keypad. 'You have got ten seconds.'

Eniko swallowed. 'I can't believe that you would really do this.'

'It doesn't matter what you believe. What matters is that you give me back the SIM card.'

'You are serious, aren't you?'

Balthazar glanced at his watch. 'Four seconds.'

'I will give it to you, but hear me out. Please.'

'Two.'

'Let's work together. We can trade.'

'We can. And the first trade is you freely walking out of the door once you have given me the card.' His voice turned cold. 'Don't push me any further, Eni.'

Eniko blinked several times, clearly shocked at his tone, reached inside her bag, took out a small plastic box and slid it across the table. Balthazar opened it. The SIM card was there. He jammed it deep inside his trouser pocket. 'What's the trade?'

Eniko said, 'We both want to know what's on the card.'

'I'm a policeman. We have people for that.'

Eniko glared at him. 'Of course you do. You can get the numbers on the card, the text messages and a record of all the calls they have made. But you would have to put in a request, and even if you didn't and someone did it for you as a favour, it would still leave a data trail on their computer.'

'So?'

She stared at him, held his eyes. 'I think you are working under the radar.'

'Why?'

She sipped her Diet Coke, put her glass down. 'There are procedures for handling evidence, especially in a murder enquiry. Something tells me they don't involve stuffing it in a bag, putting it in your trouser pocket, and taking it home.'

She was completely correct, of course, although he would not admit it. And he could not use a police technician to strip the SIM card as he was not officially on the case, Sandor Takacs had made that clear. 'Why were you going through my trouser pockets?'

'Actually, I wasn't. I was folding your clothes while you were asleep. It was half out. I saw it was an evidence bag, and naturally, wanted to see what was in it.'

'And then you stole it.'

'Borrowed it, Tazi. You have it back.'

'Thanks. Your suggestion is?'

'We work together,' she said, her voice brisk and business-like. 'Partners.'

'Why would I do that?'

Eniko reached inside her bag, took out several printed sheets that were stapled together. She handed the papers to Balthazar, who flicked through them. The first section listed all the numbers on the SIM card, the second, outgoing calls, and the third, incoming calls. A fourth section included several incoming and outgoing SMS messages. The messages, he guessed, were in a kind of code, talking about a 'birthday party'.

Balthazar put the sheets down on the table. 'How did you get these?'

'I got them.' Eniko had asked Arpi, the Keleti activist, to help her. Arpi was an expert hacker, able to get into any electronic system including high-security government networks. 'Does it matter how?'

'I guess not. Thank you. This is very useful. Well done. I'll keep this.'

Eniko shrugged. 'Fine. I have a copy.' Balthazar's telephone bleeped. He looked down at the screen. A text message from Alex:

Hey Dad – what's the plan? Can't wait to see you

Balthazar smiled, tapped out a reply.

PBF

He planned to take Alex to his favourite playground on Freedom Square, then walk up Oktober 6th Street to a new burger bar and watch a film at home in the evening. Balthazar glanced at Eniko while he waited for the reply. 'Alex.'

'How is he doing?' she asked, a wistful look on her face.

'Fine, thanks. I'm seeing him later.'

'I'm sorry...' Her voice tailed off.

'Sorry for what?'

'... that I never met him.' She looked up, paused for a moment. 'Will I?'

'Maybe. I'm quite careful who I introduce to him. His life is turbulent enough, without new people walking in, then...'

'Walking out?'

'Something like that,' he replied, when his telephone beeped again.

Park, burger, film?

He tapped out 'yes x 3', then put his telephone down.

Eniko sighed. 'OK. So what do we do next?'

'*We* don't do anything. I will continue with my investigation. And you don't do anything else illegal.'

Eniko tapped the papers. 'This is just the start. We have the numbers but we need to know whose they are, build up a network of contacts.'

She was right. But that was going to be Anastasia Ferenczy, not Eniko Szalay. 'I'll think about it,' he said.

Just as he answered, Eniko's phone rang. She glanced at the screen. It showed 'number unknown'. She placed the handset on the table and let it ring several more times before it stopped.

'Why don't you answer it?' asked Balthazar.

Eniko shrugged. 'I never answer unknown numbers on the first call. If it's important they will call back or leave a voice-mail. The phone tells me when they do.' She waited several seconds then looked down. 'Nothing.'

The handset began to trill again. This time she picked it up, said hallo. Balthazar could hear a female voice ask for

207

Eniko Szalay. The voice sounded vaguely familiar but was too distant and tinny for him to properly recognise.

'Who is this?' asked Eniko. Her eyes widened when she heard the reply. She quickly stood up and backed away from the table, her phone now pressed hard against her ear. 'How do I know you are who you say you are?'

Balthazar heard nothing of the reply, but could see that it satisfied Eniko. She glanced at him and mouthed 'Excuse me', now completely possessed by the call. Her face was set and determined, her eyes focused, her shoulders jutting forward in the mix of excitement that she was on the trail of a story and her determination to get it. He watched her walk to the other side of the room and turn her back on him. There she listened briefly and said two more words. 'Where?' and 'When?'. She hung up and walked back over to the table, no longer apologetic, but calm and confident.

'Who was it?' asked Balthazar.

'Are we working together?'

'I told you. I'll think about it.'

'Let me know when you decide,' said Eniko as she gathered up her bag. 'Then I'll think about telling you who I'm meeting.' She turned and walked out.

Prime minister's office, Parliament, 2.30 p.m.

Pal Dezeffy pressed the pause button on the browser window. The screen showed a frozen image of the man who had tried to kill Reka, lying face-down by the castle rampart. His eyes stared sightlessly while blood oozed from the hole in the side of his neck. 'That worked out well,' said Dezeffy, his voice heavy with sarcasm. He turned to Attila Ungar. 'Plan B?'

Ungar was sitting next to him, behind the large oak desk

in the prime minister's office. The Gendarme commander shrugged. 'Same as Plan A. But this time I'll take care of it myself.'

Dezeffy exhaled hard, stood up and walked over to the windows overlooking the Danube. The river sparkled merrily in the bright sunshine, its rushing waters for once almost blue. A ferry boat filled with tourists taking selfies chugged towards the Pest embankment. His back to the room, he clenched his fist, banged it hard against the bulletproof window, and his face split into a broad grin. Ungar jumped, looked around for an intruder. 'Relax, Attila, it's just me,' said Dezeffy.

He watched the tourists disembark, clambering down from the boat to the walkway near Parliament. He had hit the window in celebration. She was still alive. And she had killed the man Ungar had sent to kill her. Dezeffy had known Reka since childhood. They had grown up together in the privileged world of the Communist elite. The party had promised equality for all, but as George Orwell had noted, 'All animals are equal, but some animals are more equal than others.' The Dezeffy and Bardossy children had enjoyed the greatest inequality that the workers' and peasants' state could provide: an education in London and Paris, a childhood in pre-war villas whose lounges were bigger than many family apartments, summer houses almost as large on the shore of Lake Balaton, residences staffed with live-in housekeepers and servants, a Volga limousine with a driver permanently on call, highly paid sinecures in government ministries for their parents.

Dezeffy trusted nobody, which was how he had survived at the top of Hungarian politics for so long, but Reka was the nearest thing he had to an ally. Part of him had always admired her, although he was careful never to let that slip.

On top of that, she was very good-looking and voracious in bed. Now she had despatched a would-be assassin with a part of a shoe. The more dangerous she was, the more alluring. He closed his eyes for a moment – seeing Reka on her back on the ground, the dead man's hands around her throat, her arm whipping up into his neck – feeling a familiar hunger surge.

Ungar said, 'Prime Minister, we really need to get her out of the way as soon as possible.'

Dezeffy closed his eyes for a second, banished the images of Reka in various states of undress that were pouring into his mind, forced himself to focus, and turned around. 'Try and think things through, Attila. If she didn't do it before, by now she will have deposited copies of all her files, all the evidence about the passports and the money. Almost certainly with her lawyer, with instructions to release them if anything happens to her. That's what I would do. There are probably copies somewhere on the dark web as well. We won't be able to find them. Do you want that information to be released? Who do you think is paying for your nice new uniforms and equipment and vehicles? The national budget?'

'It was your idea to do her at the castle,' said Ungar, sulkily.

Actually, it wasn't, Dezeffy almost said. It was the Librarian's. Instead he replied, 'And it was your job to execute it. Which you failed to do.'

'I lost a man.'

Dezeffy snorted with derision. 'To a woman. A woman armed with a pair of high heels.'

'She got lucky.'

'Yes. Lucky that your man was an amateur.'

'We don't even know where his body is.'

'Boo-hoo. Try the gravel pit in Budaors.' He looked at

Ungar. 'I believe you know where that is?' he asked, his voice sardonic. Ungar said nothing.

Dezeffy walked over to his desk and pressed the play button on the browser. The rest of the footage showed Reka standing up, calling Antal, the appearance of Akos Feher, the arrival of the clean-up crew, Reka and Akos Feher leaving. 'We have this, at least,' said Dezeffy. He gestured to Ungar to leave. 'Now let me think about how to use it. We need to bring her in, make her cooperate. But we need her alive.'

Ungar stood up, pointed at the black Nexus 6 phone on Dezeffy's desk. 'Is that the journalist's?'

Dezeffy nodded. 'At least you managed to do that properly.'

'Thanks. Anything useful?'

'Nothing yet. She bricked it remotely.' Dezeffy picked up the handset, pondered the black screen. 'The technicians will try again this afternoon. She's served her purpose, but she's getting in the way, asking a lot of questions.'

Ungar smiled. 'Journalists do that.'

'Until they realise it's in their best interest to stop.' He looked at Ungar. 'I think it's time she realised that. Don't you?'

Ungar nodded. 'Absolutely.'

'Good. And use your brain this time, not your fists. We want her scared. Not dead. And not on YouTube, showing off her bruises.'

'Of course. What about the Gypsy?'

'Keleti didn't work. He met someone from the ABS this morning.'

'Who?'

Dezeffy knew about Anastasia Ferenczy. He had a mole inside the security service. Several, in fact. But he was certainly not going to share that information with Attila Ungar.

211

He would move against her too, when the time was right. But not yet. 'Someone. It doesn't matter who. What matters is that you get rid of him. Make it look like an accident. Use a knife. They like knives. Everyone will think it's some kind of Gypsy feud.' He gestured at the door. Ungar stood up to leave. Dezeffy said, 'Get going. You have a busy afternoon.'

THIRTEEN

Rakoczi Square, 2.45 p.m.

Rakoczi Square had once been the epicentre of Budapest's red-light district, avoided at night by everyone except locals and the prostitutes' customers. It now looked like a spread from an urban design magazine. The front of the space opened onto the Grand Boulevard. It was flanked on both sides by rows of newly restored grand nineteenth-century apartment buildings, each with a shop on the ground floor. The metro station entrance in the centre of the square was marked by an ultra-modern steel-and-glass pavilion with a sloping roof. The square itself was covered with grey granite tiles. The central area, where prostitutes had once strolled back and forth, now housed a fountain and a modern playground in bright colours. Stallholders sold artisan cheese and organic fruit at a small market on one side of the metro entrance. The dank bars were gone, replaced by trendy cafés. Only Balthazar's destination, the Tito Grill, sandwiched at the back of the square between an ABC grocery store and a used clothing shop, was holding out.

Balthazar paused for a moment, watching the children running around the playground, climbing in and out of the toy cars and ships as their parents on the side watched indulgently. The people too, had changed. When Balthazar was

213

growing up nearby on Jozsef Street, this part of District VIII was largely Roma, with a smattering of poor locals and a small Jewish community. Now that District VII was pricing itself out of the market for locals on modest incomes, District VIII was becoming a popular place for young families. A 100-square-metre apartment here could still be had for 80,000 euros, considerably cheaper than across the Grand Boulevard.

Balthazar checked his watch. He needed to hurry up. He was scheduled to pick up Alex at 4.00 p.m. Sarah's apartment in District XIII was fifteen minutes away on the tram. He had an afternoon and the whole evening and night with his son, which would fly by. Eva *neni* had invited them both down for Sunday breakfast. She doted on the boy, and he loved her pancakes.

Balthazar sat for a moment on a bench, suddenly hit by a wave of fatigue. The weather did not help. The sky was blue and clear with a few wisps of white cloud. The sun was hot on his face and it was warm enough for him to feel the heat rising off the ground. He wore a white T-shirt and light canvas jeans and black wraparound Ray-Ban sunglasses. The T-shirt was already sticking to his back. Balthazar knew he should be resting; his body and brain had taken a sustained shock. Both needed time to recover. Instead, he had been on the move much of yesterday evening and all this morning. Thankfully, the iron bar in his head had shrunk and almost vanished. He opened his mouth, stretched his jaw, could open it a little wider today. The paracetamol took the edge off, but he knew there was a week of stiffness and discomfort ahead, especially as the bruises came out. His back and shoulders felt as though a herd of elephants had thundered over them.

Balthazar rolled his shoulders, trying to ease out some of the tension. He had returned home after meeting Eniko, and hidden the SIM card and the list of telephone numbers under a floorboard in the lounge. After Balthazar had been targeted by Hazifiu.hu, the extreme right-wing website, Sandor Takacs had insisted that a proper security system be installed in his flat, with a camera that was connected to the Budapest police headquarters. Most of the time he did not bother activating it, unless he was overnighting somewhere else. He had very few valuables, and most of those were of sentimental rather than monetary value. In any case Eva *neni*, who kept a sharp eye on all visitors, was far more effective than an electronic system. Takacs had called Balthazar on the way home. He had seen the YouTube footage of the attack at Keleti. Takacs had ordered Balthazar to be checked over by a police doctor and move out and stay with him. Balthazar had managed to talk him out of both demands. But he had agreed to activate the flat's security system.

He shut his eyes, and took his Ray-Bans off. Who was Eniko going to meet later? Clearly a source of some kind, and almost certainly connected to the migrant crisis. Balthazar had watched Eniko work with interest in the few weeks they had been together. Journalists, like policemen, needed information and a network of contacts to provide it. But policemen, unlike journalists, could use the threat of criminal proceedings to make unwilling sources talk. Journalists had to use their wits and powers of persuasion to cajole their contacts, sometimes to reveal information that was not flattering or helpful. Which made Eniko's people skills all the more impressive. He smiled as he remembered his grandfather's advice about girls, 'don't reheat the *toltott kaposzta*, stuffed cabbage'. But the problem was, that reheated stuffed cabbage was even tastier the next day. He shut his eyes for a moment, Eva's voice resounding in his head: 'Any woman who brings you home in that state and looks after you is either your girlfriend or your wife, or wants to be.' Did she? Maybe. For now though, there were other things to focus on, such as the Gendarmes covering for an Islamist terrorist murdering refugees on his beat.

For a few moments he tried to clear his mind, listening to the soundtrack of District VIII: the happy shouts of the children playing nearby, the trundle of the tram as it rolled along the main boulevard, a siren wailing in the distance.

Balthazar was well-travelled. He had spent two weeks attached to the Metropolitan Police, had met colleagues and attended conferences in Vienna, Berlin and Brussels, marvelled at their mix of cultures. Budapest was not as cosmopolitan as western cities, but the Hungarian capital too had its hidden outposts where immigrants and foreigners gathered among their own. Arab moneychangers met in the Cairo restaurant on Garay Square, behind Keleti Station, to compare exchange rates and smoke fruit-flavoured tobacco in brass and gold shisha pipes. African students and the handful of African refugees who had been allowed to stay congregated at the Lagos *bufe*, behind Blaha Lujza Square. The Russians, especially the newly rich who were buying up prime properties downtown and in the Buda hills, favoured the ritzy bars and restaurants of the five-star hotels along Budapest's riverbank. The latest influx, of Chinese investors, was also spread out in Buda, near the British and American schools. The city's several hundred Israeli medical, dentistry and veterinary science students favoured, naturally enough, the old Jewish quarter in District VII.

But the biggest group of foreigners was probably the southern Slavs, the Serbs, Croatians, Bosnians and marooned former Yugoslavs whose country no longer existed and now did not know what they were. Tens of thousands of refugees had poured north across the border into Hungary during the wars of the early 1990s, many of them smart, young and entrepreneurial. Some had planned to return home once the fighting was over, but had eventually moved on to Vienna, London, Berlin, New York or Toronto. Some had gone back to Belgrade or Zagreb. They found their new countries awash with traumatised refugees, gunmen and organised crime. They promptly left again, many returning to Hungary, where they eventually applied for citizenship.

A handful, like the man Balthazar was going to see, were criminals themselves. Balthazar opened his eyes to see a man with a familiar face, sitting ten yards away on another bench, reading that day's *Magyar Vilag*. He took his sunglasses off to see him better. The man caught Balthazar's eye and nodded. Balthazar half-nodded back.

What was he doing here? Tamas Fekete was better known as the Hammer, several of which he liked to use in the course of his work. Fekete was in his late twenties, stocky, muscled, about five feet eight, with the over-developed physique of a regular steroid user. He wore a tight white T-shirt emblazoned with the MNF logo and blue shiny track pants. Despite his T-shirt, Fekete was a debt collector for Black George, who definitely did not meet the MNF's standards of racial purity. Which was why Fekete should not have been in Rakoczi Square. Under the terms of the agreement brokered by the Kris, Black George operated in District IX, all of which counted as his territory. District VIII belonged to Gaspar. Both groups' men were allowed to pass through either district, if necessary, en route to somewhere else. But they were not allowed to linger. Eating or drinking in a District VIII café, even hanging on a park bench, was a hostile act. Fekete caught Balthazar's eye again, deliberately this time, winked, sat back and slowly turned another page of the newspaper.

At that very moment, Balthazar's phone rang. He looked down at the screen: it was Sarah. He considered not answering. Judging by previous experience, there was only one reason why she was calling now, shortly before his time with his son. He answered, the sinking feeling in his stomach growing steadily heavier.

'I'm really sorry, Tazi. Alex can't make it this afternoon,' said Sarah, not sounding sorry at all.

Balthazar resisted the urge to hurl the telephone across the square, ideally at the Hammer. Instead he kept his voice calm. 'Why?' he asked in English.

'He's double-booked.'

'With what?'

'A children's conflict resolution workshop.'

Balthazar held the phone away from his head, staring at it as though it had just landed from outer space. 'A what?'

'We're really excited about it. It's being developed by the Gender Studies department at Central European University. There are some really interesting creative visualisation techniques about non-hierarchical de-acceleration. I forgot that I had put his name down three months ago. Alex is one of the first kids to try it.'

Alex attended the American school, a mini-campus better equipped than most Hungarian universities, far out on the very edge of Budapest. The children were a mix of expatriates whose parents were diplomats or worked for the

218

United Nations or other international organisations and corporations, and the Hungarian nouveau riche. Like every schoolboy, Alex had to cope with troublesome peers, who sometimes got physical. Balthazar's advice on conflict resolution was simple and had served him well growing up on Jozsef Street: if someone hits you, fight low and dirty and hit them back as hard as you can. So far, according to Alex, it had worked very well.

There was no point engaging Sarah on the merits of the workshop. He thought for a moment. Her usual tactic was to try and provoke him, so she could then run to her lawyers and claim he was being uncooperative or even intimidating. He asked, 'Can I talk to him?'

'Maybe later. He's asleep now.'

Balthazar brought his emotions under control. He could call Alex directly, on his own phone, but that would only annoy Sarah. He needed time to think. Sarah considered herself a smart intellectual, but her thought patterns were rigidly set in a politically correct paradigm. Which meant she was actually quite predictable. Which meant in turn that he should be able to outmanoeuvre her. The first thing was to buy some time. 'OK, Sarah. Listen, I'm tied up with something right now. Can I call you back in a few minutes?'

'Sure,' she said, clearly surprised how easily the call had gone, and hung up.

Balthazar was in the middle of a turf war apparently brewing between his brother and the most dangerous organised-crime boss in the city, but that would have to wait. Alex came first. Balthazar knew that protesting to Sarah would get him nowhere. He had to be clever, give her something she wanted. What she wanted, more than anything, was academic recognition. Sarah was still trying to finish her PhD thesis, which would hopefully bring her an assistant professor's post at CEU. Its working title was 'Gendering the domestic bio-space: A Study of inter-familial power dynamics in Roma society'. Jargon aside, the topic was actually quite interesting: how Gypsy women used food and sex to control their men. Sarah's problem was that apart from Balthazar, his family, and Maria, her cleaning lady, she did not know any Gypsies, let alone Gypsy women, and she was no longer welcome at Jozsef Street. Sarah, like many of her colleagues, lived in an academic bubble. She walked from Pozsonyi Way in District XIII across the Grand Boulevard and through District V to the Central European University each morning and back again in the evening. If she went out, it was usually to the ruin pubs of District VII. She rarely visited District VIII and had no contacts in the villages and settlements outside the capital.

Balthazar had been her ambassador. When they first got together, Sarah wanted to explore everywhere. He had taken her into the ghettoes of Districts VIII and IX, and the Roma settlements in the villages around Budapest. Swept up in her enthusiasm, he had quickly fallen in love with the vivacious New Yorker who was so fascinated by his world. But as their relationship faded, so had Sarah's passion for fieldwork. By the end, she was mostly content to recycle other sociological studies peppered with densely referenced academic jargon. Her other problem was that when she did meet Roma women, they had no idea what she was talking about. She couldn't speak Hungarian and had not even learned a few greetings in Lovari. But this was more than a language issue. After so many years in academia, her whole conceptual framework was utterly alien to them. Even Balthazar struggled to translate her questions into comprehensible language.

He had heard on the CEU grapevine that Sarah's supervisor, a ferocious Swede, had said that without more fieldwork, she would not receive her doctorate. He had also heard on his own grapevine that a group of Roma women in a village outside Budapest had recently set up a weaving cooperative – against the will of their menfolk – which would be a perfect solution for Sarah's fieldwork problem.

Balthazar glanced across the square. The Hammer had put his newspaper down and was now on the phone. Balthazar put his sunglasses back on and rubbed his neck, trying to ease a tendon which seemed to have locked solid, and thought for a moment. Maybe, much as the idea pained him, he should postpone Alex's overnight visit. It was only a day since the beating and it would take at least one more to recover. He knew he would run out of energy by the early evening. He didn't want Alex to see him like this and to worry. Plus, the situation with the Gendarmes was not resolved. Balthazar had humiliated Attila Ungar in front of his men. The attack at Keleti was payback and a warning to stay away from investigating the dead man. But he was not staying away. He was digging deeper. The Gendarmes would come back for him and the next encounter would be much worse. What if they came to his flat when Alex was there? For now, Alex was probably safer staying at his mother's. He could see him tomorrow evening, somewhere public, like the playground on Freedom Square. That was right by the American embassy. The square was thoroughly covered by the embassy's CCTV – even the Gendarmes could not interfere with that – and there were always lots of policemen around. They would be quite safe there. Balthazar glanced again at the Hammer. All that aside, why was Black George's man here, provoking him?

Balthazar picked up the phone and called Sarah. As expected, she did not pick up and the call went to voicemail. He left a message, suggesting that he meet Alex the next afternoon instead and briefly mentioned the Roma women's cooperative. He sat back and relaxed, enjoying the warmth of the sun on his face. After a couple of minutes, his phone rang. He glanced at the screen, took the call.

Sarah was friendliness itself. 'Hi, so sorry I didn't pick up. But that's a great idea to reschedule for tomorrow afternoon, Tazi. The workshop is only on this evening and Alex will have done his schoolwork by tomorrow. He can be out until eightish.'

Balthazar thanked her, said nothing for several seconds. Sarah was only helpful when she wanted something. The silence stretched out, then she surrendered. 'Thanks for the information about the women's cooperative. It sounds amazing.'

'It is.' Balthazar had taken a course in the Gender Studies department during his time at CEU. He dug into his store of English academic vocabulary. 'They are doing some pioneering work dismantling the intra-familial hierarchy and reconfiguring the domestic power dynamic.' He paused. 'And I know they want to tell their story. They are looking for funding so they need someone to write about them.'

Sarah could barely keep her hunger from her voice. 'The thing is, er, Tazi, could you... er...'

Balthazar smiled. She could not bring herself to ask for what she needed. The Roma women would be much more at ease, would talk to Sarah more openly with Balthazar there. In fact, without him, she would get nowhere. 'Sure. I can take you. Maybe next Saturday.'

'It's a date. Thank you.'

Balthazar checked the calendar on his watch. After tomorrow, he would not see his son for more than a week. 'Alex could come with us. An extra trip.'

That meant it would not be counted under the terms of his agreement with Sarah. He heard her sharp intake of breath, sensed her annoyance that she was losing control over his access to Alex fighting with her appetite for academic success. The latter won.

'Sure. That would be nice. Oh, and I meant to ask. How are you? Someone told me you were attacked at Keleti.'

'Fine, now. It got a bit rough, but nothing serious. Let's meet at Freedom square tomorrow afternoon. I'll call you.'

Balthazar hung up, then scanned his surrounds. Two more of Black George's men had appeared, one young, barely in his twenties, the other obese, in his forties. Both were strolling leisurely around the entrance to the metro station. They too caught Balthazar's eye. They smiled, sat down on two different benches, facing him from two sides, and lit cigarettes, the trails of smoke rising slowly over the square.

HEV station, Boraros Square, 3.00 p.m.

Eniko sat back in the hard plastic seat and stared out of the window as the HEV, the suburban railway, trundled alongside the Danube. Her instructions had been precise. Take the train from Boraros Square, ride it six stops to the end of the line at Csepel, where a driver in a blue Nissan saloon would pick her up. She knew where she was at Boraros Square. It stood on the edge of District IX, next to the Petofi Bridge over the Danube. Raday Street, a trendy pedestrianised thoroughfare, was nearby. The 4 and 6 trams ran over Petofi Bridge, connecting with the Grand Boulevard that looped around

223

the inner city. The number two tram also left from Boraros Square, heading back downtown, rattling north along the Pest side of the embankment, past Parliament until the route ended at Margaret Bridge.

As the HEV pulled out of the station, she realised somewhat to her shame that after almost thirty years living in the city, she had never been to Csepel Island. Born in Budapest, Eniko had grown up in District XIII, not far from where Sarah lived, although they had never met. It was a liberal, middle-class area, home to a large Jewish community, *Ulipotvaros* in Hungarian, New Leopold Town, shortened to 'Lipi' by its inhabitants. Both Eniko's grandparents on her mother's side were Jewish. They had survived the war in the flat where her mother now lived, on a street named for Raoul Wallenberg, the Swedish diplomat who had saved tens of thousands of Budapest Jews by declaring them to be under Swedish protection. Budapesters were often intensely territorial, passionately loyal to their own district. Eniko's life, like many of her peers', was defined by the 4, 6 and number 2 tram lines which cut the city into a giant semi-circle, with occasional forays into District VIII on the other side of the Grand Boulevard.

The HEV carriages were oblong, with flat roofs, trusty Soviet-era workhorses, crowded with shoppers laden down with bags of groceries. Three girls in their early teens sat near Eniko, crowding around their friend in the middle as she scrolled through her Instagram account, hooting at the photographs. A cycle path ran alongside the train track. Eniko watched a couple in their early twenties racing the train and each other, swerving in and out before nearly colliding, laughing out loud. Part of her thought that was how she should be spending her day, zipping along the riverbank, out in the fresh air, with a guy – there was one in particular who sprang to mind.

She closed her eyes for a moment and played back – again – the conversation in Balthazar's flat on the day that they broke up, hearing herself say that she wanted to end it because she was going to London, the look of amazement on his face, his protests that London was just two hours away on an aeroplane and in any case she was not moving there permanently, but only for a few months; her shake of her head, tight and determined, the dull hurt in his eyes and the heavy silence. Everything Balthazar said had been true, which was why she could not meet his eye. Perhaps she should have just told him the truth: that she was falling in love with him, as she had never done before, and that she was terrified that she would be hurt. So she had taken the coward's way out and walked away. And part of her – a large part, she realised since she had returned to Budapest – regretted that decision every day.

But if her personal life was a disaster, at least she had her work. Why did Bela Lidaki want to meet her? To threaten her, perhaps? Or to give her more information?

The latter was more likely. The damage to him was done. In most European democracies – 'normal countries' as Hungarians described them – the next step would be criminal charges, and prison. But no Hungarian politician ever went to prison, no matter how corrupt they were and how strong the evidence against them. That was the one rule of engagement that all sides agreed on, whoever was in power. That and the 80/20 per cent split: eighty per cent of the monies stolen from the EU subsidies went to the ruling party, the other twenty was divided up among the opposition. Eniko had been used as a conduit, she knew, aiding one side in an intra-party struggle. She still did not know who sent her the documents and video footage, but every source she had ever dealt with had an agenda. She had no choice but to publish the documents and video footage. As the former interior minister, in charge of both the police and the secret service, Bela Lidaki would be privy to many of the government's innermost secrets. He had been brought down by the prime minister, she was sure. What would Bela Lidaki want now, more than anything? Revenge.

Eniko felt her pulse quicken. Partly from nervousness – she was now a player in a political game with very high stakes – and partly with a familiar anticipation that a big story was coming her way. She checked her watch: it was six minutes past three. Her second appointment was downtown at 6.00 p.m., so she should have plenty of time. The journey from Boraros Square to Csepel Station only took around thirteen minutes. The train veered away from the riverbank, heading deeper into the island, stopping at the local stations. It passed over a small canal, its water brown and stagnant, through fields bordered by wire fences. An abandoned Communist-era industrial building stood by the side of the track, a grey concrete hulk covered with graffiti. Eniko felt as though she had crossed some kind of border, not just of place, but of time. Single-storey houses stood shuttered, their front gardens wild and overgrown.

The train slowed down as it arrived at the penultimate stop, Karacsonyi Sandor Street. The carriage emptied out, the teenage girls and the women shoppers chattering happily as they disembarked. A blue Trabant, now a rarity, puttered down a side street, its narrow exhaust pipe coughing out puffs of grey smoke. A young woman got on board. She looked like she was in her late twenties, skinny, with cropped brown hair and a round face. She wore black combat trousers and a white T-shirt, looked fit and very toned. She sat opposite Eniko, who smiled in greeting. The young woman did not return her smile, but gave her a stony glance. The train pulled out and Eniko took out her old Nokia, called up Balthazar's number and tapped out a message:

> On the HEV, almost at Csepel. It was good to see you
> this a.m. Hope the bruises are healing.

At least someone would know where she was. Eniko pressed send. Nothing happened. She looked down at the handset. There was no reception. This was unusual. Hungary was blanketed in mobile coverage and they were well within the city limits. Eniko glanced at the woman opposite. She looked away, as though she had been caught staring at her.

Eniko looked out of the window again, feeling increasingly unsettled, watched an elderly woman ride an ancient, heavy bicycle down the middle of the road. For a moment she thought of her Grandma Kati, remembered the story she had told about how she had survived the last, murderous winter of the war. The Arrow Cross had raided her apartment building in January 1945. The Russians were just a few hundred yards away. She could hear the shooting, the crack of the rifle bullets, the stutter of the *pe-pe-chas*, the Russians' submachine guns, their shouts and cries. Kati was half starved, shivering, standing in the courtyard of her apartment building together with her Jewish neighbours. The Arrow Cross men were about to march them to the riverbank. One of the gunmen was the parent of a friend of hers. She had been in the man's house, eaten his wife's *almas pite*, apple pie. As the line started to move out, he had pushed her back into the courtyard, so hard she had slipped over.

The train slowed, then came to a halt between the stations. Eniko glanced at her phone again. Still no reception. Was someone blocking the signal? Or maybe she was being paranoid. She looked around, damped down her anxiety. Green fields stretched into the distance. A stork flew overheard, towards the riverbank. The young woman looked out of the window, raised her right hand and slowly scratched her neck. A loudspeaker crackled in the carriage roof, apologising for the delay, which was for 'technical reasons.' Eniko watched her stand up, looked out of the window again. Two large figures dressed in black were walking rapidly towards the train.

FOURTEEN

Balthazar stood on the empty pavement outside the Tito Grill, took off his Ray-Bans, hooked them into the neck of his T-shirt, and glanced up. A CCTV camera on the outer wall pointed at the door. Where was everybody? Normally on a Saturday lunchtime, especially in the heat of an Indian summer, the place would be packed, with a queue of customers snaking back into the square. But the restaurant was shuttered and silent, the tables and chairs chained up and gathered together. A red light glowed softly underneath the CCTV lens. Balthazar stared at the camera and knocked once. After several seconds the door opened a fraction.

'Are you alone?' a male voice asked.

'Of course,' he replied.

The door opened wider and Balthazar stepped inside. A man in his thirties moved away from the door. He was short and wiry, with green eyes and two days' worth of beard. He wore a white T-shirt and a shoulder holster that held a Glock pistol. 'Hallo, Memed,' said Balthazar. They two men shook hands, and Memed gestured that Balthazar should walk across the room.

Goran Draganovic was just where Balthazar expected him to be, sitting in the far corner of the room, flanked on either side by his other two lieutenants: Vladimir, from Belgrade, and Anton, from Zagreb. Memed was a Bosnian Muslim from Sarajevo. The old multinational Yugoslavia was gone forever, but here, at least, it lived on, in Budapest's underworld. All three men wore the same shoulder holster. An Uzi machine pistol lay on the table in front of them, next to a large, full ashtray, half a dozen coffee cups, and two half-empty packets of Marlboro red cigarettes. A laptop showed the feed from the CCTV camera on the street. A clear-glass wine bottle, three quarters full of a transparent liquid, and half a dozen thick shot glasses stood by the computer.

Goran beckoned Balthazar to his table. The two men hugged, Balthazar trying not to wince at the contact. Goran gestured at Balthazar to sit down, which he did. Goran was in his late forties, over six feet tall, broad-shouldered, with sharp cheekbones, black hair, bushy eyebrows that met in the middle, and deep-set blue eyes. He had lived in Budapest for twenty years or so. Unlike many of his Serbian compatriots, Goran was not voluble. Balthazar knew he had served in both the Yugoslav and Bosnian Serb armies. Goran was a crack shot, often practised on a shooting range outside the city. There were rumours that he had been a sniper. Balthazar had asked him once about the wars. Goran had changed the subject immediately. Balthazar had not asked again.

Goran lit a cigarette, looked Balthazar up and down. '*Kak o'si?* How are you?' he asked, through a thick plume of smoke.

Balthazar had picked up a few words of Serbian on a trip to Belgrade, to investigate the murder of a Budapest gangster with Balkan connections, a few years before. '*Dobro, hvala.* Fine, thanks. Better than I look. The painkillers help.'

'That's good, because you look pretty rough.' He gestured at the bottle on the table. 'That's the best painkiller. My grandfather's *sliva*. He makes it from his own plums. Want some?'

Balthazar shook his head. 'I'm fine, thanks.'

Goran sat down. 'No serious damage?'

Balthazar pulled out a chair, sat down and shook his head. 'Only to my pride.'

'I saw it on YouTube. You did pretty well, five against one. It could have been much worse. They stopped very quickly once you were down. Did you get the message?'

Balthazar smiled. 'What message?' He glanced at the Uzi. 'Expecting visitors?'

'We already had some. They might come back.'

Goran Draganovic was the king of the region's people-smugglers. Born in Subotica, in the far north of Serbia, his family had been smugglers for centuries, outwitting every kind of authority, from the Ottomans and the Austro-Hungarians to Tito's border guards. He now operated a network that reached from Bulgaria, Macedonia and Serbia into Hungary and western Europe. Goran was not a trafficker: he did not transport young women who applied for jobs as barmaids and waitresses, then found themselves sexually enslaved to pay off a debt that could never be paid off. Rather, he considered himself a kind of travel agent. The posters around the bar advertised the destinations he offered. Anyone who paid for the journey but was stopped by border officials or did not make it was offered a full refund, or another attempt, until they got through.

Goran had worked with Gaspar, Balthazar's brother, for years, bringing young women up from the Balkans and the former Soviet states to Budapest. Some stayed to work in

Gaspar's brothels or hostess bars, others went further west. Both men soon realised that the migrant crisis was a fantastic business opportunity. The Hungarian-Serbian border, the frontier to the Schengen zone of visa-free travel and western Europe, was now, in effect, completely open. Every day, hundreds, sometimes thousands, of people just walked through into Austria. In response, Austria had reinstituted border controls. But local people – or those the border guards believed to be locals – were rarely checked. Gaspar provided the clothes for the migrants to dress as Roma, Goran took care of the transport and the bribes for the border guards.

Balthazar looked around, asked Goran, 'Where is Biljana?'

Biljana was the manager, a vivacious Serb in her late thirties, who kept the food and drink flowing smoothly even when every table was full. 'I gave her the day off. And everyone else. So what brings you back to Chekago?'

Balthazar took out his phone, showed the photo of Simon Nazir to Goran. 'His name is Simon Nazir. Did you know him?'

Goran picked up the bottle, gestured at Balthazar. 'Sure you don't want some?'

Balthazar shook his head. Goran poured himself a small measure. 'Is this official, *brat*, brother?' he asked, his voice wary.

'Yes and no.'

'Meaning?'

'A man was murdered. Once I catch the killer, he will be officially charged and sent to prison.'

Goran knocked back his shot. 'But you are working unofficially?'

'That's it.'

'Why?'

'It's easier that way.'

'Because someone doesn't want you to be on it all.'

Balthazar smiled. 'That's about it.'

'That someone being?'

'Attila Ungar. The Gendarmes have the case.'

Goran nodded. 'That means the prime minister. Why does he care about a dead migrant?'

'That is a very good question. So can we talk? Unofficially?'

Goran nodded. 'OK. I never met your guy. But his name was on our list. Gaspar must have already told you that.'

'Fat Vik did.' Balthazar took out his notebook and showed the page with the telephone number to Goran. 'Do you know this number?'

'Have you called it?'

'Not yet. I wanted to show it to you first.'

'It's good you did. It's Black George's.'

'That figures. I saw his guys outside on the square. Three of them. Very cool, very confident. They are breaking the terms of the agreement.'

Goran said, 'They've been here all week, dogs pissing in their corners.'

'But these are also your corners. Does Gaspar know?'

'Of course. He is ignoring it. He thinks it is just a provocation.'

'But you don't,' said Balthazar.

'No. Not when so much money is at stake and we are all in the same business.'

'What do you plan to do?'

'Either we go to war, or we surrender. There are no other options.'

Balthazar looked at the bottle. 'Maybe a small one.' It was three hours since he had taken his painkillers. A small shot would not hurt and would certainly help oil the conversation. Serbs, like many Balkan men, were much more open over a bottle. Goran poured Balthazar a shot and slid the glass across. Balthazar took a sip, felt the warm glow as the spirit slid down the back of his throat, the taste of the plums expand across his mouth. '*Dobro. Vrlo dobro.* Good. Very good.'

'Thanks. I will tell Grandpa.'

Goran slowly exhaled, shot Balthazar a knowing look. 'Any other reason, apart from our long friendship, why I should help?'

'To ensure a profitable business climate.'

'This business won't stay profitable for long.'

'Why not? You have hundreds, thousands of potential customers.'

Goran said, 'We also have a new partner. Not one I invited to join us.'

'Who?'

'Your friend, Attila Ungar. The Gendarmes are setting up a new border protection unit. They have off-road vehicles, night-vision goggles, heat sensors, all state of the art. And they are on a bonus scheme: 5,000 forints for every migrant they detain.'

Balthazar frowned. 'That's new.'

'Very. It starts on Monday.'

'What does Ungar want from you?'

'Twenty per cent – of our total charge. Or we get hunted. We charge five hundred euros a crossing and on a good day we move several dozen people. After expenses, we probably clear around two or three hundred euros per person. So we instantly lose a good part of our profits. That's his opening shot. You can be sure that it will increase.'

'That's why you and I should cooperate.' Balthazar leaned forward. 'First the Gendarmes shut down Simon Nazir's case. Then they will shut down the murder squad. Then the police. All that will be left is the Gendarmes. And then they will shut you down.'

Goran said nothing, stubbed out his cigarette. He opened a new window on his laptop, turned it around so Balthazar could see the screen.

The monitor showed the CCTV footage of the restaurant's dark and cramped rear office. There were two small coffee cups on the table. Goran sat at the table, another man in front of him. Hejazi. Even in the dim light it was clear that the top of his left ear was gnarled and discoloured.

'Mahmoud Hejazi,' said Balthazar. 'Why was he here?'

Goran looked at Balthazar in surprise. 'You know him?'

'I know who he is. I have never met him. They call him the Gardener.'

'Do they? We had a different name for him.' Goran looked at Balthazar, puzzled. 'How do you know who he is?'

Balthazar thought for a couple of seconds before he replied. Goran should know who he was dealing with. 'Hejazi is an Islamic radical. He's on watch lists in London, Berlin, even America. Some of his friends have been turning up in Britain, flying in on Hungarian passports.' He turned to Goran. 'What did he want?'

'Austria. No dressing up. It had to be completely untraceable, he said. Through the green border, the fields.'

'So? You do that all the time.'

'Not for him.'

'Good. This is way beyond business as usual, *brat*. Why not?'

A cloud passed across Goran's face. 'In the war, in Bosnia, I was captured by a unit of Mujahideen, foreign soldiers, Arabs

235

mostly, Islamic radicals fighting with the Bosnian army. They held us in a POW camp in Zenica. It was supposed to be under the control of the Bosnian army, but the Mujahideen were in control. We called him the Butcher. He executed two of my friends. With a knife. I was due to be next, the following day. The Red Cross arrived that morning. We were swapped in a prisoner exchange. So the Butcher is now the Gardener. Whatever he is called, I told him we had more customers than we could handle. That we could not help him.'

'And what did he say?'

'He asked if I had any partners, anyone else who could help. I told him I didn't know anyone I could recommend, but he should ask around. The side streets around Keleti are packed with smugglers.'

'Did he remember you?'

Goran pressed the play button. Hejazi slid his cup across the table, said, 'The coffee in Zenica was better.' The footage showed him walking out of the door.

'Where is he now?' asked Balthazar.

'I wish I knew. He needs to get across the border. We won't take him. The passports won't work any more. He won't trust the guys in the side streets around Keleti. So that leaves one option.'

'Black George,' said Balthazar.

'I am seeing him tonight. He is putting on one of his shows. Do you want to come? You can ask him yourself.'

Balthazar drained the last drops of sliva from his glass. 'Sure. Can you get me in?'

Goran nodded. 'If I let them know in advance.'

Balthazar thought for several seconds. 'Why do you think government officials are selling passports that end up in the hands of Islamic radicals?'

Goran laughed. 'Is that a serious question? Money. Why else? Lots of money, more than they know what to do with. They don't care where the passports end up. They just care about getting paid.'

Goran took out his iPhone, called up the *Magyar Vilag* website on his browser, and handed it to Balthazar. He had not seen the newspaper yet or checked its website. The home page showed a photograph of Pal Dezeffy shaking hands with a tall Arab man wearing a pristine white dishdasha and head-dress at a reception at the Buda Castle. The headline read: 'Prime Minister Welcomes Gulf Investors.' Balthazar speed-read the article. It detailed how a consortium of investors from Qatar, Kuwait and Abu Dhabi had promised to invest the equivalent of billions of euros in Hungary, to build new roads and railways, new docks and a port on the Danube. The investment package was the biggest in Hungary's history. It would create tens of thousands of jobs. At the same time, the residence bond scheme was to be expanded and accelerated for senior management and officials involved in the invest-ment package.

'Check the last paragraph,' said Goran.

Balthazar read through until the end. The investors would also have the right to nominate friends, relatives and associates for permanent residence. This was new. He remembered his conversation with Anastasia that morning, her explanation of how the Gulf investors wanted to use Hungary as a transit route to Europe, where they would dump their Islamic radicals. The residence bond scheme would allow the Gulf investors to set up a forward base in Budapest for anyone they wanted to bring in, then move them westwards.

Attila Ungar carefully tore the page from Eniko's black Moleskine notebook and placed it on the table between them. She looked down at the lined yellow sheet. Her handwriting spelled out his name.

'Hallo, Eniko,' Ungar said, his voice friendly and soothing. 'It's a pleasure to see you again.'

'Is it?'

Ungar smiled. 'Well, I think so.'

Eniko suppressed a shiver. She had met Ungar several times while she was with Balthazar. She had never liked him, even less when Balthazar had told her about Ungar's working methods. 'Why am I here?'

Ungar leaned forward, pushed the sheet towards her. 'Why is my name in your notebook?'

Eniko shrugged, told herself to remain calm. This was not good. Nobody knew she was here. But she had rights. Hungary was not a country where inconvenient journalists were swept off the streets and disappeared. Not yet, anyway. She looked down at her phone. There was still no reception. She asked, 'Are you blocking the signal? Why doesn't my phone work?'

Ungar laughed. 'Who knows? I'll raise it with the phone company. They are always keen to help.' His face turned hard. 'I'll ask again. Why is my name in your notebook?'

She kept her voice steady. 'I'm a journalist. There are all sorts of things in my notebook. Which you have no right to look through or read, by the way.'

Ungar's voice turned colder. '*Kedves* Eniko. I'm not a cop, like Tazi. I am a Gendarme. We can do whatever we want, by order of the prime minister. Haven't you heard? Our country is under siege. Thousands of illegal migrants are pouring across the border. We don't know who they are or where they are going. You write about them. You are a Hungarian citizen. This is a national security emergency. You might have information that can help us.'

She looked around. They were sitting in an abandoned office in the grey, graffiti-covered concrete building by the side of the train line. A calendar was pinned to the wall showing the dates for January 1994. The single window was filthy, covered with so much grime it was almost opaque. The floor was bare concrete, the walls a muddy shade of beige, spotted with large patches of mould. They sat on plastic garden chairs, across from a rickety wooden table. A rusty metal filing cabinet stood in the corner. Despite the heat of the day, the room was damp and chilly. 'If I am under arrest, you have to charge me with something. You cannot just keep me here.'

Ungar laughed. 'Who says you are under arrest? We are just having a nice, friendly chat.'

Eniko made to stand up. 'So I can leave?'

'You can indeed. But if you don't want to have a friendly chat, we can make things more... official. That will take much longer, of course. All that paperwork, forms to fill in, taking you downtown to the headquarters.'

Eniko's unease intensified. The Gendarmerie headquarters occupied a whole city block at number 60 Andrassy Way, a wide avenue of grandiose apartment houses and stately villas that ran from Heroes' Square all the way downtown. That address had been a place of fear for decades. During the war it was an Arrow Cross headquarters, its basement cellars turned into a torture chamber, complete with gallows. Her grandmother's brother, Erno, had been taken there. His body had never been found. After the Communist takeover in 1948, the building had housed the secret police. Many of the Arrow Cross torturers stayed in place, their skills always in demand. In the early 1990s, once Communism had collapsed, a new conservative government had turned the building into a museum chronicling the horrors of Communism. Eniko had visited on a school trip. She still remembered standing in one of the cells, its bare walls, a pair of pliers and a length of rubber hose on a table, and the cracked, brown-stained gutter in the middle of the floor. It was the most chilling place she had ever seen. Last year Pal Dezeffy had closed the museum, supposedly for 'technical reasons', that catch-all phrase in Hungarian. Soon afterwards, the exhibits had been ripped out. A couple of months later the Gendarmes took over. Once again pedestrians crossed the road to avoid walking past the entrance.

Eniko sat back down. Whatever this was, she needed to get it over with, as quickly as possible. 'Can I have my note-book back?'

Ungar flicked through the pages. 'When I'm ready. Let's see what you have been doing. We can start with trespassing on state property, then move on to breaching national security. What was so interesting about John Paul II Square?'

'What are you talking about?'

'You made repeated attempts to enter the square, despite being told to leave the area.'

'So? This is still a free country.'

'The square has been declared a site of national security. There is no unauthorised entry.'

'How was I supposed to know that?'

'Ignorance of the law is no excuse. I'll ask again. What did you want there?'

The woman on the train had opened the carriage door for the two men in black who had walked across the fields. The Gendarmes had stepped into the carriage and asked Eniko to go with them. She had considered her options. Several of her colleagues had been 'invited' in for a talk about their work, their sources of information. Most had gone, then stonewalled as much as they could. Those who had refused had later been arrested while covering demonstrations or other events. Several had charges pending against them of new offences such as 'insulting Hungary's national pride'. She could have run but doubted she would have got very far, especially when she saw two black vans at the edge of the field. Plus, the young woman in the white T-shirt was standing a few yards away. So she went. If nothing else, it would make a piece for the website.

'Why was the square sealed off?' asked Eniko. 'What are you trying to hide?'

'I'm not hiding anything, Eniko.' He sat back, crossed his arms. 'Are you?'

Eniko felt the weight of her Nokia burner in her pocket. She had not brought her iPhone, and her Nexus handset, which was probably in the prime minister's office, was bricked. So Ungar could not know that she had the photograph of Simon Nazir. She thought quickly. She would give him something, something bland but plausible. 'I was walking back from Keleti. I saw that there were Gendarmes moving around. I followed them. I thought something interesting might be happening. I was right, otherwise they would have let me through. You holding me here, asking these questions, confirms it. What was happening there?'

Ungar smiled. 'Nice try. Were you going anywhere special on the HEV, Eniko?'

Did he know that she was going to meet Bela Lidaki? Possibly. Probably. But there was a chance that this was a general attempt to intimidate her. Either way, it was none of his business. 'It's a lovely summer's day. I thought I'd take a ride outside the city. There was only one stop left. So you know where I was going.'

'Was someone meeting you there?' Ungar softened his tone. 'Think of me as a source, Eniko. Journalists have all kinds of sources. They tell you things. You tell them something in return. Everyone wants to trade information. Cops, refugees, Gendarmes, what's the difference?'

'My sources don't usually stop trains between stations when I am travelling on them.' She looked around the room. 'Then block the phone signal and bring me to an abandoned building in the middle of nowhere.'

Ungar slowly shook his head. '*Milyen Lipi lany*, such a Lipi girl. We're not in the middle of nowhere. We are in the middle of Csepel Island, which, last time I looked, was still part of Budapest. I grew up near here.' Ungar tapped the table with her notebook. 'Now, I will ask you once again, why is my name written here?'

'I'm interested in the Gendarmerie. I'm working on a story.'

'What?'

'I hear that there is rivalry between the Gendarmerie and the police, and also that the secret service is not your greatest fan. I was going to ask you for an interview.'

'Why me?'

'I'm a reporter. We've met. You know me. I could use a source inside the Gendarmerie. I hear that you are a rising star.'

She saw a quick flash of pleasure across Ungar's face. 'Who told you that?'

Eniko smiled brightly. Flattery. It never failed to work with Hungarian men in positions of power. 'I don't remember. But I definitely heard it. You are the man to talk to. So, can I ask you a few questions?'

'Not now. Perhaps we can set up an interview at the head-quarters.' His face turned serious again. 'How's Tazi? He looked pretty rough this morning. He's still going to that shit-hole boxer's café. I would think he could find somewhere classier to meet you.'

Eniko stopped smiling. 'Why are you following me?'

'Actually, we weren't. We were following your former boy-friend. But then you came along, so that made you a person of interest. Tending his wounds, meeting for coffee the next day. You are very devoted for an ex. Are you getting back together?'

Eniko glanced at the young woman from the HEV train. She was still standing by the door, impassive as a statue. Eniko asked, 'You know my name. I know yours. Who is she?'

'Her name is...' Ungar thought for a moment, looked at the ceiling. 'Tereza.' He tilted his head slightly, emphasising every syllable. 'Te-re-za. One of our Christian saints. After all the terrible things that happened here, I can see why some... *people* might want to take a Christian name.'

Eniko's unease turned to fear. Her mother was called Tereza. Like many Jewish families who survived the Hol-ocaust, Eniko's grandparents had deliberately given their children names that were not recognisable as Jewish. Eniko stood up, made ready to leave. This was enough now. Either he would let her go or arrest her. She gambled that if he wanted to take her downtown, she would already be in a black van. 'It's your call. I'm leaving now. I'll try and set up that interview. My notebook?'

Ungar slid it across the table, when his telephone beeped. He looked down at the screen, frowned in mock concern. 'Gosh. That's a shame. Poor Bela.'

'What happened?' asked Eniko, guessing the answer as soon she asked.

'Bela Lidaki is dead. He stepped off the road in front of Csepel Station and a car appeared from nowhere and hit him.' Ungar shook his head as though in wonder. 'Apparently it was a migrant. They have already arrested him. One minute Bela *bacsi* is alive and with us, walking' – Ungar paused, stared at Eniko – 'talking, then he's gone. Shame for his family.' Ungar stood up, gestured at Tereza who stood aside from the door. 'It was a pleasure to meet you, Eniko.'

She stood up and slowly walked towards the door, her heart thumping, wondering if she was going to step through it, or be taken downtown. Tereza stared at her for several seconds, then reluctantly moved aside. Ungar said, 'Do take care out there. I hope they catch him. These migrant drivers, they're not used to city driving. They go way too fast, appear from nowhere and then disappear. It's been a pleasure seeing you again, Eniko. I hope you will let me give you some advice.'

She stood in the doorway. 'Which is?'

'Take the Szilky job.'

FIFTEEN

Balthazar read through the form once more, printed his name, signed and dated it. It was a one-paragraph declaration that the signatory would not film, record or discuss with any third parties what he or she was about to witness, and that he or she would not leave the area until authorised to do so. He handed the paper to a wiry, shaven-headed security guard wearing a black T-shirt and black combat trousers, holding a two-way radio. The guard added the paper to pile of sheets in a plastic tray next to a standing U-shaped metal detector, the same size and type used in airports. A large poster, professionally printed, was affixed to the wall nearby. It showed pictures of a mobile phone, a hand-held video camera, a microphone, a knife and a pistol. All the images were scored through with a thick red line. A second graphic in the lower half of the poster showed the camera followed by an equals symbol and a burly man standing above a prone figure, his right foot raised above his head. This was the second security check. Another security guard, at the entrance to the building, had already checked Balthazar and Goran's names against a list of several dozen entries.

The shaven-headed guard gestured at Balthazar to step through the metal detector. It instantly beeped loudly, a green light on the top flashing. The guard held up the radio and spoke in a rapid burst of a language that Balthazar guessed was Albanian. He understood nothing except the mention of his name and the word '*polici*'. A second of silence, a burst of crackle sounded and more words in the same language.

The guard nodded, gestured at Balthazar's rope chain. Balthazar unlocked it, placed it in a plastic tray, walked around the metal detector and through it again. This time the machine stayed silent. He turned around, picked up his chain, looped it back around his neck. Another guard gestured for him to step aside. Balthazar waited while he waved a metal detector wand up and down his chest and back, around and inside his legs. The guard nodded, and Balthazar walked towards a rusting double metal door. There he waited for Goran, his eyes scanning the long queue waiting to pass through the metal detector.

Most of Budapest's underworld was here: Tomi *bacsi*, the Hungarian-Romanian from Transylvania who ran the pickpockets and bag-dippers who worked the tourists downtown and in the Castle District; Lajos, the Hungarian Harvard graduate whose upmarket brothels in Districts II and XII were all extensively wired with sound and video recording equipment that, according to one rumour, fed straight to the prime minister's office; and a few yards behind them, Rita, a Hungarian originally from Slovakia, who bussed in the beggars who prostrated themselves on the Grand Boulevard and shuffled back and forth by the five-star hotels, pretending to be disabled. Other than Rita, who was accompanied by her two sons, the crime bosses were surrounded by lissom young women in tight dresses, giggling excitedly. The only notable figure missing was Balthazar's brother, Gaspar. And not all the customers were criminals, Balthazar noticed. A gaggle of Buda housewives wrapped in designer dresses, tottering on high heels, talked over each other with excited voices. Their husbands were a few feet ahead, talking among themselves. Balthazar saw the boss of a national supermarket chain, a well-known industrialist, one of the country's biggest landowners and several high-ranking officials from the Ministries of the Interior and Justice. Balthazar nodded at a short, rotund Roma man with long, black slicked-back hair, dressed in a green and gold tracksuit. Lajos Kolompar was a city politician, a distant cousin who delivered the District VIII and IX Gypsy bloc vote for the Social Democrats. Kolompar, Balthazar knew, was somehow enmeshed in the prime minister's business network and was also working with Gaspar. Kolompar nodded back, raised an eyebrow, as if surprised to see Balthazar there. Balthazar had spoken with Sandor Takacs before he had gone out, telling him where he was headed, when and how long he planned to stay. Takacs had wanted to send a plain-clothes squad to keep an eye on Balthazar, especially after the attack at Keleti. But Balthazar had talked him out of it. Black George would have spotted the officers immediately and in any case the event was strictly invitation-only.

It was surprising that Goran was on the list. During the Yugoslav wars many commentators had opined about the supposed 'ancient ethnic hatreds' between Serbs, Croats and Muslims that were driving the slaughter. In fact the hatreds were comparatively modern, re-animated unfinished business from the Second World War. Serbs, Croats and Bosnians had gone to war then and again in the 1990s, but they still spoke variations of the same language, ate the same food, laughed at the same jokes, even married each other. It was the animosity between Serbs and Albanians that was visceral, reaching back to 1389 and the battle of Kosovo Polje, the Field of the Blackbirds, between the advancing Ottomans and the Serbs. The Ottomans won, opening the door for the Turkish conquest of the Balkans. The war in Kosovo in the late 1990s, the atrocities and massacres, were merely the latest chapter in a long chronicle of conflict that reached back to the fourteenth century. But Balkan crime knew no borders. Gangsters of all stripes had worked together in all the Yugoslav wars. Militias had sold each other weapons across the frontlines, ran cigarette-smuggling operations from Greece to Austria. Goran and Black George were both Balkan criminals operating in Budapest, with networks that reached far south, so it made sense to keep the lines of communication open. But that did not mean that they, or their people, liked each other.

Balthazar watched Goran step forward, hand his form to the guard. He glanced down at the paper then glared at Goran with barely concealed hostility. 'Go,' he said, pointing at the metal detector.

Goran stepped through the machine. It stayed silent. He waited to be frisked and checked again, then walked up to Balthazar. The two men stepped through the double doors. The warehouse stood at the centre of a long-abandoned industrial estate in District X, a mile or so from the city's international airport. The concrete floor was rough and pitted, here and there bisected by sections of rusting tramlines that scavengers had failed to dig out for scrap. The roof had collapsed in places, the glass skylights had all shattered. The warm air was damp and heavy, thick with perfume, cigarette and cigar smoke, the acrid smell of marijuana, and an underlay of mould and decay. There were several dozen people inside, standing in small groups, smoking and passing hip flasks between themselves. Balthazar spotted numerous off-duty policemen, all of whom avoided catching his eye. He ran his index finger over the brick wall. The mortar was decaying, so soft with mould that he could dig it out with his fingernail. A generator hummed in the corner, providing power for the halogen lights strung around the ceiling. Despite the dingy surroundings, the huge space crackled with excitement.

Teams of security guards, all dressed in black T-shirts and combat trousers, patrolled the ground floor, with two-way radios in hand. More guards walked up and down the air bridges that criss-crossed the roof area. The exit, Balthazar saw, was chained and barred. A large, square metal cage, its sides about twenty feet long, stood in the middle of the space. The walls were ten feet high, made of chain-link fence, and a door was cut into one side. Standing near the front of the cage, flanked by his bodyguards, was the man Balthazar had come to see.

Gresham Palace Four Seasons Hotel, 7.05 p.m.

Five miles away, Eniko and her companion were ensconced in a corner table of the café of Budapest's most glamorous hotel. Both women stopped talking as the waiter arrived. A small black bag, slightly larger than a mobile phone, rested on the polished dark wood surface. Eniko moved it aside to make space as the waiter put down two coffees and two mineral waters. He was in his late twenties, slim but well-proportioned in a tailored white shirt and slim-cut black trousers. Like his colleagues, male and female, he was notably good-looking. Eniko glanced through the picture windows as the waiter arranged the drinks, watching the traffic sweeping around the large green space of Szechenyi Square, onto the Chain Bridge and across the Danube. The bridge was lit up, the lamps draped along the sides glowing orange over the water.

'Can I bring you anything else?' asked the waiter, his large brown eyes sweeping over the two women, holding their gaze. Both shook their heads. Eniko smiled. He really was handsome.

Reka Bardossy saw Eniko watching the waiter as he walked away. 'His name is Hunor. He's very pretty. But not very smart.' She smiled. 'That doesn't always matter, of course. I can introduce you if you like. They know me here.'

Eniko flushed pink. 'That obvious? Thanks. But I'm focused on work at the moment.'

'And you are right to be. Where did they hold you?'

'An abandoned building, in the middle of a field. Somewhere near the Csepel HEV station.'

'Did they get rough with you?'

'Not physically. But I was threatened.'

Reka needlessly adjusted the blue-and-gold silk scarf around her neck. 'I know that place. You were lucky to get out in one piece.'

Eniko glanced at Reka's neck and hands. Why was she wearing a big scarf and black leather gloves indoors? 'Luckier than Bela Lidaki, Madame Minister.'

'Yes. We will talk about that. But why don't we get to know each other a little bit first. You do good work, Eniko. I'm a fan. And please call me Reka.'

Eniko told herself to ignore the flattery. Reka had invited Eniko to meet, so she wanted something. But Reka was right, there was no need to rush to business. Even in transactional relationships, the human connection was important. The two women chatted for a while, talking about their schools in Budapest and scholarships and foreign universities, their shared love of London, their favourite bars and restaurants. Eniko was surprised at how easily the conversation flowed. Reka was the minister of justice. Which meant that she was in charge of the legal system that tolerated, even facilitated widespread corruption. It was Eniko's job to expose that, shine a light on the hidden channels where the dirty money flowed back and forth. Despite that, Eniko realised, somewhat to her surprise, Reka was also very good company. She was witty, funny, and an interested, engaging conversationalist, dropping snippets of gossip about high-profile politicians and minor celebrities. In exchange, Eniko gave her an inside account of her date with Tamas Nemeth, which Reka relished. In another universe, Eniko thought, they could easily have become friends.

After a while, when the two women began to relax in each other's company, Eniko looped the conversation back to work. 'Who do you think killed Bela Lidaki?'

Reka Bardossy looked down at her coffee, stirred it before she answered. 'I know who killed him. His name is Gabor Kozminsky. He is part of the prime minister's security detail. His driver, in fact. He was trained in Moscow. It was Pal's order. Our prime minister is tidying up his loose ends. Or trying to.' Reka paused. 'But it doesn't always work.' Reka unwrapped the scarf around her neck, then unpeeled her gloves and splayed her hands on the table.

Eniko stared at the dark red marks around Reka's neck, the torn nails and cuticles, her eyes widening. 'He tried to kill you?'

Reka laughed derisively. 'Not personally. But he ordered it.'

'How do you know?'

'It was a Gendarme.'

'Maybe someone else hired him.'

Reka shook her head. 'That's not possible. They are all extremely well paid. They have complete legal immunity. Pal personally micro-manages their operations. They don't step out of their headquarters without his say-so.'

'Oh.' Eniko looked down at the table before she spoke. 'But I heard that you were... er...'

Reka laughed. 'Yes. I was. We were. So it was a crime of passion.'

Eniko felt the familiar adrenalin rush. This story just got bigger and bigger. She took out her notebook and started scribbling. 'Can I use what you just told me?'

Reka smiled. 'The politician and the journalist. Why don't we wait until the end of our conversation, Eniko? Then we can talk about the terms and conditions, what you want to use, and how.'

Eniko knew she was being played. 'Terms and conditions', as Reka put it, were usually defined at the start of a discussion, not afterwards, otherwise a source could let something slip and then say that it was off the record, not to be used.

Sometimes, though, it was worth bending the rules – and this was one of them. But that did not mean that tough questions went unanswered. 'OK. But why did Dezeffy want you dead? And why did he have his former interior minister killed?'

Reka glanced at her watch. 'It's well after seven, Eniko. I'm coffeed out and I won't be able to sleep if I have any more. How about a proper drink?'

Eniko was about to say no. She was exhausted. She had been taken off a train, detained and threatened. The man she was supposed to meet earlier in the day had been murdered. The minister of justice, sitting with her at the same table, had just survived an assassination attempt and was feeding her the kind of information journalists dream about. Eniko needed a clear head. But it was also important that Reka felt comfortable. Nobody wanted to drink cocktails on their own. She glanced at the circular bar in the centre of the room, where a tall barman ladled ice into a gleaming cocktail mixer and shook it back and forth. Eniko said, 'OK. Whatever you are having.' She watched Reka summon the handsome waiter.

'A gin and tonic, please.' Reka said, glancing at Eniko, who nodded. 'Make that two.' He took their order and walked over to the bar. Reka turned back to Eniko. 'You were saying?'

'Bela Lidaki. Why was he killed?'

'He was unfinished business. A loose end. A loose end who knew too much.'

Eniko tried to process what she had heard. Part of her was beyond excited, part incredulous and another quite terrified. She closed her eyes, took a deep breath. For a moment she was sitting in a circular rubber raft, white-water rafting on a summer holiday in Slovenia, the currents spinning the boat around as she fought the undertow that almost crashed her into the river bank. But the waters had calmed, and she brought the raft back under control. 'And he also tried to kill you?'

'Yes.'

Eniko asked, 'Aren't you scared? I know I am. This has been the scariest day of my life.' She looked at her watch. 'And there are still more than four hours to go.'

Reka looked into the distance. 'Sometimes, I am, yes. But this has started, and now it has to finish.'

Warehouse, District X, 7.10 p.m.

'Good evening, Detective Kovacs,' said Black George. He gestured at the two women standing on either side of him. 'Have you met Bettina and Dorentina? They are twin sisters. From

253

Prizren, in Kosovo.' Both women were wiry and toned, with dark eyes, full lips, long, raven hair pulled back from their faces and walnut-brown skin.

Balthazar smiled and wished the bodyguards good evening. They did not answer but stared at him with cool, assessing glances, taking in his physique, body language, and the bruises and scratches, quickly deciding he was not a threat. They wore heavy perfume over the tang of fresh sweat. Like Black George himself, the two women were Gypsies. Balthazar knew that their knives were concealed, but would appear the instant they thought that Black George was in any kind of danger. The blades would be wielded faster than any man's fists. Black George continued speaking. 'It's going to be a great evening. But before the entertainment starts, we should clarify something.'

'I signed your form,' said Balthazar.

'Someone called Balthazar Kovacs signed it, but who? The policeman, or the brother of the city's biggest pimp? The Gypsy from the backstreets of Chekago, or the diligent student at Central European University?'

Balthazar shrugged. 'All of them.'

'Where is your brother?'

'He's not coming. He doesn't approve.'

Black George laughed, reached into his back pocket and took out a brass knuckleduster. It had a short, pointed blade at one end, encased in a leather sheath. 'A pimp with a conscience.'

'A pimp with an agreement with you, brokered by the Kris.'

Black George slid the sheath from the weapon and touched the end of the blade with his fingertip. A small dot of crimson appeared on the skin. Black George nodded approvingly, handed the blade to Bettina. 'The time of the Kris is finished,

Detective Kovacs. The whole world is in chaos.' He squeezed his fingertip until the crimson dot swelled and burst, then licked his finger. 'Look at poor Bela Lidaki. One minute he is the minister of the interior, the next he is dead.'

Black George was a well-built man of medium-height in his mid-forties, with the dark complexion of a southern Balkan gypsy. He wore a skin-tight black vest, black jeans and trainers. The sides of his head and most of the top was shaved, apart from a backwards triangle of black hair which was gathered into a topknot. Both of his hands and arms were covered with tattoos of eagles, the symbol of Kosovo. Another bird was tattooed on the back of his neck, its wings reaching around to his cheeks, its talons down his back. His eyes, which gave him his name, were his most compelling feature, black as obsidian, they seemed to glow in the dark. He exuded a coiled, menacing energy, and was, Balthazar knew, capable of extreme violence on a whim. Bela Lidaki's death in a hit-and-run earlier that day was all over the news. The reference to Bela Lidaki was a thinly veiled threat.

Black George had first arrived in Budapest in 2000 after the war in Kosovo, claiming to be a refugee from Prizren. He had lived there for a while, but he was born in Albania, in a slum outside the capital Tirana. By his mid-twenties he controlled much of the downtown capital, running prostitutes, pickpockets and selling adulterated fuel. But the Kosovo war brought new opportunities. Suddenly the city was awash with aid workers, reporters and spies. He quickly hired more prostitutes, trained more street children to pick pockets. His empire grew rapidly. Several of his rivals were found dead. Then the borders opened to let the Kosovo Albanian refugees flee. Black George walked into Kosovo from Albania and there linked up with a column of refugees fleeing to

Macedonia, where he secured false papers. With those, he flew to Hungary and claimed asylum. On that trip, he kept a low profile, gathering intelligence about crime in the city. Budapest, he decided, would be his springboard into operations across western Europe, where the real money was to be made.

A slim young blonde woman in a red dress walked up, holding a silver tray. Three lines of white powder were laid out next to a polished silver tube. 'Will you join me, Detective?' asked Black George, his tone only slightly mocking.

'No, thanks,' said Balthazar.

Black George looked down at the tray, 'Do you mind if I...?'

'Not at all.'

The young woman held the tray as Black George inserted the tube into his nose and bent forward.

Black George sniffed up the two lines, one after another, exhaled hard and shivered with pleasure. 'The best. Pure Colombian.' He held the tray out to Balthazar. 'There's enough left.'

'No, thanks.'

'You want to talk?' Black George looked down at the tray. 'Then try it. You are safe here. There are no cameras.'

Balthazar dipped a finger in the white powder and dabbed it on his tongue. A strong chemical taste flooded his mouth. His tongue fizzed for a second, turned numb. The drug was so pure that he felt a kick. 'As you say. Very good.'

Black George gave him a quizzical look. 'You intrigue me, Balthazar Kovacs. The Gypsy detective. Why do you spell your name with an "h"? Why not Baltazar, like the Hungarians?'

'My mother changed it. She liked that version better.'

Black George laughed, his eyes creasing. 'If that was a disguise, it didn't work. And look where it gets you. Why do you bother? You can arrest us, your cousins, your brothers, all day and night. You will still be a *budos cigany*, a filthy Gypsy. Why not come and work for me? I can pay you much more than you will ever earn as a policeman.' He lifted up Balthazar's rope chain, looked him up and down, taking in his close-fitting T-shirt and jeans. 'I think you would fit right in. This Gaspar business, we can sort it out, fix things amicably. And there are other benefits.'

Black George gestured at his bodyguards, nodded at Balthazar. Bettina came to stand close to him on one side, Dorentina on the other. He felt the soft weight of their breasts on his arms, the warmth of their breath on his neck. 'They like you, Bal-tha-zar,' said Black George, mockingly emphasising each syllable.

Two hands slid up and down his spine, fingers pressing gently on his back, a further two sliding down to his backside and under his crotch. Balthazar blinked, tried to ignore the wave of pleasure running up and down his body.

Black George dropped Balthazar's neck chain, smoothed it back in place. 'Such fun and no complications.' He sniffed, flicked a smudge of white powder from the underside of his nose. 'None at all. And you would be protected. No more fights at Keleti. No one would dare. You, me and Gaspar. Partners, the three of us, what do you say?'

'I'll think about it,' replied Balthazar, stepping forward, away from Bettina and Dorentina. 'But we need to talk. Alone.'

'Police talk?'

'Friendly talk. A few questions. Let's see if we can cooperate.'

'OK.' Black George gestured at his bodyguards to leave him. The two women began to protest. His voice dropped and his eyes suddenly glittered. 'I said, leave us.' The women immediately stepped aside. Black George stepped into the crowd. It parted instantly as he led Balthazar to a corner of the room.

The two men stood in the corner. The generator hummed and coughed. Balthazar took a sheet of paper from his back pocket, a printout of the photograph of Simon Nazir. He unfolded it and showed it to Black George. 'Do you know him?' he asked.

Black George shook his head. 'Never met him.'

'But you know who killed him?'

'Maybe. Maybe not.'

'The killer's name is Mahmoud Hejazi.'

'Is it?'

'You were going to take Hejazi across the border. With a passport issued by the Ministry of Justice.'

'Was I really?' asked Black George, his tone bored.

'Yes. There are three ways out of here. With Gaspar and Goran, but they won't take him. Through the green border with one of the guys who hang out at Keleti, but that's way too risky. Or with you.'

Black George slid a finger back under Balthazar's rope chain, lifted it up and down again. 'Partners?' Balthazar said nothing. He dropped Balthazar's chain, started walking back to the seats in front of the cage. 'Think about it, Detective Kovacs. But first, let's watch the fun.'

Ungar home, Bimbo Way, Buda hills, 7.10 p.m.

Attila Ungar put his can of beer down and pressed the pause button on the television remote control as his phone rang. The football match, a Budapest derby between Ferencvaros and Ujpest, froze on the sixty-inch television screen that dominated the room, the Ujpest goalkeeper suspended in mid-air.

Ungar had been divorced for a decade. He lived alone in a new luxury development in the Buda hills. The flat had a large wraparound terrace and a panoramic view of the river, but he rarely ventured outside, and kept the blinds down. There were three bedrooms with en suite bathrooms. One was kept for his teenage son, Henrik, complete with an Xbox and flat-screen television. The boy rarely visited and had never stayed over. The flat had a fully fitted American-style kitchen diner, most of whose equipment was unused. Ungar scrabbled around among the beer cans and empty pizza boxes on the coffee table until he found his phone. The ring tone, the Hungarian national anthem, meant one particular caller. One who definitely needed to be answered.

'Did the journalist get the message?' asked Pal Dezeffy.

'Of course.'

'How long did you hold her?'

'Long enough.'

'Then why is she ordering gin and tonics with Reka Bardossy in the bar of the Four Seasons?'

Ungar shook his head, exhaled hard, put his can of beer down and glanced at the screen, a wave of nostalgia for simpler times washing through him. He had come a long way from his childhood in a cramped tenement flat on the outskirts of the city, with a cowed mother and an alcoholic father who regularly beat him half-senseless. He had learned to fight on the Ujpest terraces, had been a founder member of the Ultras squad. By the time he was fourteen he had learned enough to hit back against his father, who had not beaten his son again. Some of Ungar's former brawling partners had been recruited to the Gendarmes. Others were dead or in prison. A few were still there on the terraces. He looked harder at the screen, thought he could even make out their faces. Or maybe it was wishful thinking. 'What do you want me to do?'

'Deal with her.'

'A few hours ago, you told me no violence.'

'Just shut this down, Ungar. You have a station almost next door. How many people are on duty?'

'Around a dozen.'

'Is that enough, or shall I send reinforcements?' His voice turned sarcastic. 'There are two of them. They might be wearing high heels.'

Ungar grimaced. 'I got it. And Reka?'

'Leave her. Once the journalist is out of the way, she'll get the message.'

'OK, boss. I'll deal with it myself.'

SIXTEEN

Hunor the waiter reappeared and placed Reka and Eniko's drinks on their table. The drinks were served in tall, frosted balloon glasses with large, transparent ice cubes and a semi-circle of lime. The two women clinked their glasses. Neither noticed Hunor walk out of the main area and into a small service annex.

Eniko took a small sip of her drink and put the glass back down. It was delicious, ice cold with a bracing taste of lime and juniper. But she was very definitely still at work, so a sip was enough. An American couple in their sixties walked by. Eniko waited until they had gone before she answered. 'There are rumours at Keleti, some of the migrants say that it's possible to buy a Hungarian government passport.'

'That's true.'

Eniko braced herself. She was probably about to ruin what was turning into quite an enjoyable evening, and burn a potentially excellent contact. But she had no choice. 'Do the passports come from your ministry?'

'Yes.'

Eniko thought for a moment. 'But you are the minister of justice. If you know this, then why don't you do something about it?'

261

Reka picked up her cocktail and took a longish drink. She closed her eyes for a second. 'The cocktails here really are unbeatable.' She put the glass down. 'I am doing something about it. I am telling you.'

'It took you a while.'

Reka smiled brightly. 'Better late than never. Do you want this information, Eniko, or not?' she asked, a hint of steel in her voice.

Eniko scribbled in her notebook, her heart thumping as she held her pen in her hand. 'Yes, of course. Can you say that on the record?'

Now it was Reka's turn to hesitate. She had thought about this all day. The words she was about to say could not be unsaid. Even if Eniko did not write the story – which she thought highly unlikely – the information, or a version of it, would soon be flying around the city's bars and cafés and up and down the corridors of power. No journalist could keep something like this to themselves. Budapest, or at least the insiders' part of it, was a very small place. Pal Dezeffy would come for her, again. But he was going to anyway. The choice had been made for her. 'I can say that on the record and more. Much more, but not all of it tonight. Let's spend some time together, get to know each other a bit. See how we can help each other.'

Eniko nodded warily. 'Sure. That makes sense.'

Reka continued talking, 'But before that, I have a question for you. About how the media works. As I understand it, the time to frame a story, to shape how it is covered, is when it is first reported. Is that correct?'

Eniko nodded. 'Broadly, yes. The way it is projected stays in people's memories. That is how they perceive it. But any story can go in different directions afterwards. Once it's out, it's impossible to control.'

'Of course. But its *initial* impact, the first impression – that can be managed?'

'To some extent, yes,' said Eniko, now thoroughly intrigued as she started to understand the trajectory of the conversation. She put her notebook down. 'Reka, why don't you tell me what you want.'

'I want to help you, Eniko, to report what is happening in the highest reaches of our government. But Bela Lidaki is dead. I am lucky to be alive. So we have to be smart, and careful.'

'Is that why you have brought a bodyguard?' asked Eniko. A tall, broad-shouldered man with buzz-cut blond hair had accompanied Reka into the café. He now sat nursing a still mineral water two tables away, a Bluetooth earpiece in his right ear, and a noticeable bulge under his left armpit.

Reka nodded in his direction. 'Yes. Zsolt. Zsolt and his colleagues.'

Eniko looked around. Now she noticed that another man of similar build and appearance was sitting by the door to the café. Another bodyguard stood outside, by an Audi 6 saloon parked at the hotel entrance. The Four Seasons took up a whole city block. A small private road ran in front of the building, crowded with hotel cars and taxis. Eniko recognised the government vehicle, low on the road, heavy with armour plating. The Audi pointed at the flow of traffic into Szechenyi Square, gauzy grey smoke drifting from its exhaust pipe. The windows were tinted black, but there was surely a driver inside, keeping the engine running.

Eniko looked down at the table. 'And that's why our phones are in a signal blocking bag?'

'Yes. But it's very important, crucial, for our future cooperation that your report is accurate and' – Reka paused, looked for the right word – 'fair.'

Eniko understood instantly what Reka was offering. Reka was a journalist's dream: a high-level source, a cabinet minister privy to the innermost reaches of the government. But she wanted if not to control, then at least to shape her reporting. What was fair to a government official was not necessarily fair to a reporter. Even now, more than twenty-five years after the change of system, numerous government officials demanded to see the whole article in which they were mentioned before it went online. Eniko never agreed. Nine times out of ten, they still spoke to her afterwards. She smiled as she thought of the poster in the 555.hu newsroom and the quote from H. L. Mencken about journalists and politicians, dogs and lamp posts. That was all very well, but the real world was transactional. Lamp posts were not very good sources.

Eniko sat up, her voice businesslike now. 'I cannot give you copy approval. Nor can I show you the article before it's published.'

Reka tilted her head to one side, smiled. 'Eniko, please. I'm not asking for that. I would like us to have a mutually productive working relationship. And that any article reflects my point of view and gives weight to my perspective. I trust you to do that. And that you check any direct quotes with me.'

'I can do that. My next question is: did you know that passports issued by your ministry were ending up in the hands of traffickers?'

'Yes, I knew that passports, issued by my ministry, were being sold. Some of them ended up in the wrong hands. British officials have arrested several Islamic radicals at airports, posing as Hungarians.'

Eniko scribbled in her notebook. This story just got better and better. 'How many? Where? Can you give me more details?'

'We are agreed. Accurate and fair?'

Eniko nodded. Whatever. She could negotiate the details later. Hunor the handsome waiter appeared, hovered near the table, looking questioningly at the two women. Reka smiled, said, 'We're fine, thanks.'

Reka waited until he walked away, and leaned forward. 'This is the key point, Eniko. It was a sting operation. The passports were bait to draw out the traffickers. Obviously it was all highly confidential. Only I and a couple of my most trusted officials knew about it. Now that we know who the traffickers are and how their networks operate, my officials are preparing a dossier to share with the British, European and American authorities.' She sipped her drink, carried on talking. 'You can use that. It's all on the record. I can see the headline now: "Hungarian Officials Run Sting Operation to Catch People-Traffickers." What do you think?'

Eniko continued writing. Was that really the headline, that Hungarian officials had run a sting operation to catch traffickers? She would think about that later. This was part of the story, she thought, but not all of it. There was something else here, she was sure. Reka's phone buzzed. She looked at the screen, mouthed 'My husband' to Eniko and took the call, turning away as she dropped her voice.

Eniko sipped her gin and tonic while Reka spoke. It was delicious, certainly the best she had ever tasted, the ice cold spirit exploding on her tongue with tiny juniper taste bombs as the alcohol coursed into her bloodstream, mixing with the adrenalin. The synapses in her brain crackled and snapped. Dead ministers. People-traffickers. Passports for terrorists. Islamic radicals. Still, there was something else, something more here, she was sure of it. It could not be a coincidence that all this was happening as a massive influx of money was pouring in from Gulf investors. She remembered a report she had read in the *Economist*, about the shadowy figures in the Gulf who were secretly funding Isis in Iraq and Syria. There had already been questions in Parliament about the residence bonds, the ease with which Arab investors acquired them. When opposition MPs had raised the matter at a meeting of Parliament's national security council, Dezeffy's allies had all walked out, thus preventing a quorum and any further discussion. What if the Gulf investment came at a much higher price? A price that only Pal Dezeffy knew about. It seemed a wild idea, too wild to be feasible. But it also made perfect sense and explained why Simon Nazir had been killed.

Eniko waited until Reka finished speaking and put her phone away. 'Tell me what else the Arab investors get for their money?'

'Oh, that's easy,' said Reka. 'Transit. Transit for whoever they want.'

Warehouse, District X, 7.35 p.m.

Black George beckoned Balthazar to sit down. Four white plastic chairs had appeared a couple of yards in front of the cage. The Kosovar sat at the end of the row, Bettina next to him. Balthazar sat between her and Dorentina. He was the guest of honour, it seemed. There were no other seats. The rest of the audience stood, craning forward for the best views. The lights dimmed and a ripple of anticipation ran through the crowd.

A tall man with long brown hair pulled back in a pony-tail stepped forward and climbed up the short staircase that led to the cage. He wore a black tuxedo and trousers and a crimson bow tie over a white dress shirt, and held a cordless microphone in his hand as he stepped through the door. He walked into the centre of the stage and a single spotlight bore down on him. The talking stopped and the crowd fell silent, the air electric with anticipation.

'Good evening, ladies and gentlemen,' he announced in Hungarian, English, Russian and Albanian. 'Tonight we have a fantastic show for you, with a special prize for the winner.' He reached into his back pocket and pulled out a small burgundy booklet. 'A passport.' The crowd murmured its approval. The MC cupped his left hand to his ear. 'I'm sorry, I can't hear you.' The crowd shouted louder. 'That's better. Because this is not just any old passport.' He paused, opened the document and showed a blank page. 'It's a *Hungarian* passport. Ready and waiting for a name and a photograph. And if the winner has a family, they all get one as well.'

The crowd roared, shouting, '*Hajra Magyarorszag! Hajra Magyarorszag!* Go Hungary! Go Hungary!'

'*That's* better. Because this is going to be an amazing evening. Eight fighters. Each bout will be a single round of three minutes. The four winners will go through to the semi-finals, then the last two will fight in the final. Now, before we start, a quick recounting of the rules of the ring.' He put the passport back in his jacket pocket, turned and looked across the warehouse, a long sweeping gaze that took in every corner of the room, a solemn expression on his face. He stood still for several seconds, before his face split into a wide grin. '*There aren't any!*' The audience roared. The MC smiled. 'Except these: no tearing, gouging or biting. We are not animals. Just good, clean, dirty fun. And please, dear fighters, try not to kill each other. Dead bodies are *so* inconvenient.'

Balthazar half-watched as the MC ran through his routine, remembering what he knew about Black George. Even his nickname was a deliberate provocation. Karadjordje, the original Black George, was a nineteenth-century Serbian nationalist leader, regarded as the founder of modern Serbia. The Albanian Black George had returned to Budapest a few years after the Kosovo war. District IX, he decided, would be his base. The quarter had been run by Karcsi *bacsi*. Karcsi had been a distant cousin of Gaspar and Balthazar's, an old-school crime boss in his seventies, overweight and with a heart problem. He had run streetwalkers and pickpockets, and provided protection for local bars.

There had been a comfortable modus vivendi between Karcsi, the locals and the police. Karcsi was preparing to hand over to his son, Karcsi junior, and retire. Despite being one of the poorer areas of the city, District IX was comparatively crime-free. The pickpockets operated downtown. The prostitutes used cheap hotel rooms, not back alleys or playgrounds after dark. There were no condoms or syringes on the pavement. The bars were protected. Until Black George had arrived. A spate of muggings had erupted, bars and cafés were smashed up or set on fire, prostitutes found beaten half-senseless. The cheap hotel near Boraros Square that doubled as Karcsi's brothel had been burned down.

Soon afterwards, Karcsi junior had disappeared. So did six of Karcsi's highest-earning prostitutes. Karcsi, Gaspar and Balthazar had used every contact they had to try and locate Karcsi junior and the prostitutes. All they could discover was that they had been bundled into vans and driven away. After three days, the call came. The prostitutes were found stripped naked, freezing, dehydrated and hungry in the warehouse where Balthazar was now talking to Black George. Karcsi junior was nearby, unconscious and barely alive. He had also been stripped naked, beaten severely, forced to stand against the wall while his hands were nailed into the brick-work. Such an assault was enough to trigger an all-out war. Gaspar and the bosses of Districts V, VI, VII and XIII had all pushed for a ferocious response, even hiring a hit man from the Balkans or Ukraine to take out the dangerous new inter-loper. But Karcsi seemed to lack the heart to take revenge. He had then received a series of photographs of his wife, sons, daughters and numerous grandchildren leaving their homes, playing in the park and going to school. He handed control over to Black George, and died soon afterwards of a heart attack.

Did Black George know where the Gardener was? Almost certainly. His offer might even be genuine. But the partner-ship would soon turn into a takeover. Gaspar would lose his business and Black George increase his empire. In any case, Gaspar would never agree to go into business with Black George to help Balthazar solve a murder case. Balt-hazar watched the spotlight fade, then move to the back of the warehouse, where it stayed for a couple of minutes, before following the two fighters as they stepped forward.

Gresham Palace Four Seasons Hotel, 7.40 p.m.

'I think that's enough for now. I'm fading,' said Reka. 'You have a murder, an attempted murder, a passport sting and a government providing transit facilities for Islamic radicals in exchange for foreign investment.'

Eniko nodded. Reka was right. Her head was reeling and not from the gin and tonic. She needed to go home, type up her notes, make a pot of coffee and work out what to do next. Reka caught Hunor's eye and made a scribbling motion with her hand. He nodded. The drinks would be charged to the ministry's account. She left a thousand-forint note on the table, put her jacket on, and adjusted the silk scarf around her neck. Zsolt, her bodyguard, stood up and strode rapidly towards the table. 'We have to leave, Madame Minister, and now.'

Eniko glanced at Reka, then out of the window. Four black Gendarmerie vans were approaching the hotel. The Four Seasons had three entrances: one in front and two side entrances on Zrinyi and Merleg streets. A Gendarmerie van forced a path between the hotel taxis and tourist buses on the narrow road that ran in front of the building, stopping behind Reka's Audi. A second reversed down the same road, stopping in front of the Audi, boxing the vehicle in. The other two vehicles blocked the entrances on Zrinyi and Merleg streets. Four squads of four Gendarmes spilled from each vehicle, advancing on the front entrance, barging the startled tourists out of the way.

'We really do have to leave now, Madame Minister,' said Zsolt.

Reka said, 'Give me a moment, Zsolt. And Eniko, you stay close.' Reka turned to Zsolt. 'She is with us, OK?' Zsolt nodded. Reka reached for her iPhone. 'I need to make a call.' She quickly scrolled through her numbers until she found the one she was looking for, and pressed the dial button. The call was answered after three rings. 'Sandor, it's me. We have a problem.'

Warehouse, District X, 7.40 p.m.

Balthazar watched the spotlight track the first fighter as he walked across the warehouse into the cage. 'Go West', the 1980s hit by the Pet Shop Boys, suddenly boomed through

270

the space. He was a giant of a man, at least six feet four inches tall, shaven-headed, with dark brown eyes, his heavy-set muscles oiled and gleaming. He wore a pair of shiny black nylon shorts and a blue lycra singlet. He stepped through the gate and the MC announced, 'Ladies and gentlemen, Ahmed, better known as the Baghdad Brawler, and a former captain of the Iraqi Olympic wrestling team.' The giant grabbed the chain-link fence, baring his teeth, roaring out loud and shaking it hard. The sound of rattling metal triggered another cheer from the crowd.

The spotlight remained on him, while another light followed the second fighter as he emerged from the shadows. He was considerably smaller, about five feet eight, with rope-like muscles and a large lion tattooed on his back. He also wore nylon shorts and a singlet, had a boxer's nose, badly straightened where it had been broken, and he bobbed up and down on his toes. Balthazar thought he looked fast and light on his feet. 'And on the other side of the ring, ladies and gentlemen,' said the MC, 'Memet, better known as the Kurdistan Killer, for reasons we don't need to discuss here.'

The MC, who doubled as the referee, brought the two men together to shake hands. The giant tried to grab his opponent and pull him towards him. 'Naughty, naughty,' said the MC. 'Wait until the bell.' The giant released his opponent. The MC stepped back into the corner. The bell sounded and the crowd cheered.

Both men circled each for several seconds, their hands up, looking for an opening. The giant moved first, rushing towards Memet, trying to use his weight and mass to force him into a corner of the cage. Memet seemed to allow himself to be swept forward. Once the two men were in the corner, the giant tried to grab Memet, who dodged sideways. Balthazar watched

271

as his left leg flew out, sweeping hard behind the wrestler's leg. He aimed for the back of his knee. The blow would have dropped the giant instantly but the giant crouched down as the kick connected. Memet's foot hit his thigh then slid off.

Even so, most men would still be floored by such a move. The giant laughed and remained immobile. Now Memet was off balance, grimacing with pain as the force of his failed leg-sweep ran back up his leg. The giant grabbed for him again and this time succeeded. He wrapped his arms around Memet and raised him up, trapping his arms, ready to throw him to the ground. The crowd cheered. Balthazar looked around. It wasn't just blood lust that was running high. There were rhythmic movements in the shadows, gasps and moans as well as cheers.

Memet drew his head back then slammed his forehead forward into the giant's nose. The crack was audible. Blood erupted from his face, pouring over the two men. The wrestler staggered back, then hurled Memet against the wall of the cage. Memet landed on his side just as the wrestler rushed at him. Memet scrabbled back up from the floor, instantly jumping forward with his left leg, scissor-kicking with his right into the giant's groin. The giant's face twisted in agony. He staggered back, tried to right himself, then collapsed sideways in a heap, blood still pouring over his torso from his broken nose.

Memet walked over to him, looked down at his defeated, half-unconscious opponent. 'Kill him, kill him,' echoed around the warehouse. The MC walked over and held Memet's hand high. 'Bout one goes to the Killer from Kurdistan.'

Black George turned to Balthazar. 'Not bad. Less than a minute.'

Balthazar nodded. The Baghdad Brawler was a wrestler. He knew how to grab and throw and lock down. But the Kurdistan

Killer was a street fighter and the result had never been in doubt. There were another six bouts of this to go. He had no desire to watch the parade of desperate men fighting and injuring each other for the chance of a passport. He looked around the audience. Goran was huddled in a corner with a Croatian gangster who smuggled stolen cars out of Hungary into the Balkans, from where they were shipped to South America. The two men were deep in conversation, their body language friendly and animated. Balthazar smiled. In crime at least, the old Yugoslavia lived on. But what he wanted, more than anything, was to see his son. Or at least to speak to him. Goran had given Balthazar his car keys in case he wanted to use his phone. Balthazar turned to Black George. 'I need to make a call. I'll be back in a few minutes. Is that OK?'

Black George said, 'Bored already?'

'Not at all. But I need to speak to someone.'

'Your colleagues? You calling in a team to shut us down, arrest us?'

'Of course not. Gaspar should know about your offer.'

'Where's your phone?'

'In my car.'

'OK. But she goes with you.' He nudged Dorentina, who stood up. 'And come back quickly. They'll let you in again.'

Balthazar stood up and stepped around the crowd, Dorentina following him. The second set of fighters were walking into the cage. One was African, tall and lean with the build of a Somali or Ethiopian. The other was shorter and heavier-set with olive skin and slicked-back hair. The African man looked vaguely familiar, then Balthazar realised where he had seen him before: it was Samuel, the South Sudanese man to whose family Balthazar had given the supplies at Keleti, and who had helped him when he had been beaten up. The cheering started again as the two men faced each other. This was one fight that he definitely had no desire to see. Balthazar quickened his pace, stepping out of the main warehouse into the front area. The security guards moved forward to block his path, receding when they saw Dorentina escorting him.

Balthazar stepped outside and stood for a moment, taking deep breaths of the cool night air. He looked up, watched an aeroplane climb slowly, red and green wing lights blinking as it banked westwards towards Vienna. He walked over to Goran's car, a battered blue Lada Niva four-by-four, and leaned against the door, taking the keys from his trouser pocket. A light breeze washed over him, carrying the smell of green fields. Headlights swept back and forth on the road in and out of the city. The only sounds were the distant hum of the traffic and the wind blowing through the trees. The exhaustion was hitting him in waves now. He had not taken any painkillers since lunchtime. His back and shoulders were a mass of aches and the iron bar had reappeared in his head. He reached into his pocket, still leaning against the car door, found a packet of paracetamol and dry-swallowed two tablets, the bitter taste of the medicine flooding his mouth. He fought to stay awake but the tiredness briefly won and he dozed off for a few seconds, until he smelled a heavy perfume and felt a touch on his arm. Dorentina said, 'Wake up, this is not a place to sleep.' Her voice was soft, but laced with warning.

He thanked her and she watched him as he opened the car door and took his phone from the glove compartment. She stepped away, pretending at least to be out of earshot. Balthazar started to dial Alex's number, pressed the first five digits, then stopped. Black George doubtless knew that he had a son, but there was no need to let his bodyguard listen in on the conversation. Even standing at a distance, she would be able to hear Balthazar speaking. But more than that, his son would ask him where he was. He could not tell him, that was obvious, and he did not want to lie to the boy. He was already manipulating Sarah to get access and an extra visit next week. He felt no guilt about that, none at all, but there were enough secrets and unsaid things in his family. His relationship with Alex was one that he intended to keep open and honest. He could at least text him. Balthazar tapped out a couple of lines, explaining that he was working and that he was really looking forward to seeing him tomorrow and that he loved him. All that was true. A few seconds later the telephone beeped that a message had arrived.

I love you too Daddy. We will have fun tomorrow.

Balthazar smiled, leaned back against the door and closed his eyes for a few moments. However chaotic his personal and professional life was, he had his son. And nobody would ever take that from him. He suddenly had a craving for a cigarette. He had smoked, only socially, for years. Gypsy family gatherings were usually accompanied by a fog of tobacco smoke. It seemed easier to smoke his own cigarettes than passively inhale his relatives'. After Eniko had left, he was soon up to half a packet a day. One morning, he had lit his first cigarette before he even got out of bed. He had met Alex later that day. After his son told him that he smelled of cigarettes, he had stopped completely. The craving was not overpowering, but he needed, he realised, a reason to stay outside while the desperate men inside pummelled each other senseless. He opened the car door again. There was a half-empty packet of Marlboro Lights in the side compartment of the driver's door. He reached inside and took the crumpled box out, but realised he did not have a light.

He smelled perfume again, turned around to see Dorentina standing next to him, lighter in hand. She moved like a ghost. He offered the packet to her. She shook her head. He took out a cigarette from the box. It was bent and the paper was cracked, but it would do. Her thumb slid across the top of the lighter and a small flame caught. He leaned forward and inhaled. The tip of the cigarette glowed red in the darkness. He coughed. The tobacco was dry and stale and the acrid smoke caught in his throat. Now he remembered why he had given up.

Dorentina watched him for several seconds, then said, 'Boy or girl?'

'That was Gaspar. He texted me. We'll talk later.'

Dorentina smiled. 'I don't think so. You aren't going into business with Black George. And you can see Gaspar whenever you want. That was someone else. Someone who fills your soul, who softens your face.'

Balthazar laughed. Gypsy women. They knew everything. He could lie with a straight face to any *gadje* and be believed, but never to his own. 'Maybe it's my wife.'

Dorentina took the cigarette from his hand and dropped it on the ground. 'You don't want this. And you aren't married.' She picked up his left hand. 'No ring.'

Balthazar felt a current pass through him as his fingers rested on hers. 'Maybe it was my girlfriend.'

Dorentina shook her head. 'No girlfriend either.'

'How do you know?'

Her eyes glowed in the dark. 'I just do. You are lonely. So, boy or girl?'

'Boy. Almost thirteen. You?'

She looked away, let her fingers slide from his. 'Son. He is five. We don't live together.'

'That's hard. Where is he?'

'I don't know. Here, I think. I see him a few times a year. He is brought to me.'

'By who?'

She turned around to Balthazar, pain written on her face. 'Who do you think? I heard your conversation with Black George. How much do you want this Hejazi?'

'He is a killer. I'm a cop. So, very much. Do you know where he is?'

'No. But I know where he will be tomorrow evening.'

'Where?'

'Can you help me get my son?'

Balthazar thought before he answered. The likelihood of him being able to locate and rescue Dorentina's little boy was remote. But not impossible. 'I cannot guarantee anything. But we could try.'

Dorentina looked at him. 'Good. Then I can tell you this.' She stood very close to him, spoke for some time, then asked, 'Is that enough?'

'Yes. But how do you know all this?'

'Black George speaks freely in front of us. He trusts us with his life. We know everything about him.' She paused. 'My son?'

Balthazar laid his hand on her arm, feeling the hard muscle underneath. A distant cheer sounded across the fields. 'I will try. I give you my word.'

'I believe you. Then let's go back.'

Gresham Palace Four Seasons Hotel, 7.45 p.m.

The Four Seasons doorman tried to protest but was quickly pushed out of the way as the Gendarmes stormed into the hotel entrance; his hat flew from his head. For a second, Attila Ungar seemed lost in the enormous space, with its vaulted ceiling, tiled walls, stained glass windows and sleek wooden reception desk with vases full of orchids. He glanced back and forth then ordered his men towards the café, pushing their way through a crowd of startled tourists. A Japanese man held up a smartphone and started filming. Ungar grabbed the handset and hurled it against the wall. It smashed into pieces. 'Would anyone else like to film us?' he demanded. The Japanese man jumped back and quickly left.

A short, dark Spanish woman in her forties stepped out from behind the reception desk and stood in front of Ungar. 'This is an outrage. You have no right to behave like this on private property.'

Ungar walked up to the reception desk and slowly pushed one of the vases with his forefinger until it reached the edge.

'Who are you?' he asked.

'Carmen Esperanze. The manager. And I must ask you to leave.'

A Gendarme stepped back into the foyer. 'She's not there, boss,' he said to Ungar.

Ungar pushed the glass vase an inch further. It fell off the reception desk and shattered on the floor, spilling water and flowers all around. Ungar looked at the manager and said, 'Ooops.' He gestured at another Gendarme, then at the staff behind the desk. The Gendarme grabbed one of the receptionists, a redheaded German in her twenties, and dragged her out from behind the desk, her face twisted in pain as he held her hair in his fist.

Ungar turned to the manager. 'You can help us, or we can take her into one of the vans. Where are they?'

'Where are who?'

The Gendarme yanked the redhead's hair. She shrieked in pain. Ungar said, 'Reka Bardossy. You know who she is. And you know where she is.'

'I don't,' said Esperanze.

Ungar stepped forward, an inch from her face. 'Don't waste any more of my time.'

The manager glanced at her employee. She shook her head, her face set in determination. Esperanze thought quickly. 'Tower Suite. Fifth floor.'

Ungar smiled. 'OK. I'll send up my men. If she's not there, we'll take you in and all your staff.' The Gendarme yanked the receptionist's hair again. This time she flinched but stayed silent.

There was movement on the other side of the foyer. 'Behind you,' said Esperanze, her face like thunder. 'She's behind you.'

At that moment Reka appeared, accompanied by Zsolt, Eniko and her two other bodyguards. Reka walked into the foyer, as poised and calm as though she was entering the gates of her ministry, all eyes on her, and knowing it. 'Are you looking for me?' she said to Ungar.

Ungar gestured at the Gendarmes. 'Take her in.' He glared at Eniko. 'What are you doing here? Are you deaf or stupid?'

Eniko said, 'Neither,' as Zsolt stepped in front of Reka and drew his pistol.

'We're not going anywhere,' Reka said. 'Take a look outside, Attila. Because neither are you.'

Warehouse, District X, 7.50 p.m.

Balthazar walked back across the field with Dorentina into the warehouse and they took their seats. The atmosphere had changed, the bloodlust fading. Samuel was standing inside

279

the cage, his tall body shining with sweat, blood seeping from a cut on his cheek. In front of him, semi-conscious, lay a dark-skinned man in his late twenties. The MC stepped forward, held Samuel's arm in the air. 'Ladies and gentlemen, the winner, the Sudanese Strangler. Three knockouts in a row, all within one minute. Soon to be an honoured citizen of Hungary.' The crowd cheered. The cry went up, '*Fekete bajnok*, black champion.' Samuel gave a tight-lipped smile.

Balthazar watched, pleased for Samuel, but also ashamed. The sooner he could get out of here, the better. 'You missed all the fun, Detective Kovacs,' said Black George.

'It's over?'

'Yes. That man is a machine. Perhaps I will give him a job. Did you speak to your brother? Are we going to be partners?'

Balthazar shook his head. He had not called Gaspar. There was no need. They both understood what a 'partnership' with Black George would mean. 'No. That's not going to happen.'

Black George said, 'Then you may leave. I hope you enjoyed the evening. There is nothing more to talk about.' He walked off into the audience, Dorentina and Bettina beside him, the crowd instantly making way for him.

Except there was something to talk about, although Black George did not know it. Balthazar still had not mentioned Islamic terrorism, the involvement of western intelligence services, or broached Anastasia Ferenczy's offer. He looked around. The black-clad security guards had moved out of sight. The lighting was back on. Some of the spectators were preparing to leave. Others had formed small groups, discussing the fight and the further rounds planned later. Pretty hostesses were circulating with trays of finger food and drinks. The atmosphere was more relaxed but the blood-lust would soon be running high again, Balthazar knew. He was done for the evening and could not wait to get out. He could see Goran standing on the other side of the cage, now talking to a Hungarian businessman who he knew was trying to start up a budget airline. Balthazar stood up and walked over to the door, waiting for his friend.

Gresham Palace Four Seasons Hotel, 7.50 p.m.

It is usually an eight-minute drive from the District V police station on Szalay Street, four blocks behind Parliament, to the Four Seasons Hotel. The six cars that roared out of the station car park made it in under three minutes, although they did go the wrong way down several one-way streets. The two vehicles that flew out of the District VI police station, on Szinyei Mersze Street, were further away but had an easier route, straight down Andrassy Way, sirens blaring, then on to Jozsef Attila Street. The District V cars split into two groups of three. One squad blocked in the Gendarme vehicle on the Zrinyi Street side of the hotel – one police car in front, another behind and the third parallel-parked – and the second trio blocked in the Gendarme vehicle on the Merleg Street side. The District VI cars split into two groups. One drove onto the narrow road in front of the hotel and boxed in the Gendarme vehicle behind Reka's Audi, while the second police car carried out the same manoeuvre in the front. The Gendarmerie vans were now trapped.

Four police officers spilled out of each car. Each group executed the same manoeuvre. Two carried sledgehammers, two utility knives. The officers with the sledgehammers swung them hard against the locks of the empty Gendarmerie vehicles. The locks shattered and the doors buckled inwards. The policemen with the sledgehammers gave the locks a couple more blows. There was no way to open the doors now. Then they smashed in the windscreens. At that moment, a Polish tour bus parked in the road in front of the hotel, its passengers staring in amazement at the scene unfolding in front of them. The policemen with the utility knives rapidly slashed each tyre of the Gendarmes' vehicles, ran into the hotel and formed a ring around Reka and the others, protecting them from Attila Ungar and the gendarmes.

Reka greeted the policemen, then looked at Ungar. 'Attila, you were saying?'

SEVENTEEN

Balthazar was dozing off in Goran's car when it slowed suddenly, waking him. Goran had parked in a far corner of the parking field at the warehouse, then had got stuck behind a procession of SUVs leaving the fight. The spectators and their vehicles had been checked by Black George's toughs at the exit as well. Balthazar and Goran were the last ones out. It had taken the two men more than forty minutes to leave. Balthazar stared through the windscreen, watched a car's headlights flash on and off in the distance. They were driving down a narrow access road, little more than a muddy path, that led through the fields back from the warehouse and onto the road that would take them into downtown Budapest. The blackness was almost total, the only other lights the glow of houses a mile away and headlights on the distant highway. To the left stood a small copse of trees. The curl of tension in his guts started to tighten again. What was this?

A light rain had begun to fall and the windscreen wipers scraped back and forth leaving a greasy smear on the glass. Goran flicked his cigarette out of the window, then held the steering wheel with both hands, suddenly alert as the Lada carried on down the path. The lights came on again, brighter and more powerful now, full in their faces. Goran grimaced, flashed the Lada's headlights back. The lights dropped down. Balthazar still peered ahead, his tension easing somewhat when he saw the two police cars pointing forward, parked in a V-shape across both lanes that blocked the road. They were brand-new Toyota SUVs, white and spotless, fancier and more powerful than the police's usual Volkswagen Golfs or Opel saloons. A policeman stood by the side of each vehicle; one was tall and lanky, the other shorter and tubby.

Goran slowed down, pulled over to the left of the two police cars. The tall policeman walked up, wished Goran and Balthazar a good evening.

'Good evening,' said Goran. 'What's happening ahead?'

The policeman peered inside the vehicle, nodded at Balthazar and smiled, his manner easy and polite. He looked to be in his early thirties, pale, with dark-brown hair. 'Nothing to worry about, sir. There's been an accident. No through traffic until the road has been cleared. You might have to wait a little while. Probably best to turn your engine off. No need to waste petrol.'

'How long?' asked Goran, keeping the engine running.

'As I said, sir,' the policeman replied, his manner a degree less cordial, 'as long as it takes. You can switch your engine off.'

Balthazar glanced at the short policeman. He was younger, in his late twenties, with small eyes and greasy black hair. He walked right up to the car, staring hard at Goran and Balthazar, then checking the number plates. His uniform was so new it was still stiff and shiny. Balthazar looked ahead, his unease growing. There was no sign of a road-block, but the road began to curve leftwards about ten yards ahead and it was impossible to see further. He did not recognise either of these officers, but there were several thousand police officers in Budapest and he had not worked on many cases in District X. He checked the Velcro name pad that was attached to the tall policeman's uniform: Janos Kovacs, John Smith, then looked over at the short policeman. Janos Kovacs, again. The name patch was crooked. Neither of the officers had asked for Goran's driving licence or to see the car papers. That was automatic whenever a police officer engaged with a driver.

The short policeman pulled a handheld radio from his waistband. Standard police-issue radios were small and grey, clipped to the jacket uniform. This was green. The same model that the Gendarmes had, Balthazar knew, that used restricted military frequencies. Balthazar heard the radio crackle, but the short policeman turned away, speaking into a cupped hand. The two policemen, he saw, had black special-forces-issue knives in sheaths on the sides of their belts. Balthazar watched in the mirror, his back rigid, fully awake and alert now, the adrenalin starting to course through him. Four more headlights were heading towards them, two more police cars, he realised, one next to the other, blocking the road behind them. He glanced again at the knives. No policeman openly carried a bladed weapon.

Balthazar slapped Goran on the thigh, '*Go!*'

CIA safe house, Filler Street, Budapest, 8.45 p.m.

Five miles away, on the other side of the Danube, in a once-grandiose villa high in the Buda hills, Celeste Johnson waited until Reka Bardossy had finished talking. The British diplomat let the silence hang in the air for several seconds, then gave her a cool, appraising look. 'Why would we agree to that?' she asked, before glancing at the man sitting next to her.

He was in his early fifties, Reka guessed, with thinning grey hair, round shoulders, a pasty complexion, thin lips and watchful grey eyes. He wore a white shirt with a button-down collar that was stretched tight over a substantial paunch, crumpled cream chinos and dirt-streaked white leather trainers. Celeste had introduced him as 'Brad, a colleague from the American embassy'. Brad – if that was his name – had apologised for not having a business card, but Reka thought it was pretty clear who he worked for. So far, Brad had not said a word. Next to Brad sat a tall, blonde Hungarian woman. She had showed Reka an ID from the state security service: Anastasia Ferenczy. These were two more people than Reka had planned on meeting, but it was rapidly becoming clear that she was not in control here.

'Because I've done nothing wrong,' said Reka, while mentally telling herself to stay calm, credible and persistent. 'Pal Dezeffy is the villain here, not me. I'll give you everything I have on him. In exchange you guarantee my safety and freedom.'

Celeste reached inside her shoulder bag and took out two Hungarian passports. She laid them on the heavy oak table. 'Really? Then how do you account for these? Passports issued by your ministry.' Reka picked up the document, flicked it open to the photograph page, then the second and third. Zsolt Szabo, in whose name it had been issued, was very dark and lean like a Bedouin.

'Or this?' asked Brad, as he slid another passport across the table, open at the photograph page. Reka looked down at the name under the picture. Attila Hegedus had tight, black curly hair and light brown skin and looked like he was from Morocco or perhaps Algeria. 'Zsolt Szabo, or whoever he is, is now being held at Yarl's Wood Immigration detention

286

centre,' said Celeste. She glanced at Brad. 'Mr Hegedus is helping us out not far from JFK airport, somewhere in New Jersey,' he said, in his Midwestern twang, 'while we find out who he really is.'

Celeste said, 'You might have got away with it if they had stayed in the Schengen zone.'

Celeste was right, thought Reka, although she was not about to agree. It was still a source of amazement to her that it was possible to travel from the Hungarian border to the Atlantic coast overland without showing any identity documents. Even airport checks were cursory within the Schengen zone. Schengen fuelled the rapacious demand for Hungarian and all EU passports. Without it, she would only have been able to charge of a fraction of the price. Often the only people to open passports were airline staff at the gate, whose priority was to get the passengers on board, not to run security checks. Except when travelling to Britain, which was not part of Schengen, and which zealously guarded its borders. As far as she knew, the traffickers had been specifically ordered to tell their customers not to use the passports for entry to either Britain or the US. It was unfortunate that they had not listened.

Reka had called Celeste on a burner telephone, asking for an immediate meeting, even before she'd left the Four Seasons. Celeste had agreed. A second wave of police reinforcements had arrived a few minutes after the first. Attila Ungar had backed off, although barely able to control his anger. She could only imagine the level of his fury when he saw what had been done to his vehicles. She had made a very dangerous enemy. And this meeting was not going well.

Reka had wanted Celeste to come to her house. There Reka would have been on home territory and more in control. Celeste had declined, citing 'security and confidentiality issues'. That was understandable. Celeste Johnson was instantly recognisable: there were not many tall, black women in Budapest, and certainly no others working for the British embassy. Nor did Reka want it known that she was meeting British and American officials. But she had to move quickly. She glanced involuntarily at the thin, white dress gloves on her hands that covered the scars, and shivered. Celeste had already stared curiously at them – Reka had told her she suffered from eczema, made worse by the heat, although this house was anything but warm.

The villa was enormous, two wings over three floors, divided by a central staircase. But even now, after two months of a powerfully hot summer, the place felt damp and musty, so Reka had no need to explain the silk scarf around her neck. They had entered through the back door, a small servants' entrance, but it was clear that most of the rooms had not been entered for months, if not years. She had glanced inside the large reception room where white dust sheets were draped over the heavy, dark wooden furniture. They were sitting around a large wooden table in a kitchen that looked like it had last been used some time before the Second World War. A Hungarian nobleman with a long waxed moustache, seated on a horse, stared out of a murky oil painting, two Vizsla hunting dogs sitting nearby.

Brad asked, 'How is it in our interest, in the interest of the United States and the United Kingdom, to allow you to get away with selling passports to people-traffickers that end up in the hands of Islamic militants?'

Reka replied, 'As I said, Brad. It was a sting operation. That is what I agreed to. Pal Dezeffy told me the aim was to draw out the traffickers and their networks. Once we had a clear picture, we would hand all the information over to you both. He is the prime minister. I had to take him at his word.'

Brad looked her up and down, considering her words. 'You have that in writing? Some kind of evidence that Dezeffy told you this was a sting operation?'

Reka shook her head. 'No.'

Brad asked, 'Emails? Recordings? Anything?'

'Not about that.'

Celeste drummed her long, slim fingers on the heavy oak table. She wore a black Polo shirt and grey linen trousers. 'Then why should we believe you? We could charge you in the UK with aiding and abetting terrorists, then request your extradition under a European arrest warrant. You are looking at a very long prison term indeed.'

'Or we might do the same,' said Brad. 'Find you a nice, cosy cell in a super-max prison.'

Celeste continued talking. 'It seems to me, Madame Minister, you are in no position at all to make any kind of deal. In fact, we expect that you might soon be facing a murder charge here.'

'Meaning?' she asked, although she already knew the answer.

Celeste took an iPhone from her pocket. The screen showed a video file. Celeste pressed play. The footage showed Reka on her back at the Castle, the would-be assassin sitting on her, her hand flying up to his neck, the man toppling sideways, Reka scrabbling to get to her feet. Celeste said, 'Neat move, by the way. You could probably get away with self-defence if this comes out. You would even have public opinion on your side. I can see the headlines now, "The Stiletto Killer". You might be able to walk free from court. But you might not. Either way, it would be the end of your political career. Which I am guessing you're not planning yet.'

'It was self-defence. And no, I don't plan to retire from politics yet.'

Brad asked, 'Then what use to us are you, Reka? What have you got? Because if it's not good enough, there's no deal. And you won't be walking out of here.'

Unmarked road, District X, 8.50 p.m.

Goran yanked the steering wheel hard to the left as he slammed his foot down on the accelerator. The Lada bucked and jumped forward, clipping the tall policeman on his thigh as it screeched away. He shrieked in pain and collapsed on the road. The force threw Balthazar back in his seat as they bounced across the fields. He looked at Goran in wonder. The Serb was clearly enjoying himself. The Lada Niva was a trusty workhorse, could traverse the roughest terrain, manage potholes and steep banks, but was not known for its speed.

Goran turned to him, laughed out loud and slapped Balthazar's leg. 'Turbo-charged, *brat*. They don't stand a chance. Who were they?'

'Gendarmes, I think. They had the Gendarmerie radios. And no municipal cops have cars like that.'

'Or knives.'

'Those too.'

'Then where did they get the uniforms?'

'They can get anything.'

'How did they know we were here?'

'Black George, I guess. He wanted to go into partnership with Gaspar.'

'You said—?'

'No, of course.'

'*Picka ti materina*, that motherfucker.' He glanced in the driver's mirror. 'We have a problem, *brat*.'

Balthazar turned around to see the two Toyota SUVs careering across the fields. 'I think so. They are catching up with us.'

Goran glanced in the mirror, then gestured at the glove compartment. 'Open that and give them to me.'

Balthazar reached inside and took out a set of military-grade night vision goggles. The equipment resembled a camera, with two eyepieces at the back and a long external lens in the front, with a headset attached. He passed the goggles to Goran. He yanked the gearstick, dropped down into second gear. 'Steer.'

Balthazar leaned across the gearstick and took control of the steering wheel. Goran switched the goggles on, placed them on his head and adjusted the sights. Once the goggles were properly in place, he switched the car's headlights off and took the steering back under control, heading towards the copse. Balthazar felt as though they were hurtling blindly through the darkness, and would soon crash into the trees, but Goran seemed serenely confident. He flicked a switch on the dashboard. 'Brake lights off. We are almost invisible.'

Balthazar thought back to the fake police vehicles. 'But they might have night vision goggles as well.'

Goran nodded. 'I hope so.' He lightly side-punched Balthazar's arm. 'Don't worry, *brat*. We'll be fine. But let's have some fun on the way.'

Balthazar watched the trees rush towards them, a dark army marching out of the gloom. He winced, almost braced himself for impact, when the Lada lurched to the left, skidded and stopped ten yards from the side of the copse. Goran kept the engine running as the two Toyota SUVs roared towards the Lada, one on either side of the vehicle, facing in the same direction. Just as they approached, Goran switched the headlights back on and reversed at full speed between the moving vehicles. A loud crack sounded across the field and the Lada shuddered for a second.

Balthazar looked at the right side of the vehicle. Goran laughed, grabbed the shattered wing mirror, now hanging on by a sliver of plastic, yanked it hard and hurled it into the darkness. The Toyotas spun around and roared across the fields, catching the Lada in their headlights.

'What now, *brat*?' asked Balthazar.

Goran kept driving, now headed in a wide arc around the SUVs. 'Firstly, now they know that we are here, we can put the music on.'

Balthazar knew what was coming. 'Boban?'

'Who else?' Goran pressed a button on the ramshackle CD player. The Boban Markovic Orchestra filled the car, a blast of brass instruments with a thumping rhythm. Goran glanced at Balthazar. 'Feel at home now?'

Balthazar laughed. 'Totally.' The band was the best-known Gypsy orchestra in the world. For a moment he was back at home on Jozsef Street, a teenage boy listening to his older brother Melchior as he explained how during the Ottoman empire Gypsy musicians had marched into battle alongside the soldiers, which was why, even now, bands like Boban Markovic had a distinctly martial rhythm.

A set of headlights cut across the field, illuminating the car. 'Now what?' asked Balthazar. He trusted Goran. But he also needed to know that the Serb actually had a plan. Balthazar had no desire to end the evening in police custody, or even worse, with Attila Ungar or any of his underlings.

'We have a couple of choices. Option A, which is somewhere

down here,' Goran said, as he kept one hand on the steering wheel and rummaged in the door side pocket, 'where are you, *mojo mala draga*, my little darling? Aha, got you.'

Goran pulled out a Glock pistol. 'Option A.'

'No,' said Balthazar. 'Definitely not.' Gunplay, even just a couple of shots in the air, would not end well.

'Really?'

'Really. No guns. What's option B?'

Goran looked disappointed but put the gun back. He spun the steering wheel, cut behind one of the Toyotas and sped back towards the copse. He pulled in close to the trees and quickly took off the night vision goggles. He stretched across Balthazar and reached into the glove compartment again. He took out two grey metal cylinders, each six inches long and three inches wide. There was a ring pull on the top of each lid.

Goran passed one to Balthazar, kept one in his hand. 'Get out of the car. When I say "now", pull the ring, count to three, and throw it at the cars coming towards us. Shut your eyes and cover them, drop down behind the car and stay there until you hear the second bang when I throw mine. The light will blind them. It wrecks the sensors in the night vision goggles. It's even worse if they aren't wearing them.'

Balthazar got out and looked across the field. The cars were about fifty yards away and closing in fast. Goran shouted, 'Now!'

Balthazar pulled the ring and threw the canister. He dropped down and covered his eyes, but his left leg gave way from under him. He landed badly and his right hand flew out to break his fall. His palm scraped along the rough ground, taking off the skin. A loud bang thundered across the field. The flash of light was so strong he could see the outline of his fingers against his eyelids. A second explosion sounded and then another flash. Two seconds later another loud bang sounded, deeper and longer, followed by the noise of crunching glass and metal. Balthazar stood up, steadied himself, and looked across the field. One Toyota had spun around and was now facing in the opposite direction. There was a massive dent in the right front side, the bonnet was open and bent almost in half, and steam poured from the engine. The other car was still pointing towards the Lada, its front crumpled and its windscreen shattered. The sounds of moaning and swearing carried across the field.

Balthazar ignored the pain in his hand and started to walk towards the vehicles. Goran placed his hand on his arm. 'They will be fine. Those cars have airbags, crush-zones, everything. An ambulance will be here soon.'

'I don't care about that. We need their phones and their radios.'

'No, Tazi,' said Goran as he directed him back to the Lada. 'We're done. And we need to get out of here.'

CIA safe house, Filler Street, 8.55 p.m.

Reka reached inside her Prada handbag, extracted two sheets of paper and placed them on the table. They were bank statements for a numbered account in the Seychelles, and showed a steady stream of six-figure payments coming in, and nothing going out.

Celeste picked up the sheet, scanned the details and the figures. 'Pal Dezeffy's offshore bank account. So what? We've known for a long time he's been taking pay-offs from Gulf investors.'

She passed the sheets to Anastasia, who flicked through the papers and shrugged. 'We already have this.'

Reka took out another document, several sheets of close type stapled together. 'Maybe you do. But you don't have this. And you don't know what he secretly promised the Gulf investors in exchange for their money.' She handed them to Celeste who read through the first few paragraphs. Reka could see that she was interested. 'These are transcripts of what?' she asked.

Reka said, 'Dezeffy's pillow talk.'

'With who?'

Reka said, 'Do I really need to answer that?'

'No,' said Celeste. 'You have the recordings?'

Reka flushed pink. 'Of this, yes.'

Brad asked, 'Where did you meet?'

'At home. My home, obviously.'

'He didn't sweep the place?'

'Yes. Thoroughly.'

'So how did you make the recordings?'

Reka smiled. 'His head of security is on my private payroll.'

Brad shot her a sideways glance, clearly more impressed than he let on.

Reka said, 'Take a couple of minutes, please. Go through the transcripts.' She laughed, a little nervously. 'Don't worry. There are only the parts that would interest you.'

Reka watched Celeste carry on reading. She had typed them up a few days ago. There was enough there to finish off Dezeffy for good. She had recordings of him admitting that there was a secret annex to the Gulf investors' deal: transit for Islamic radicals, recordings of him saying it was 'not his or Hungary's problem as long as they went west', that a number of potential terrorists had already passed through Keleti and he had deliberately taken no action to stop them. That more were coming. A second copy of the transcripts and the bank account records were suspended in cyberspace. If Reka failed to log on to a specific website by midnight, the transcripts would be sent by email, first to Eniko Szalay, then, a day later, to every media outlet in Hungary and the foreign press corps, together with a recording of her telephone call with Celeste Johnson arranging this meeting. The nuclear option was no guarantee, but would doubtless trigger enough of a shake-up that she could negotiate something. But before the nuclear option, she had one final card to play.

Celeste, Brad and Anastasia left the room for several minutes. Reka stood up and walked around. The kitchen was like time travel, back to her own house, her childhood before the change of system. She ran a finger along the layer of dust on top of the dark wooden sideboard, bent down and opened the door. A Zsolnay dining set was stacked up inside. If she shut her eyes, she could almost see her grandmother sitting at the head of the table, calling the live-in servants to bring the soup for Sunday lunch.

The door opened and she turned to see the trio walk back inside. This was it, the moment of truth, in the biggest gamble of her life. She would either leave with a deal, her fate assured. Or she would be handed over to the Gendarmes or God knows who. Her heart was thumping, her hands sweaty inside her gloves. She stood still, pleased to see that they remained steady.

Brad said, 'Sit down, please, Reka.'

She did as he asked. His voice was calm but his eyes were glinting. 'So what we have here, is proof that you knew that your prime minister was allowing Islamic terrorists to transit through Hungary. You talked about it in bed. Isn't that the case?'

Reka nodded, a sinking feeling spreading through her stomach. 'Yes, but I...'

'But nothing, Reka. You have facilitated travel for international terrorists. And you failed to notify the authorities.'

'I am telling you now. I was running a sting operation.'

'They move people, Reka, because you took bribes and helped them.'

'But you caught them.'

Celeste leaned forward, her voice tight with anger. 'We caught some of them. We don't know who else has got through or where they are or might be. Thanks to you. Who knows where they are or what they are planning? You have blood on your hands, Reka.'

The sinking feeling in Reka's stomach turned to nausea and fear. 'I have nothing on my hands. What I do have are all the records and documentation to show that I and my colleagues used Pal Dezeffy to run a well-planned sting operation to track and unravel an international jihadi network. And I have said that I can turn everything over to you.'

Celeste said, 'You will do that, Madame Minister. As soon as we are done here. Because you are done. Your career is finished. And so is your time as a free woman.' She glanced at Brad, then Anastasia. 'How do you want to do this? We are in Hungary and she is a Hungarian citizen. You have first rights.'

Anastasia considered her answer before she spoke. 'The best place to hold her for initial interrogations would be at the Gendarmerie headquarters on Andrassy Way. The Gendarmes have isolation cells there.' She looked at Brad. 'Like one of your super-maxes.'

Brad said, 'Sounds good to me.' He looked at Celeste, who nodded.

Reka tried to beat back her rising sense of panic. The isolation cells were grey concrete cubicles, barely larger than a child-sized bed, with a bucket for a toilet. The lights were left on twenty-four hours a day. Isolation prisoners were not allowed to mix with other inmates or take exercise, even in their own cells. She had several times asked Pal Dezeffy about their function, pointed out that they were illegal under EU human rights laws. Dezeffy had refused to answer her questions, but a couple of days later the Gendarmes' interrogation manual had been left on her desk, with a sticky note pasted to the section on Grade One beatings. She stopped asking.

Reka closed her eyes, ignored the fear surging inside her. She had to stay in control. She would stay in control. For a second, she was back on the walkway at the castle, as the man sent to kill her advanced towards her, on her back as he tried to strangle her, saw him toppling over with the heel rammed into his neck. She opened her eyes, summoned every iota of her courage and began to speak. 'Thanks to me, you know that the prime minister of Hungary is secretly taking bribes from some very questionable people in the Gulf. Thanks to me, you know that Gulf investors have set up a base here to move potential terrorists. Thanks to me, you will soon know how the networks operate, how the traffickers move people, how the dirty money flows. Thanks to me, a major terrorist route westwards can be closed down.' She paused. 'Thanks to me, we are all just a little bit safer tonight.'

Brad said, 'Nice speech. But not nice enough.' He turned to Celeste and Anastasia. 'Shall we proceed?'

The two women nodded. Anastasia said, 'Sure. I'll make the call.'

Reka leaned forward. The last card would have to be

played. 'Wait. There's something you need to know.' The three turned to her. Reka continued talking. 'You have CCTV on this house?'

Brad nodded. 'The whole of the street is covered.'

'Call it up. There is an Audi A4 parked three doors down.'

Brad took out his iPhone, tapped on the screen. He placed the handset on the table so that Celeste and Anastasia could see. The image showed Filler Street, a long, leafy avenue. There was no traffic and the pavements were empty. Brad zoomed in on the Audi. 'I see it.'

Reka asked, 'Can you see the driver?'

The image showed a broad-shouldered man with a shaven head and deep-set blue eyes.

Brad said, 'Sure. Who is he?'

'His name is Antal. He works for me.'

'That's nice,' said Brad. 'But you won't be getting any visitors.' He turned to Anastasia. 'Now, let's proceed with what we need to do.'

Reka sat back, forced herself to sound more confident than she felt. 'The thing is, Brad, Antal has film on his phone of all three of you coming in here, and of me.'

The three intelligence officers glanced at each other. She had their full attention now. 'We know all about your safe houses. It was easy to guess where you would want to meet.' This part at least, was true. Reka continued talking. 'If I don't walk out of here by 11.00 p.m., that film will be posted to YouTube. You will be identified as the chief of station for the CIA, Celeste as the equivalent for MI6, and Anastasia as an operative for the ABS, all part of an operation to illegally detain a lawfully elected minister of the Hungarian government.'

This was a lie: there was no film. Antal refused to use a smartphone. He had an old Motorola flip-top without a camera. But there was no way the three intelligence agents would know that. Reka turned to Brad and Celeste. 'You will be – what's the term? – "burnt", I believe. You will certainly be declared persona non grata. Your bosses will protest but they will pull you both out. Your careers won't recover for a long time, if ever. That film will follow you around the internet. *Forever.*'

Reka then addressed Anastasia, her tone harsh now. 'And you, *kedves* Anastasia, you will also have to leave the country, probably for a long time, especially once your personal details are all over hazifiu.hu. You certainly won't ever work for our security service again.'

Brad asked, 'Are you threatening us?'

Reka shrugged. 'Of course not. How can I threaten you? I am just helping you understand the local operating environment.'

Brad picked up his phone and started to call a number. Reka said, 'Before you call your security team, you should know that Antal has several webcams in the car, covering the street and the inside of the vehicle, all set up to live stream on Facebook if anyone approaches the vehicle. Plus we have another team in a nearby house watching him, also ready to film and live stream. So your operatives, whoever they are, can also book their tickets home.'

This was a complete fantasy. There were no webcams installed in the vehicle and nor did Reka have another team. The only part that was true was Antal was there, sitting in a car nearby. Would that be enough to convince the trio? Reka watched the three intelligence agents carefully. Brad sat back for a moment, exhaled slowly. The two women looked at each other. There was nothing spies hated more than the prospect of having their names and faces made public. Their bosses would be furious. Their operational careers would certainly be over for good. If nothing else, Reka had taken control of the encounter. She was not out of the woods yet, she knew, not by a long way, but the atmosphere in the room and the power balance, she sensed, was shifting in her favour. She still had the nuclear option – releasing the transcripts to the press – in reserve, but there was no going back from that. She wanted to negotiate, not leave a trail of wreckage.

Brad exhaled slowly, scratched his stomach, then gestured to Anastasia and Celeste. The two women stood up. He turned to Reka. 'We'll be back in a few minutes. Don't leave the room.'

Reka smiled. 'Why would I?'

The trio returned two minutes later and sat back down at the table. Reka made sure not to show her nervousness. The isolation cells were probably an empty threat, she had decided. Too many people would see her arrive and would know she was being held at 60 Andrassy Way. But she had no doubt at all that Brad and Celeste could, if they chose, make her disappear and guide the media to come up with a plausible reason for her sudden absence. Or even arrange an 'accident'. This was a high-risk game she was playing. But she also knew that she had no choice.

Brad spoke. 'If we accepted your explanation that you were running a sting operation – *if* – your documentation would be helpful. But it's not enough. You have left out one of the most important players. Give us everything you have on him, and you'll walk free.'

'Who?' asked Reka, for a moment genuinely puzzled. 'Dezeffy is the key person. I have given you everything I have on him. Really, everything.'

'We know that, and we believe you,' said Brad. 'But there is someone else. Someone deeply involved in all of this. We need all the details of his role as well.'

Celeste spoke, her voice softer, more encouraging now. 'Of course, we understand that is a difficult step for you to take. It will have a cost, a personal cost. But it will be worth it. We can help you, Reka, help you get the prize you have wanted for so long. And when you move into that lovely corner office, with the view over the Danube, we can help you stay there.'

Reka asked, 'How?'

'We are in the information business,' said Brad. 'We tell you things, you tell us. But it all starts with one man.'

Reka felt the relief coursing through her. They were offering a deal. She was safe. *Kez kezet mos.* Ten, even five years ago, they would not be negotiating with her. But now Budapest was back on the map, which meant they needed her. International crime gangs had set up their headquarters in the city, reaching east to Moscow and west to London, New York and Los Angeles. The banks were awash with dirty money pouring in from the former Soviet Union and the Middle East. Britain and the United States all had boosted their intelligence operations. The city was full of Russian spies. Budapest was a gateway to the west for everyone from the Triads in Hong Kong to corrupt American corporations – and now jihadists.

Reka had no qualms about sharing that kind of intelligence with London and Washington DC. In return they would supply information that could dispose of any opponent whenever she wanted. Reka was a Social Democrat. The party was in power and so had the most access to EU funds and controlled their disbursement. But every group in Parliament, from the minuscule, unreformed Communists to the ultra-nationalists, had their fingers in the till. The only question was how much they could extract. But the relief was mixed with puzzlement. Who were they talking about? And then the dread rushed through her as she realised they could only have one person in mind. Someone who, for all her betrayals, she had always tried to protect.

Reka asked, 'Who?'

Brad said, 'Your husband.'

EIGHTEEN

Dob Street, 10.05 p.m.

The unmarked police vehicle, a black Toyota saloon, dropped Balthazar off right in front of his building. Just as Sandor Takacs had promised, there was a regular police car parked right outside the front door, a Volkswagen Golf in the white-and-blue livery of the Budapest police, with two officers inside. He raised his hand to them in greeting and they nodded in return. A second Volkswagen was parked on the corner of Klauzal Square, just behind the rack of green Bubi bikes, also with two policemen inside. A third vehicle was positioned ten yards further up Dob Street, near the corner of the Grand Boulevard. All three were fitted with a roof-mounted CCTV unit slowly sweeping back and forth. It would be impossible to approach the building without being noticed. The CCTV feed, Balthazar knew, would go straight back to the Budapest police headquarters. Any threat, or even a hint of one, would trigger a fresh armada of vehicles and probably a helicopter.

Usually, at this time on a Saturday night, this corner of District VII was still jammed. But there were no crowds of revellers strolling past, making a raucous path from ruin pub to ruin pub. There were no teenagers drinking and smoking in the Klauzal Square park and definitely no smell of marijuana wafting over the fence. The Irish pub was quiet and shuttered. A row of empty green beer bottles and tiny clear palinka bottles was lined up on the window sill of Csaba's ABC but the drinkers had long gone. If nothing else, Sandor Takacs's display of force had brought the residents a rare night of quiet.

Balthazar watched the black saloon slowly drive off. The vehicle would circle the area for three hours, before another took its place. He had called Sandor Takacs on his way back from District X. His boss had heard on the police grapevine about an incident near the cage fight. The details were very hazy but the crashed cars in the field had been found by chance by a local police patrol. Takacs already knew that the vehicles were not police cars. The two Gendarmes had been taken to hospital, where they would soon be charged with impersonating police officers. Even so, Takacs still tore a strip off Balthazar, reminded him of his instruction to stay under the radar. He then despatched two carloads of regular riot police to pick up Balthazar and Goran. The Serb had been escorted back to one of his many apartments. Balthazar had been taken to the police headquarters on Teve Street, to wait in safety while Takacs despatched the local police in District VII to check out his flat and the surrounds.

Once they gave the all-clear, Balthazar was allowed home. Takacs had also arranged for regular foot patrols from the local stations from Districts VI and VIII to Dob Street. The Gendarmerie would back off, for now, Balthazar thought, especially after the incident at the Gresham Palace Hotel, which was all over the news and the internet. The new force might have state-of-the-art vehicles, weapons, equipment and legal carte blanche but they were barely three hundred strong and far outnumbered by the regular police – and numbers counted, especially as the struggle between the two was turning ever nastier.

Yet for how long? Attila Ungar was a thug, to be sure. But a thug with highly developed political antennae. Balthazar walked up to the door of his building, his mind running back over his conversation with Anastasia Ferenczy earlier that day. The involvement of the western intelligence services was a game-changer. Hungary was a small country, of just ten million people, fewer than the population of London and its surrounds. If America, Britain and Germany wanted to crash the economy, wreck the forint, release compromising material on Pal Dezeffy, they could. They might not even need to act to bring down his government. Dezeffy had created a praetorian guard. But praetorian guards had a habit of turning on their creators. A more interesting question was how long would Ungar stay loyal to Dezeffy?

The door buzzed open before Balthazar had the chance to key in his entry code. The kitchen of Eva's ground-floor flat looked out onto Dob Street. She had been waiting for him to come home, he guessed. He walked up the stairs, holding onto the metal banister for support, his legs feeling as though they were about to give way. Eva was standing in the entrance foyer by the open door to the her flat. She beckoned Balthazar to her, staring at him for several long seconds. 'You look terrible.' She looked down at his right hand. 'More fighting? You need a doctor?'

He shook his head. 'No, I slipped. It's nothing. Just a graze. I don't need a doctor. I just want to go to sleep.'

'You can sleep. But not yet. We have company.'

Balthazar stiffened, a sense of dread rushing through him. Were the Gendarmes here already, inside the building? Had he put Eva *neni* in danger?

She sensed his unease, laid her hand on his arm. 'Come, Tazikam. There's nothing to worry about.' They stepped into her kitchen. The small room was familiar and curiously comforting. Eva *neni* invited him down for a meal once or twice a month, sometimes with Alex. The orange wall units, spotless gas cooker and formica-topped table dated back to the 1970s. Framed pictures of Eva *neni*'s family, sepia-tinted formal photographs of her parents, sister, colour snaps of her daughter and grandchildren stood on the window sill. Eniko sat by the table, hunched over her laptop. She looked up at Balthazar as he walked in. Her eyes were red-rimmed. 'I'm sorry, Tazi. I can't go home. I didn't know where else to go.'

Eva *neni* shook her head in mock exasperation. She had met Eniko several times while she and Balthazar were together. Eva had made it clear that one, Balthazar needed to get married again and have more children, and two, Eniko would be a good choice. 'She's all yours. She wouldn't eat anything, would barely have a cup of tea, and spent all her time looking at her watch or her computer, waiting for you to get home.' She smiled mischievously. 'And you can be sure there was no word from that actor. Now can you two lovebirds leave an old lady to get her beauty sleep, please? And by the way, where is Alex?'

Balthazar smiled. 'At his mum's. He's coming next weekend.'

'OK. You get pancakes tomorrow anyway. But not too early.' She reached for a small green plastic bottle on one of the shelves and handed it to Balthazar. She turned to Eniko. 'You'll look after him?' It was a statement more than a request. Eniko nodded. She picked up her laptop, thanked Eva *neni*, kissed her on both cheeks and followed Balthazar into his apartment.

'Shall I make us some tea?' asked Eniko. Balthazar nodded, almost too tired to speak. He put the Betadine down on the coffee table. While Eniko was in the kitchen, he walked through to the small room. The bed was made up with clean sheets and pillowcases, waiting for Alex. It would do for Eniko. But why was she here?

He stepped back into the lounge, flopped down on the sofa, his hand throbbing, the fatigue washing through him in waves, dozed off for a minute or two. Eniko brought two mugs of tea on a plastic tray, which she placed on the coffee table before sitting down next to him. She looked at Balthazar uncertainly. 'Strawberry. It's all I could find.' She picked up her mug. 'So here I am again,' she said, smiling brightly.

Balthazar gave her a wary look. Was this some kind of mind game? He didn't think so. Her smile, like her voice, was brittle. She was not only exhausted, but frightened. 'Strawberry is fine, Eni. You can stay here as long as you need.'

She gave him a wan smile. 'Thanks. I saw the police cars. All three of them.' She glanced at his neck. 'You are wearing your chain. It makes you look like...' her voice trailed off.

'Like a Gypsy mafioso?'

Eniko flushed red. 'That's not what I meant and you know it, Tazi.' She glanced at his hand. A thin brown crust of blood had dried on the fleshy part of his palm. Eniko said, 'You're hurt. Go and wash your hands. Or have a shower. I'll find something to clean you up.'

Balthazar walked into the bathroom, turned on the warm water and stepped into the shower. Dirt and dried blood fell away and spiralled down the plughole. The warm water stung against his raw skin. He ran the water as hot as he could bear for several minutes, feeling the tension in his back and shoulders begin to drain away, then switched to cool. He dressed quickly in a clean T-shirt and loose trousers and walked back into the lounge.

Eniko was sitting on the sofa, a clean white T-shirt in her hand. It looked small, certainly too small to be one of his. For a second he thought she had found it among his son's clothes. Eniko looked up at him, as though reading his mind, a bashful expression on her face. 'It's mine. I forgot to take it back. I kept it with Alex's stuff. Emergency clothing if I stayed over without planning. Come,' she said, glancing at the space on the sofa next to her.

Balthazar sat down, presented his right hand. 'But you will spoil it. The Betadine won't come out,' he said.

'It doesn't matter, Tazi. We need to clean you up. It's only a T-shirt.' Eniko opened the bottle of Betadine, squirted some of the thin, dark-brown liquid onto the white cloth, dabbed it onto Balthazar's palm. He winced a little as the iodine stung. Eniko reached for his other hand, her fingers soft and warm on his skin as she dabbed at his skin. He sat back, holding his hand out so the Betadine could dry.

'Thanks.' He paused, gave her a quizzical look.

Eniko smiled wryly. 'What?'

'It's nice to see you, Eniko. But what's happened? Why can't you go home?'

She swallowed, exhaled hard. 'Have you got something to drink?'

He looked around the room. Unlike many Hungarians, Balthazar was not a big drinker. A beer or two on the weekends, a glass of wine at family dinners or on a rare date. But there was a bottle of barack, peach-flavoured palinka, somewhere, home-distilled by one of his mother's neighbours in her village in the far north-east of the country. If ever there was a day for palinka, it had been today. He got up and rummaged in the cupboard across the room. The bottle was stashed at the back, behind a pile of his old university essays. He took it out, found a couple of dusty shot glasses, sat down, and poured them both a measure, a larger one for Eniko.

They clinked glasses with the traditional Hungarian salutation, '*Egeszsegedre*, to your health.' He drank half, Eniko downed all of hers in one. She shivered as the alcohol hit the back of her throat, closed her eyes for a few seconds, stared at Balthazar and burst into tears.

Kenyermezo Street, 10.20 p.m.

At that moment the most-wanted man in Hungary was pacing back and forth in a dark, cramped studio flat on the top floor of a dilapidated apartment building on Kenyermezo Street. The street, on the very edge of District VIII, ran from Republic Square to Rakoczi Way, five hundred yards south of Keleti Station. A narrow iron bedstead with a sagging mattress took up most of the room. A cheap plastic kettle and two-ring electric stove, thick with grease, served as the kitchen. There was no bathroom or shower, just a cracked sink in the other corner, with a single cold tap. Empty pizza boxes and kebab wrappings were jammed into a rubbish bag under the sink.

The room was hot, the air stale and humid. The heat was even worse at night. He had barely slept and the yellow nylon sheets and thin brown blanket were crumpled up at the end of the mattress. A blue cotton baseball cap rested on top of the thin pillow. The hotel across the street had been tolerable, a palace of luxury, in fact, compared to this place. But the Gendarme commander had said he needed to move here for security reasons. He would manage; he had endured far worse. And soon he would be in London, in a duplex apartment overlooking Hyde Park. He watched a cockroach scuttle across the floor towards the food remains, raised his shoe and slammed it down. There was a cracking sound. He lifted his foot. White gunk oozed from the cracked carapace. He rubbed the sole of his shoe on the floor, feeling a growing sense of disgust. He had been forbidden to use the shared facility along the corridor and had been told to empty his bowels into the plastic bucket under the sink. He could urinate into the sink, but using the bucket was beyond him. After three days holding back a diet of pizza and kebabs, he was now severely constipated and constantly suffering stomach cramps.

He had been told not to stand by the window or open it. He had disobeyed once, but opening the window brought no relief, just the thick stench of exhaust fumes from Thokoly Way and the greasy stink of fatty, roasting meat from the Turkish kebab restaurant on the corner. The window was coated with a layer of ancient grime, but if he stood to the side he could see Keleti Station and Baross Square. The forecourt was still packed with sleeping bodies, a human wave that spilled down the side of the station, almost to the taxi rank and across the patches of grass. Here and there, tiny red embers glowed and moved, the cigarettes like beacons in the night. A small group, a family, he thought, huddled around the sputtering blue flame of a camping stove.

Hejazi reflexively checked his shirt pocket once more, knowing that the search was hopeless, and was suddenly back at the square where he had lost it. It was Nazir's fault. Why had that fool followed him? Revenge? What did he think he would achieve in the backstreets of Budapest? They were a long way from Aleppo, almost in western Europe. If

Nazir had stayed in the station, he would still be alive. Hejazi had spotted him almost immediately. The streets were almost empty at that early hour and Nazir had barely bothered to use any cover, if he even knew how to. The Gendarmes had arrested him almost immediately, marched him into the half-demolished building.

Nazir had gone berserk when he saw Hejazi, clawing at him, trying to punch him. That was when the SIM card must have fallen out. The Gendarme commander, the thuggish one they called Attila, had tasered Nazir. Tasers were not supposed to be fatal, but this one had been. Perhaps it was the stress and trauma of Nazir's journey. Or seeing again the man who had removed his fingers and was ready to take some more off. Either way, Nazir had gone into cardiac arrest. The Gendarme had even tried to save him, administered CPR. But it was no good. Nazir had died. In any case, it almost counted as a mercy killing. He would have taken Nazir somewhere quiet and safe, found out what how much he knew. He excelled at such work now, even enjoyed it.

A mobile phone rang, the sound clamorous in the cramped space. He picked up the cheap red Alcatel burner and waited. The handset rang five times, then stopped. He waited a few seconds, then the phone rang a second time, again stopping after five rings. He was to call the fifth number on a list of six. All the numbers on the list were the same, apart from the last digit which ended in one to six. He tapped out the digits. The number rang twice.

'The birthday party is set for tomorrow afternoon,' said a male. Hejazi recognised Attila's voice.

'Good. When does it start?'

'At three o'clock. Be at the pick-up place. You are definitely invited.'

The phone went dead. The code was Hejazi's idea. If someone was listening in, they would likely assume that some sort of terrorist attack was planned in Budapest at three o'clock tomorrow. The authorities would waste considerable energy and divert resources trying to discover what was planned and foil it. There was something planned, a kind of 'spectacular', but for once no bombs or guns were involved, and there was no way that the Hungarians, or anyone else, could stop it.

Balthazar's flat, Dob Street, 12.25 p.m.

Balthazar watched Eniko cry softly for several seconds, her head in her hands. In his heart he instantly wanted to hug her. It would be an easy, natural move, the simple response to another human being in distress. His head, colder, more distant, said not to. He knew where a hug was almost certain to lead. He had picked up Eniko's mixed signals, knew by now that she was conflicted about her decision to break up with him, and was still attracted to him. Her arms would wrap around him, he would respond, their bodies press together. Their emotions were running high, both were ready to take comfort where they could, especially familiar comfort. It was after midnight and she was obviously staying the night. Part of him wanted nothing more. Then he imagined the scene the next morning: her embarrassed explanations, her rapid dressing and hurried exit. He had built a wall around himself after Eniko left, for a reason. This was not the time to think about it dismantling it.

Balthazar looked around for something to give her to wipe her face. There was nothing in sight, apart from the iodine-spattered T-shirt. He handed it to her. She blew her nose on it and dabbed her eyes. 'Sorry, Tazi. I'm not usually like this.'

She looked at the T-shirt, now thoroughly stained and crumpled, laughed wanly. 'At least we're getting good use out of it.'

Balthazar smiled but kept his distance. 'Do you want to tell me what happened? The last time I saw you, a few hours ago, you were rushing off to meet someone. A secret source. You wouldn't even tell me who he or she was, unless I agreed that we should work together. The next thing I see is you all over the internet at the Four Seasons with Reka and her bodyguards, facing down the Gendarmes, then leaving with a police escort.'

Eniko laid the T-shirt on the table. There was no point holding back now. She wiped her eyes, gestured at the bottle. 'Pour me another one. A small one.'

He did as she asked. This time she sipped the drink. The day poured out in a torrent of words – the HEV, Csepel Island, her interrogation in the strange concrete building, Ungar's threats, the killing of Bela Lidaki, her meeting with Reka Bardossy and their escape from the Four Seasons.

'Congratulations,' Balthazar said. 'You have a lot of scoops: the prime minister is running a travel agency for Islamic radicals, has murdered the former interior minister, tried to kill the justice minister while she has confessed to selling passports to people-traffickers.' He picked up his glass, sipped the palinka. 'But why is she telling you all this?'

'She's playing hardball, trying to bring down Pal Dezeffy. For that she needs to get the information out.'

'Why you?'

'I was there. Because I'm on this. Because I'm a good reporter.'

'Sure. But what else does she want?'

'To shape the media narrative. To frame the story.'

'How?'

'The passport operation was a long-term sting, planned and run by her, to draw out the traffickers so their network could be dismantled.'

Balthazar exhaled sharply. At least Gaspar's name was somehow staying out of this conversation. But his brother's and Goran's operation across the borders was small beer compared to the passport channel. 'She's smart, I'll give her that. Do you believe her?'

That was the million-dollar question on which her future career would probably turn. 'I don't know.' She paused. 'I believe that I have to report what she tells me.'

'What are you going to do?'

'Think about it.' She smiled, wryly. 'But probably not too much. Everyone has an agenda. Mine is to report the news.'

There was silence for several seconds, then Balthazar's stomach growled. The palinka, he realised, had made him ravenous. He had eaten nothing since a snatched lunch of a Turkish shawarma sandwich. 'Aren't you hungry?' he asked.

Eniko nodded. 'Actually, yes. I was too nervous to eat while I was waiting for you. Besides, there's never anything in your fridge or your cupboards. And I guess we aren't going out for dinner.'

'No, we are not. We are not going anywhere.'

Eniko shrugged. 'So?'

Balthazar picked up his phone and called Sandor Takacs's number.

'What is it, Tazi? More car crashes? Gendarmes again?'

'No. Nothing like that. Everything is fine, except I'm hungry. And the cupboard is bare.'

Takacs laughed. 'OK. There are at least six cops near your front door with nothing to do. I'll send one of them. What do you want? Pizza? Burger?'

Balthazar looked at Eniko, mouthed pizza or burger. She whispered 'burger'.

Balthazar returned to his phone call. 'Two burgers and a pizza.'

Takacs laughed. 'Two? You must be hungry.'

'Not just me.'

'She is still there. That's good. It's the best place for her.'

Sandor Takacs had met Eniko a couple of times, at work social events when colleagues were leaving or celebrating birthdays. He approved of her. Eniko had been charming, sociable company and had not tried to leverage her connection to Balthazar to get information from his colleagues. Takacs's voice turned serious. 'Work with her, Tazi. We'll protect her. Share everything.'

Balthazar looked at Eniko, idly leafing through a copy of *Newsweek*, pretending not to eavesdrop. For a moment he was back at her mother's sunny flat on Pozsonyi Way, sitting down to Sunday lunch on a bright spring day, before retiring to a book-lined lounge with a piano in the corner. There had been Sacher torte for dessert and a Schubert recital. Her mother had welcomed him immediately. Eniko told him later how outraged she was at the pointed remarks the next day from her neighbours that there was a Gypsy in the house.

'I will,' said Balthazar. 'What about her mother?'

'There's a car already outside her house. Call me in the morning. Call 112 if there is any trouble. You are in the system. There is a city-wide instant response alert on you and your flat. Keep Eniko there.'

Balthazar asked, 'Is it starting? At Keleti?'

'The rumours are flying. It looks like it.'

'Thanks, boss.' Balthazar hung up and put his telephone on the table. He had no doubt that someone, somewhere, was listening to the call. But Ungar should know that Eniko and her mother were now protected. It would at least buy them some time.

Eniko asked, 'Whose mother?'

Balthazar sat down, making sure that their legs did not brush against each other or touch. 'Yours. That was Sandor Takacs. There is a police car outside her house. It will stay there, until all this is over.'

'Thank God. So we are safe.'

'For now. The food will be here in twenty minutes or so. Let me know if you need anything else.'

Eniko walked across the room to the bookshelf and stared at the silver-framed photograph of the pretty green-eyed young woman she had seen yesterday. 'Tell me, Tazi. Who is she?'

'I already said. One of my zillions of cousins. Why are you so interested?'

She turned to look at him, gave him an appraising look. 'I know a quite a lot about you and your family, Tazi. But I don't think you ever mentioned her. What's her name?'

And there is so much more you don't know, and hopefully never will, he almost said. 'I had it framed recently. Her name was Virag.'

Eniko picked up the picture. 'Was?'

'Yes. She's dead. She was my cousin. Third cousin, but we were very close.'

'I'm so sorry, Tazi. That's so sad. What happened?'

'She was killed. Murdered.'

'Did they catch him?'

'Yes.'

'How long did he go to prison for?'

'He didn't.'

She looked away from the photograph and at Balthazar. 'Oh. Is that why you became…?'

'Partly, yes.'

'Do you miss her?'

'Sometimes,' he said. 'A lot lately.' More since you left, he thought, but would never say so.

Eniko put the photograph down, sat back down on the sofa, took off her hair band, released her pony tail and closed her eyes. Balthazar watched her face relax, her hair spilling around her shoulders. She leaned back, her head high, her arms at her side. He watched her chest rise and fall as her breathing steadied, dozing off, then looked across the room at the photograph of Virag. She would have been thirty-four now, a few years older than Eniko, her beauty fading, probably with half a dozen children, stretching out her welfare payments, trying to keep them in school, a feckless husband and a pile of unpaid utility bills. Or getting a handout from Gaspar on Envelope Friday, when she would not have to queue because she was family. But she wasn't thirty-four. Thanks to him, she wasn't anything. Or partly thanks to him. He could never decide how much her death was his fault. But one thing was certain: all the murderers that he arrested would never bring her back.

He picked up his shot glass, drank the rest of his palinka, and walked out onto the balcony. Klauzal Square was still and silent, the benches empty, the playground deserted. The night was warm and still, the apartment buildings quiet and shadowed. He thought of the stories Eva *neni* had told him, of the bodies stacked up in the winter of 1944 and 1945, the Arrow Cross militiamen prowling and hunting, the terror and starvation. He thought too of her relatives who had escaped the deportations in Pecs and made it to Budapest, and his cousins from the villages nearby who had not.

A large black saloon was driving along Dob Street towards his apartment building. As it drew nearer, he could see that it had Gendarmerie number plates. He watched it slow to a crawl as it went past the police car on the corner then turn left down Klauzal Square. The black vehicle went around the square again, then parked a few yards from the police car in front of his house.

He sensed movement behind him. Eniko walked across the room and then she was standing next to him. The air turned thick and charged. She looked at him, the light playing on her face, her expression a mix of trepidation and something else. Hope, he realised. The entrance buzzer rang and the moment was gone.

NINETEEN

Balthazar's flat, Dob Street, Sunday, 6 September, 9.30 a.m.

The knocking on the front door was light but persistent, waking Balthazar from a deep sleep. He scrabbled for his watch on his bedside table, checked the time and sat up slowly, gingerly waiting for the assault on his muscles to begin. Today there were no sharp pains, just a general ache and an all-encompassing stiffness, from his shoulders down to his calves, as though he had been strapped to an ironing board. He winced as he reached for his drawstring trousers, slipped them over his boxer shorts, and walked to the bathroom. He had slept decently, certainly better than on Friday night, although he remembered being woken around dawn by some light noise in the lounge. He had called out to Eniko, asked if she was OK, and she had replied that she was just coming back from the bathroom. He had immediately gone back to sleep. The knocking started up again. He shouted that he was on his way, splashed his face with cold water, quickly brushed his teeth, and walked to the front door. The door to Alex's room was half-open and he could hear Eniko gently snoring.

He looked through the peephole. Two women stood waiting expectantly. One, with a tray of pancakes in her hand, was short and elderly. The other was neither. Balthazar opened the door. Eva *neni* marched in, Anastasia Ferenczy behind her. Eva looked around at the mess in the lounge and shook her head, tutting then gathering up the pizza box and polystyrene burger containers. She pointed at several cold chips and a single slice of pizza on a greasy plate. 'It's a shame to waste food, Tazi. I should make you finish them before you get these,' she said, making space for the tray of pancakes.

'I'm sorry, Eva *neni*,' said Balthazar. 'We did the best we could.' The door to Alex's room opened. Eniko poked her head around, her eyes widening as she saw how many people were in the room, then quickly retreated, closing the door firmly behind her.

Eva *neni* put down the pancakes, gathered up the mess, and left. Anastasia stood in the middle of the room, a half-smile playing on her face. She wore a close-fitting green scoop top that matched her eyes, and pale-blue skinny jeans. 'I hope you don't mind me dropping in.'

Balthazar shrugged. She was really quite attractive. 'Why not? Everyone else is. Are they still outside?' he asked.

Anastasia's smile widened. 'They are all there, Balthazar. The cops. The Gendarmes. Our British and American friends. God knows who else.'

'And your people?'

'Oh, definitely us as well. We do like to keep an eye on things.' She looked at the sofa. 'Aren't you going to invite me to sit down?'

Balthazar opened his hand towards the sofa. 'Please do.'

Anastasia picked up Eniko's T-shirt, still stained brown from the Betadine, looked at it quizzically, put it aside, and made a place for herself. 'How was the fight?'

There was no point asking how she knew about it. 'Horrible.

Desperate men pummelling each other to stay in Europe. I knew the winner, Samuel. He helped me out at Keleti.'

'Who's Samuel?' asked Eniko as the door to Alex's room swung open. She stepped out. Anastasia stood up. Balthazar watched the two women introduce themselves. Eniko warily assessed the new arrival, taking in her clothes, her figure, and her confident body language. 'Sorry,' said Eniko, not sounding very sorry at all. 'The door was open. I couldn't help overhearing.'

Balthazar said, 'Anastasia works for the ASB.' He turned to Eniko, 'And Eniko, as you know, is a journalist.'

'Of course,' said Anastasia. 'I know your work. I am a fan.'

'Thanks,' said Eniko warily. Beyond the spark of jealousy, something else about Anastasia nagged Eniko. Her face, her upright posture, was familiar. 'Have we met? I'm sure I've seen you before.'

Anastasia gave her a bland smile. 'Possibly.'

'Retro-kert,' said Eniko, her voice confident now. 'Friday at around 9.00 p.m. You were downstairs. While I was upstairs with my editor. He was nervous. He kept looking down and I couldn't figure out why. It was because of you, wasn't it?'

'I don't know. People get nervous for all sorts of reasons.'

'Were you meeting him?'

Anastasia did not answer, her smile still fixed.

Eniko continued talking. 'And before that, I saw you at Keleti, several times, at the taxi drivers' stand.' Eniko leaned her head to one side, shot Anastasia an assessing look. 'Is that part of your cover?'

Anastasia nodded slowly. 'Yes, Eniko, it is. Was. But I would be grateful if you didn't write that.'

Balthazar looked down at the tray of pancakes. There were at least a dozen, piled one on top of another, dusted with lemon zest, oozing *turos*, and four lemon quarters. 'Why don't we eat first, then we can get to know each other. It's going to be another long day.'

'OK. I'll make some coffee and get some more plates,' Eniko said and walked into the kitchen.

Anastasia waited until Eniko had left the room. 'I didn't know that you had a guest. A reporter.'

'I didn't know I was supposed to tell you.'

'You weren't.' Anastasia added, sotto voce, 'Black George?'

Balthazar shook his head, made sure to hold her gaze. 'He won't help.'

'You passed on my offer?'

'I did. He said he was not interested.'

'You explained the consequences to him? That this goes far beyond criminal business as usual?'

'He doesn't care. He won't help. He thinks he is invulnerable.'

'Then we'll have to show him that he's not,' said Anastasia.

Balthazar was surprised at how easily the lies came. Easily and guilt-free. Anastasia was easier to deceive than Dorentina. 'Let's do that. Once we have Hejazi.' The ASB could save Gaspar's business, if all went well, and never even realise.

Eniko walked back in with three plates, sat down and placed two pancakes on each. 'Coffee on the way.' She looked at Anastasia, then at Balthazar, trying to work out what was happening.

Balthazar sat in an armchair and the two women perched on the sofa, their plates on their knees as they ate Eva's *turos palacsintas*. He squeezed his quarter lemon over the pancakes. The atmosphere was uncomfortable. The two women neither liked nor trusted each other, that was clear, but he was beginning to enjoy himself. For once, he was on home territory and in control. Anastasia wanted something, but she was here in his flat, had come to him. He knew Eniko well enough to recognise her initial flash of jealousy.

Balthazar turned to Anastasia. 'So how can I help?'

Anastasia put her plate down. 'The SIM card. You have it?'

'Yes. I have that. And a proposal.'

Anastasia leaned forward, her voice brisk. 'This isn't Lehel Square market, Balthazar. This is a matter of national security. International security.'

'So you say. But if this is so important, then why doesn't my boss know about your visit? Where is the inter-agency liaison request? There is a protocol for this. Impromptu meetings in my flat on a Sunday morning are not part of it.'

'Neither is keeping vital evidence in your personal possession. This is an emergency, Balthazar. We are sidestepping protocols.' Anastasia glanced at Eniko, clearly uncomfortable about speaking in front of a reporter, then looked back at Balthazar. 'What do you want?'

'Two things. One, the file on Hejazi.'

Anastasia reached into her shoulder bag and handed a plastic folder to Balthazar. He opened the file. There were several sheets of typewritten paper inside and a photograph of him clipped to the front. 'OK.'

Balthazar glanced through the contents. 'Thanks.' Eniko, he saw, was staring hungrily at the papers. He gathered them together, closed the file and placed it on the coffee table.

Anastasia asked, 'And two?'

'Samuel. The South Sudanese refugee who won the cage fight last night. He was promised Hungarian passports for himself and his family, his wife and two children. Make sure he gets them.'

'OK. Four passports.'

'Proper passports. Genuine passports. And IDs, tax numbers, healthcare numbers, everything. Citizenship.'

'We can do that.'

'*If* I give you the SIM card—'

'When you do.'

'*If* I do, you will immediately strip it, source and analyse the numbers, and make a network of the connections.'

'Yes. It will go straight to our analysis department.'

'I'd like you to share that information with Eniko.'

Anastasia looked aghast. 'With a reporter?'

'Not *a* reporter. This reporter,' said Balthazar, nodding at Eniko. She looked oddly embarrassed, he thought, but guessed it was just the general tension in the air.

He stood up, walked across the room, lifted up the rug and used a twenty-forint coin to lever up the parquet slat where he had hidden the SIM card and the call list. The floorboard was much looser than when he had left it and it moved easily. Too easily. The space underneath was empty.

Shamsi family home, Rakoczi Way, 9.40 a.m.

Maryam sat on the brown fake-leather sofa in the money-changers' office on Rakoczi Way, staring at the tattered poster of Damascus, wondering what to do with the rest of her life. She had been here for two days now. The Shamsi family had been very kind, checking on her every hour or so, inviting her to join them for meals, treating her like a welcome guest. She sat at the table, grateful for the company, and glad not to be sitting in the dust and dirt of the forecourt of Keleti Station. The food they served was delicious: tender kebabs, crisp salads, spiced rice, a taste of home. She pushed it around her plate, without a trace of appetite. The hours passed like sand through a sieve, one grain at a time.

The shock of Simon's death had worn off, but the pain only seemed to intensify. She had not slept, had spent the nights staring at the ceiling. The worst was that she did not know what had happened to Simon, how he had died or where his body was. The reporter had been kind, in her way, but Maryam, in her grief and shock, had forgotten to ask her to send a copy of the photograph. Sometimes she thought this was all a bad dream, some kind of hideous nightmare, that Simon would walk through the door, take her in his arms. Then she glanced at their two rucksacks, and the list of unanswered calls on her phone.

This horror, a life bereft and empty, a sick weight in her stomach every waking moment, was her new reality. She had two options, she supposed. She could go back to Keleti, somehow find the strength to continue their journey westwards, and try and ensure that Simon had not died for nothing. Or she could go back to Syria. Her parents, and many of her friends and relatives, were still in Aleppo. Refugees, yes, driven from their homes by the bombing, but at least there she would be among people who knew her and some who loved her. She glanced at the piece of paper on the table, the last word she had from Simon: *bustani*, the Gardener. The man who had tortured her husband, and who, if he had not personally killed him, had caused his death.

And then she realised. She had a third option. She walked over to Simon's rucksack, reached inside and pulled out a large Swiss army knife. She opened the biggest blade, ran her finger carefully along the edge. It was extremely sharp. For a moment, she imagined the knife in Hejazi's throat, the expression of surprise as the blood sprayed, the fear and the realisation that he was dying.

At that moment Amal, the Shamsis' youngest daughter, who had first served her coffee when Maryam had arrived, knocked on the door. Maryam put the knife into her rucksack and told Amal to come in. Her smooth-skinned face was alight with excitement. 'Come quickly,' she said. 'Something is happening at Keleti.'

They walked into the lounge, where the family was gathered watching the BBC international channel. The local correspondent was explaining how rumours had been swirling around Keleti Station for more than a day that the refugees and migrants had decided to walk to Austria. 'We have had enough, we are not animals to be caged here,' said a tall man in his twenties, clearly agitated. 'We have no proper food, not enough toilets or water. We will leave. And nobody can stop us.' The reporter nodded, turned to the camera. 'Hungarian authorities have refused to comment on these latest rumours, but it seems unlikely that they will seal off the station. For many Hungarians, the sooner the refugees and migrants leave, the better.'

Maryam watched the report until the end. The camera showed small groups already packing up, poring over maps. She walked back to the office and sat on the brown sofa, deciding what to do. After a couple of minutes she got up, found Simon's passport in his rucksack, placed it in hers together with the roll of banknotes, and went to explain to the Shamsis that she would be leaving later that afternoon.

Balthazar's flat, Dob Street, 9.45 a.m.

Balthazar leaned forward and stared down at the space. There was nothing there. He ran his hand around the inside, just to make sure. An indentation in the packed dirt, the edge of the supporting wooden floorboard underneath, but that was all.

He frowned. The SIM card and the printout were definitely there yesterday afternoon. Had he been burgled? The Gendarmes were outside, lurking in the square, driving their vehicles around, but it was almost impossible for someone to break into the flat, especially after Sandor Takacs had deployed three police cars nearby. But the flat had been empty for several hours the night before while he'd been out at the fight. There was the security system linked to the Budapest police headquarters, but nothing was completely secure. There was one agency that specialised in domestic break-ins. It had a team of experts that was renowned for getting into the most difficult places. He turned to Anastasia. 'They're not there.'

She looked alarmed. 'Then where are they?'

'I have no idea. Your colleagues?'

'No. Of course not. Why would I be here now if we already had it?'

This was a fair point, Balthazar had to concede. So where was it? He suddenly remembered the noise that had woken him soon after dawn, a scrabbling sound, asking Eniko if she was OK. He looked at her. She was staring down at her coffee cup and had turned pink.

'Eni?' he asked.

She looked away, flushed and embarrassed. 'I meant to put it back. I just wanted to check if there was anything else, if you had something new. Then I panicked when you called out to me. I thought you were going to get up and see what was happening. Then I overslept and it was too late because you were up.'

Balthazar stood up, walked back to the armchair, feeling a

familiar mix of disappointment and vindication that he had not let events take another course last night. 'Why didn't you just ask me?'

'I don't know. I should have. I should have trusted you. I'm sorry, Tazi.'

Anastasia leaned forward. 'I hate to interrupt this therapy session,' she said, her voice lightly ironic, 'but the SIM card?'

Eniko reached inside her shoulder bag, took out the evidence bag and the printout of the numbers. Balthazar reached for them, took them from her hand. Eniko looked hopefully at him, waiting for him to remind Anastasia of his request to share the information with her.

'You're on your own now, Eni,' he said, as he turned to Anastasia.

Balthazar kept hold of the SIM card and printout. 'There is one more thing.'

Anastasia sighed. 'What?'

'You found Jozsi. The gypsy kid at Republic Square.'

'I did. Are you going to arrest him?'

'No. Of course not. Just send me his full name and address.'

Anastasia held her hand out. 'Sure. As soon as I can get back to my office with the SIM card. Is that it?'

Balthazar nodded, gave her the SIM card and papers.

Eniko said, 'You'll share the network analysis with me?'

'That depends.'

'On what?'

'We have a lot of interests in common, Eniko. You have spent a lot of time at Keleti and other places. You know all sorts of interesting people. And we are both in the information business. *Kez kezet mos.*'

Eniko looked down at her hand. Some things could never be washed off. 'I'll think about it.'

Balthazar's phone rang and he glanced at the screen. It was Sandor Takacs. He took the call and stepped away on the balcony.

Takacs said, 'You're very popular today.'

Balthazar laughed, looked out over Klauzal Square. The police cars were still parked nearby. The black Gendarmerie vehicle was slowly turning onto the square. A stocky man in his forties was sitting on a park bench near the Bubi bikes, reading *Magyar Vilag*. Another, younger man, was inside the park, watching the playground. ABS or Gendarmes?

'Not with everyone. How am I going to get out?' asked Balthazar.

'I'll take care of that. Get ready, you need to come in for a briefing. The rumours are already flying around Keleti.'

Balthazar said goodbye and walked back into the lounge. The two women looked at him expectantly. 'Finish your breakfast. I need to go to work. And so do both of you.'

Keleti Station concourse, 3.05 p.m.

Maryam stood in front of Keleti Station, her rucksack on her back. She had left some of her clothes behind, together with most of Simon's, but the bag was still heavy on her slight frame, already sticking to her top. She wiped her brow for a moment, glanced at the station entrance. The line of riot police had vanished. A few officers stood here and there, wearing their summer uniforms of blue trousers and white polo shirts, chatting and smoking. An overweight man in blue shorts carrying a Hungarian newspaper walked through the gate, but none of the migrants or refugees were trying to get into the station.

The tension, the sense of desperation, had gone. Instead, the atmosphere was excited, almost festive. She watched a family of four – mother, father, two toddlers – pack up their meagre belongings in two canvas bags, pick up their children and walk out. Two teenage boys, bottles of water in their hands, were shouting, '*Yalla, yalla*, let's go, let's go,' waking those still asleep. A CNN reporter, a blonde American woman in her forties, was interviewing a skinny young man, perhaps eighteen or nineteen, as his friends crowded around him, nodding and gesticulating. 'We won't stay here any more. We are going west to Germany, west to work,' the boy declared, to cheers and whoops from those nearby.

All around her, hundreds of people were gathering their possessions and streaming across the forecourt, heading across the road onto Thokoly Way, blocking the traffic. For a moment, she felt as though she was back in Syria, watching the long columns of wretched humanity fleeing the fighting with everything they could carry, or in the refugee camp in Turkey. At least here nobody was shooting at them. She touched the pocket of her jeans, where the Swiss army knife bulged.

Tents, once the most precious possession, stood abandoned across the forecourt. Empty water bottles, sandwich packets and nappy wrappings littered the ground. Even blankets and bedrolls had been left behind. There seemed to be no leaders and nobody was giving instructions or orders. The police were making no effort to stop the migrants leaving, and were even holding up the traffic to let the migrants cross Thokoly Way in safety. Volunteers mixed among the crowd, wearing light-blue baseball caps, handing out bottles of water and packets of biscuits. For a moment she glimpsed a man in his thirties, handsome, dark-skinned, with striking green eyes. He stood on the edge of the crowd, watching, then he disappeared into the mass of people. He wore a T-shirt and jeans, carried a small rucksack on his back. At first glance he might have been an Arab, or from Afghanistan, but his body language was very confident and he did not seem at all agitated or excited, like the other migrants and refugees.

The man stepped away, into the throng of people. Simon's absence hit her like a punch in the guts. This was the moment they had been waiting for. The moment when they would leave together. Except he was not here. Would never be here. A stream of people was coming up from the Transit Zone and the entrance to the underground station. A middle-aged woman in a white headscarf appeared with her daughter, perhaps ten years old, both blinking in the bright afternoon sunlight.

'What is happening?' asked the woman in Arabic. She had a round, intelligent face and clear brown eyes.

Maryam recognised her Damascene accent and replied in the same language.

'I don't know exactly. People are going to the Austrian border.'

'How? On foot?'

Maryam looked across the road. The column of people now filled one side of Thokoly Way down to Baross Square and was heading down Rakoczi Way towards the Elizabeth Bridge and the Danube. 'I think so, yes.'

'How far is it?'

'About a hundred miles, I think. Three days, maybe four.'

'But where will we get food? Where will we sleep?'

She took her decision. This is what Simon would have wanted. There was no going back to Syria. Maryam smiled. 'I don't know. God will provide.'

A cry went up in English, 'Freedom, freedom, Ger-man-y, Ger-man-y.' Maryam felt the tears well up and wiped her eyes.

'Why are you crying?' asked the woman.

'My husband is dead.'

'So is mine, her father,' the woman said, gesturing at the girl.

Maryam introduced herself to the woman. 'My name is Nur,' said the woman, 'and she is Raina.' Maryam said hallo to Raina. She looked at her shyly, but did not answer. 'She does not speak any more,' said Nur.

She reached for Maryam's hand. 'Come. We will walk together.'

Kenyermezo Street, 3.10 p.m.

Mahmoud Hejazi stood by the side of the window in the squalid apartment and watched the column gather in front of Keleti Station before walking down Thokoly Way. There, leading the procession, was a one-legged man in a wheelchair, being pushed by a rota of people walking alongside. Hejazi's instructions were to stay about fifty yards behind him, keep his baseball hat and sunglasses on, his head down, and to wait for further instructions. The baseball cap covered the burn marks above his left ear. Personally, he had never favoured this plan. He had wanted to take his chances at the green border or with the smugglers. That had brought him this far.

But the Gendarme commander had insisted: the borders were on full alert and Hejazi was on an international watch list. Hiding in plain sight was the best option. After a few hours, once the column reached the outskirts of the city, the Hungarian authorities would lay on a fleet of buses. Then they would open their side of the border and simply dump the migrants a few yards from the Austrians. The Austrians, good-natured and naïve, would be overwhelmed and take in everyone. There would no identity checks and he would be in the west. And Hejazi had to admit the organisation was impressive: first a few dozen, then a couple of hundred and now several thousand people were walking towards the river, watched warily by the police. The Gendarme commander had promised him that their plan would work. They had planted agents and agitators at Keleti for days, spreading rumours, ramping up the tension. Perhaps it could work. He opened the window and the shouts carried up on the wind: 'Freedom, freedom.'

TWENTY

Keleti Station concourse, 3.10 p.m.

Balthazar waited at the top of the staircase that opened onto the forecourt of Keleti Station, ignoring the persistent urge to touch the tiny earpiece he was wearing. Before he had left his flat, Balthazar had outlined to Anastasia and Eniko what Dorentina, Black George's bodyguard, had told him on Saturday night, when the two of them had stepped outside the cage fight. Hejazi was staying near Keleti, in an apartment owned by the Gendarmes. She did not know the address, just that it was somewhere nearby. Gendarmes and other operatives, posing as refugees at Keleti, were spreading rumours that the Hungarians were going to open the Austrian border.

The plan was to trigger a mass exodus of thousands of people who would start walking to Austria. Hejazi would slip into the crowd. There would be thousands of dark-skinned Arab-looking men on the move. It would be impossible to find him. Even if the security services were looking for him, he would be hiding in plain sight. Anastasia had suggested that she contact Sandor Takacs and that the ABS and the police set up a proper operation. Takacs had immediately agreed. It was now very clear that capturing Hejazi was not something that Balthazar could achieve on his own, working under the radar.

Balthazar's gaze wandered over to the station's entrance. Keleti was part of the city's backdrop, a place to pass through, en route to somewhere else. He had never really looked at the building before. But the yellow walls were full of grandeur, a throwback to an age when the station was at the epicentre of one of the world's most powerful empires. Sunlight streamed through the glass roof inside. Four pillars at the entrance propped up an ornate balcony, where statues on pedestals overlooked the forecourt. The entrance doors were made of glass and green ironwork that flowed in intricate floral patterns. And somewhere nearby, among thousands of Middle Eastern men, was Mahmoud Hejazi.

The earpiece crackled and he heard Sandor Takacs's voice. 'Anything?'

'Nothing,' murmured Balthazar. 'At your end?'

'Nothing. There are hundreds of them. It's almost impossible to... er...' Takacs's voice tailed off.

'Tell one from another?' said Balthazar helpfully.

'Something like that. Keep looking, Tazi.'

Takacs was in the operations room at the Budapest police headquarters, watching the CCTV feeds. Keleti was covered, as was Baross Square, but there was no more coverage on Rakoczi Way until Blaha Lujza. There the road was under surveillance all the way down and onto Elizabeth Bridge. There had been some discussion as to how to proceed. Once the CCTV network was brought into play, some of Takacs's colleagues had to be informed what was happening. His deputy, a veteran of thirty years' service called Tamas Meszaros, had argued that there should be a city-wide alert out on Hejazi and that his photograph should be circulated to all officers. That was what the rule book said, and Meszaros was always a stickler for the rules.

But Balthazar had argued against this and Takacs had agreed. As soon as they went wide with the information that they were hunting Hejazi, the Gendarmes would hear. And they would certainly have a Plan B and probably a Plan C as well. Plus Hejazi was a highly experienced operative. He would quickly realise that the squads of police all over the city looking for someone were almost certainly looking for him and he would go back into hiding. Meszaros had settled for increased security at the border and Hejazi's photograph being circulated there. The CCTV team was kept as small as possible and informed that they were not to discuss anything about the operation.

Balthazar's eye alighted on two Arab women with a young girl. One of the women wore a green headscarf. The other was notably beautiful, with sensuous Levantine features and black curly hair that flowed freely over her shoulders. She looked extremely sad. Balthazar glanced again, tried not to stare. For a moment he was back in his apartment with Eniko after she had played the recording of Maryam talking.

'Very beautiful. Long black curly hair halfway down her back. She's a Christian so she doesn't wear a headscarf.'

It was her, he knew. Balthazar had got nowhere on Friday when he had tried to interview Maryam at the moneychangers' on Rakoczi Way. He could take her aside now and ask some questions, he supposed, but his instinct told him not to. She would certainly become emotional, draw attention to herself and Balthazar. He knew who he was looking for. And what he needed now was to blend in. But he would definitely keep an eye out for her.

Mahmoud Hejazi waited inside the door of the apartment building as the column of migrants and refugees headed down Rakoczi Way. The blue baseball caps worn by volunteers wove in and out of the crowd as they handed out water bottles and bananas. The one-legged man in the wheelchair was at the front. The whole of Keleti's Transit Zone looked like it was on the move: a father wearing a singlet and flip-flops carried a toddler on his shoulders; a plump mother with a blue hijab ushered three children in front of her while, behind her, half a dozen men in their twenties wearing jeans and T-shirts laughed and joked as they headed towards the Danube.

He waited until they had passed, then stepped out onto the pavement, a small nylon rucksack on his back, the tiny pistol strapped to the holster on his right ankle. The only downside was the large number of reporters, interviewing, filming and excitedly talking on their mobile phones. Whoever had planned this operation had not factored in that it would send dozens of international journalists, all thoroughly bored with spending hot, listless days at Keleti, into frenzies of excitement. But there was no turning back now. He pulled his blue baseball cap down lower over his sunglasses and walked into the throng.

Sixth floor, 2 Jozsef Boulevard, 3.20 p.m.

A hundred yards away, Goran Draganovic stared down the telescopic sight of the Dragunov sniper rifle, the wooden stock resting against his shoulder. The weapon felt comfortable in his hands. The Dragunov was a familiar workhorse,

338

the standard sniper rifle used by all sides in the Yugoslav wars before the dissolution of the Warsaw Pact, with a range of almost nine hundred yards. The trigger rested against his right index finger, sprung and ready, the barrel on a small, collapsible bipod. From his eyrie in the onion dome on the top of the roof he could see all the way to Keleti Station, well within range, and down Rakoczi Way to Elizabeth Bridge. To the right, he had the Grand Boulevard covered until Oktogon, where it met Andrassy Way, and to the left, way past Rakoczi Square almost to the Petofi Bridge. There was no better eyrie in the city. He glanced at the photograph of the target lying on the floor next to him, but the man's features were seared into his memory.

The instructions were to shoot to kill, on sight. As usual, there was no fee, just a promise that his travel agency would continue to work unimpeded. He had no ethical problems about the target. And this time, he had a personal stake in the man's demise. The difficulties were technical, not moral. It would be a tricky shot, as the target would likely be moving and surrounded by innocent bystanders. But one shot should be enough. He glanced at the small pouch of ammunition next to the gun. The 7N1 bullets were produced especially for the Dragunov. They had a steel core and a hollow spot in the nose with a lead knocker. The bullet was unstable on impact, spun around inside the body and caused massive internal damage. Even a shot to the shoulder would be fatal.

The only disadvantage was that a few yards below was a room full of some of the best reporters in the city. That, and the thick dust which covered the space. He suppressed another sneeze. But the onion dome on the top of the roof was almost inaccessible, and could only be reached by a small metal spiral staircase. There was no reason for anyone to come up here and, in any case, he had locked the door on the inside.

Goran keep his breathing steady, adjusted the telescopic sight, zoomed in on the column as it marched down Rakoczi Way. The scope filled with the faces of the marchers: grimy, exhausted, hungry but with their faces set and determined. A small girl, perhaps five or six years old, was being carried by her father, half-asleep on his shoulder. She had a bob of black hair and wore a pink top. For a second, she seemed to wake up and stare right into the telescopic sight, before she fell back to sleep.

Goran swallowed hard, closed his eyes for a moment and let his finger slide away from the trigger. He opened his eyes, forced himself to focus, and resumed his search.

Third floor, 2 Jozsef Boulevard, 3.15 p.m.

Eniko stood on the balcony, watching the column walk across Blaha Lujza Square and head south towards Elizabeth Bridge. She felt a powerful mix of excitement and frustration. Excitement because the biggest story in the world at that moment was unfolding a few yards in front of her. And she had the inside scoop, information that no other reporter had. Frustration because she could not yet report what she knew. Balthazar had made it clear that if she stayed in the room while he told Anastasia what he knew about Mahmoud Hejazi – that he was hiding in Budapest, was connected to Pal Dezeffy and would join the exodus – she could not write anything about it until the day had played out and Hejazi was caught. And even then she would have to liaise about what she could reveal. Or, she could leave the room. She stayed, of course, now overflowing with information that she could not use.

Then, amid the crowd, she spotted a young woman with long, black curly hair. Was it her? Yes, it was Maryam, about twenty yards away, heading towards Blaha Lujza. About ten yards behind Maryam she thought she saw Balthazar. Then he disappeared into the crowd. Either way, she could not stand here watching any longer. She picked up her notebook, walked briskly through the newsroom, down the stairs, and stepped out onto Rakoczi Way, when she saw Attila Ungar.

Rakoczi Way, 3.15 p.m.

Mahmoud Hejazi kept a steady pace. Nobody showed any particular interest in him and nobody asked any questions. There was no reason why they should. He was just one of thousands of desperate people heading for Austria. He kept his head down, his sunglasses and baseball cap on. The man in front of him was carrying a small girl on his shoulder, half-asleep. She had short black hair and wore a pink top. All around him people were carrying their children, or helping the elderly and infirm. The cry went up again, 'Ger-man-y, Ger-man-y, free-dom, free-dom.'

*

Attila Ungar instantly recognised Eniko and quickly walked further into the crowd to move away from her. The Gendarmes had Hejazi in a box: Ungar had a team of eight plain-clothes officers tracking him: two in front, two behind and two on either side. So far, Hejazi was following his instructions: to blend in and keep a low profile. Ungar allowed some of the tension to drain out. There was a carnival atmosphere, a great wave of relief and celebration that finally, the thousands

341

of people marooned at Keleti were on the move. The chants of 'Germany' and 'Freedom' grew louder, so much so that they woke the little girl in the pink top. Ungar watched for a moment, yawning, then saw Hejazi. He smiled at her. She reached out, grabbed the baseball cap from his head, and started to wave it like a flag. Ungar immediately muttered into his earpiece, alerting his team that they had a problem.

*

Twenty yards behind Hejazi, Maryam and her companions were walking steadily when Maryam noticed a disturbance ahead. A man was talking to a young girl in a pink top. The girl was holding tight onto a blue baseball cap. She heard his voice asking for the cap back, looked at his face and her stomach turned to ice.

Maryam checked the Swiss army knife in her pocket and turned to Nur. 'I think I know him, from Aleppo. I'll be back in a couple of minutes.'

'OK. But be careful.'

Maryam eased her way through the crowd, staring at the man. He was still trying to persuade the young girl to give him his baseball cap back. His ear was scarred and mangled. The child placed the baseball cap on her own head and started laughing. The girl's father intervened. 'It's very hot, she's a child. Can't you just leave it with her?' he asked. The man reached for the baseball cap. The girl's father caught his hand, pushed it away. 'Leave us.' He gestured at the crowd where several dozen volunteers wearing the same headgear were walking around, giving out bottles of water, snacks and bananas. 'Ask one of them. I am sure they have many.'

'Please,' said the man. 'I need it. I already had heatstroke yesterday.'

Maryam reached into the back pocket of her jeans, took out the Swiss army knife, and carefully opened the largest blade, concealing it in her hand so the other people around her would not see.

The man reached for the baseball cap again, trying to take it from the child's head. She thought it was a great game and grabbed his sunglasses. Maryam stared, felt the rage and hatred well up inside her. The Gardener. The man who had tortured her husband then led him to his death. His hair was shorter and greyer. But it was him.

By now some of the other migrants had noticed what was happening. It was unheard of in Muslim culture to harass another family's child. A tall man in his early twenties, his face twisted in anger, started pushing Hejazi, ordering him to leave the girl alone.

Maryam edged closer to Hejazi, advancing on him from behind, trying to keep out of his field of vision. Hejazi felled the man with a hammer punch, driving the air from his solar plexus. The man collapsed, retching, and his friends advanced on Hejazi, shouting angrily. Maryam was now standing right next to Hejazi. She leapt sideways, slashing at his throat with the knife. Hejazi saw the movement from the side of his vision. He parried the blow, caught Maryam's arm, twisted her body around in front of him and the knife was at her throat.

*

The angry crowd muttered and swore at Hejazi but the space around him cleared. Balthazar walked through, holding his police ID, right up to Hejazi. Hejazi was pulling Maryam towards him, the blade glinting in the sunlight against her skin. Her eyes were wide with fear and fury.

'Let her go,' said Balthazar. 'Take me.'

'No. Take one more step and she will die.' He slid the knife lightly across the side of Maryam's neck. A thin crimson line appeared. Maryam grimaced in pain, said nothing. The men around Hejazi were growing steadily angrier, starting to step forward. Balthazar could see that in a few seconds they would charge Hejazi. The jihadi would not leave the square alive and neither would Maryam. Balthazar raised his arms, shouted, 'Police, police, back off.' The men moved away. Lives spent in one-party states and dictatorships had left a legacy of fear of the authorities.

'What do you want?' asked Balthazar.

'The Gendarmes. They promised to take me to Austria.'

'OK. We can talk about that. But let her go. You can take me instead as your hostage.' Balthazar started to walk towards Hejazi.

Hejazi shook his head. 'Stop. I will let her go.' He looked around. 'In exchange for her,' he said, pointing at the child wearing his baseball cap.

The girl's father shrank back. The child started crying. At that second Maryam's right hand flew up. She slid her fingers around the blade and yanked down as hard as she could. She screamed with pain as the blade cut through her flesh almost to the bone, but kept pulling. As the knife moved away from her throat she stomped down on Hejazi's right foot.

For a second Hejazi lost his balance. Hejazi pushed Maryam away, dropped down and reached for the pistol in his ankle holster. A forest of hands reached for Maryam, dragging her away into the crowd as blood streamed from her fingers. Balthazar leaped forward.

Attila Ungar watched as the migrants backed away and the space around Balthazar and Hejazi widened. Balthazar landed on top of Hejazi and grabbed his hand, trying to take control of the gun. But the barrel of the tiny pistol was too small to hold. Hejazi brought his knee up and flipped Balthazar over onto his back, trying to punch him in the head with his left hand while his right hand attempted to steady the pistol.

Balthazar deflected the blows with his left and grabbed Hejazi's gun hand with his right hand, extending his elbow and locking it. The gun was now pointing at the sky. He slid his index behind the trigger guard and around the trigger, pulled hard again and again until the magazine was empty. The crack of the bullets tore the air. The migrants fled in every direction, shouting in fear. Balthazar raised his hips and slammed his right knee into the small of Hejazi's back, so hard he felt the vertebrae shift. Hejazi cried out and flew forward over Balthazar's face and chest. Hejazi's grip on the pistol loosened. Balthazar flipped him over. The back of Hejazi's head hit the road and his arms fell away to the side. Balthazar lifted Hejazi's head and banged it hard against the road, then stood up.

'Mahmoud Hejazi, I am arresting you for the murder of Simon Nazir,' he said. He turned Hejazi over and handcuffed him. Balthazar stood with one foot on his back. Hejazi groaned, face down on the road, his eyes fluttering.

A voice sounded in Balthazar's ear. 'Nice work, Tazi. Reinforcements on the way.' Sirens wailed in the distance, getting louder by the second.

A loud crack sounded across the square. For a second Balthazar lost his balance as Hejazi's body jerked sideways.

He stepped away and looked down. A pool of crimson was slowly leaking out from under Hejazi's chest.

*

Twenty yards away, Attila Ungar nodded to himself. The gunshot was no surprise. Hejazi was a liability. The operation had turned into a major clusterfuck and needed to be shut down. And that was impressive work by Balthazar. His former partner still had it. Perhaps he could recruit him. Everyone had a price. The only question was how high it was, and how to persuade people to pay it.

Ungar heard the voice in his ear. 'Stand down. I repeat, all Gendarmes to stand down.'

TWENTY-ONE

Budapest police headquarters, Teve Street, 6.00 p.m.

EXCLUSIVE TO 555.HU:

MINISTER OF JUSTICE RAN 'STING OPERATION' TO CATCH PEOPLE-TRAFFICKERS AND ISLAMIST RADICALS

By Eniko Szalay

Sandor Takacs sat back and scrolled through Eniko's story. He smiled as he read:

> Ms Bardossy is said to be fully cooperating with the relevant Hungarian and international authorities. 'Her information is proving extremely useful and will help us close down a major route westwards for Islamic radicals and terrorists,' said one western official.

Reka had won, which did not surprise him at all. She was a superb operator, and she played for very high stakes. She had somehow outmanoeuvred Pal Dezeffy. Takacs knew the line about a sting operation was nonsense, but he guessed she was giving 'western officials' enough inside information about the passport channel to remain useful. The only question was whether Eniko actually believed the spin, or if it was some kind of trade-off with her. But that was the reporter's business. He could give her a much better story. Perhaps he would.

The police's money-laundering and organised crime department had been investigating the Bardossy family's wealth for several months. The Gulf connection had raised multiple alarms. Takacs had opened enquiries with police forces in London, Paris and New York. He had not told Balthazar yet, nor that the Budapest police dealing with money-laundering had also been investigating the connection between Gaspar, Goran and Reka. If Reka had lost, Balthazar's brother would be in a whole lot of trouble. But she had won. That case, he knew, would now be put aside, or at least 'de-prioritised', but the information would be preserved. Hungarian politics was a very volatile arena. Reka's star was up now, but who knew where she would be in a month or a year?

Takacs was halfway through Eniko's second article, a dramatic first-person account of Balthazar's arrest of Hejazi and the shooting, when his telephone rang. It was Gundel, the restaurant where he had booked Erzsi's leaving party.

'Yes, this is Sandor Takacs,' he said. 'Thanks for calling back. No, it's not a cancellation. I still want the booking, thirty people in the private dining room. But it's an anniversary party now, not a leaving one. Yes, we still want a cake, with Erzsi's name on it. Look, why don't I send you an email with all the details.'

Ministers and prime ministers had fallen, and far more important to Takacs, Ilona, his unwanted new PA, had resigned. Erzsi had agreed to return to work immediately – doubly pleased when he told her she could keep her retirement package and start with a new contract. For now at least, Takacs knew he had a blank cheque. The Gendarmes had lost their roof. Reka would take the side of the police. But Attila Ungar was a wily and dangerous foe. The police had won this battle but the war would continue.

Prime minister's office, Hungarian Parliament, 6.15 p.m.

Reka ran her right index finger across the rectangle of green leather in the centre of the desk. Part of the surface seemed shinier, more polished than its surrounds, but perhaps that was her imagination, or her memory playing tricks. She felt a pang, of regret perhaps, a slight sense of wonder at her own ruthlessness, wonder that was soon replaced by pleasure. She smiled, sat back and looked around. The rug could stay but not the paintings. All these dark, gloomy portraits of old men in suits would have to go. Reka wrote a quick note to herself, to call the young female owner of the trendy art gallery she had found the other day, on Brody Sandor Street. That part of District VIII – what did they call it now? – the 'Palace Quarter', was getting really lively. She sat back and poured herself some more coffee from the blue and gold antique Zsolnay jug. For a moment she thought of the billboard she had seen on her way into Parliament, with the picture of Pal Dezeffy and his ministers enmeshed in a spider's web. Hers was the only female face. *Kirugjuk a komcsikat!*, Let's kick out the commies! Her father's face flashed through her mind, together with the instructions he gave her on his death-bed. So, no, not while she sat in this chair.

Reka savoured the taste of the coffee and the moment as long as she could before she decided what to do about her husband. She had negotiated a breathing space – a whole week

349

– with Celeste and Brad before she had to take her decision. A week was long time in politics, as a British politician had once said. A very long time, especially in Hungary at the moment. Pal Dezeffy had already taken a short conference call with London and Washington D.C, in which the new political reality had been explained to him. He had been given Sunday evening to draft his resignation statement. Reka's appointment would be announced tomorrow. The exit procedure was well honed: an enquiry would be announced into Dezeffy's Gulf connections. It would last for several years, enough time for the matter to be forgotten, then reveal nothing of any import. He would leave Hungarian domestic politics for good. In a couple of years' time he would find generous donors for a new think tank, write his memoirs, perhaps, if he cooperated, even win a safe seat as a member of the European Parliament.

The telephone on her desk buzzed. A female voice said, 'You have a visitor.'

'Send him in,' she replied.

The double door to her office opened. The Librarian walked in, ash drooping from a cigarette in his mouth, holding something in his right hand. She stood up and greeted him with the most respectful honorific, trying not to breathe the stale, musty smell that hung over him like a cloud. '*Tiszteletem*, I honour you.'

'Hallo, Doshi,' he said.

He placed a small black memory stick on the table. 'I brought you something. There's a video file on this. I think you will enjoy watching it.'

She knew what it was without asking. 'I've seen it.'

His voice hardened. 'Then I suggest you see it again.' His pale-blue eyes were fixed on hers. His psoriasis was worse than ever. White flakes of skin were peeling off around his eyebrows. 'Call me when you have finished watching.' He turned on his heel and walked out.

Reka waited until the door had closed, sat back down in her chair and closed her eyes for several moments, controlling her breathing and calming herself. There was a USB port on her desk, connected to her computer. She slipped the memory stick in, opened the video file and clicked play. The screen showed her lying on her back, her would-be killer's hands around her throat, her right hand flying up to his neck, the dead man toppling off her.

She watched through to the end. Just as she expected. This footage also showed Akos Feher appearing, Antal's arrival, the clean-up operation. This was a problem, certainly. But every problem had a solution. The Librarian wanted to control her, not bring her down before she had even taken office. She suddenly remembered a phrase from her history books: *Quis custodiet ipsos custodes*, Who guards the guardians? She buzzed through to her private office. Her chief of staff picked up immediately. Reka asked, 'Akos, please call the number now, on the secure line.'

She waited until the line began to ring. A female voice answered after the third ring. Reka said, 'This is Reka Bardossy.'

State Security headquarters, Falk Miksa Street, 6.20 p.m.

Anastasia Ferenczy turned the blue-and-white SIM card over in her hands and glanced once more at the colour-coded spreadsheet of names and telephone numbers on her computer screen. The SIM's network analysis had yielded a rich harvest of connections. She closed that window and opened another. A dense mesh of coloured lines appeared, tracing connections between people, companies, bank accounts and countries. A rich and troublesome harvest, mainly because of the frequency with which the name of Peter Bardossy, Reka's husband, and his associates, appeared.

She sat back in her chair and looked out of the narrow window in her office on the fifth floor of the ABS headquarters on Falk Miksa Street. It was a small, narrow space at the end of a long, gloomy corridor. The walls were off-white, the floor covered with grey linoleum. At times like this she felt the room was closing in on her. The window was long and narrow, but still offered a view of the street. She looked down to watch a gaggle of tourists staring into the antique shop on the other side of the road. A rotund, grey-haired lady strolled by, walking a spaniel on a lead. A boy and girl in their early teens were ambling home from the nearby park, perhaps.

She watched the boy take the girl's hand. She smiled shyly and did not remove it. Some tasks were indeed quite simple. Anastasia picked up her mobile phone and scrolled through the sent messages folder until she found the one she wanted: a photograph of Simon Nazir on the ground and the words '26 Republic Square'. Anastasia looked at the picture for some time, then pressed 'delete'. She then called up WhatsApp and opened one of the sent messages. The message's contents were almost identical, but included the letter 'B'. It too quickly vanished.

A few moments later her mobile phone rang. The number calling was not displayed but she had a good idea who it was. Anastasia waited until the third ring, then answered.

Freedom Square, 7.00 p.m.

Balthazar sat on a park bench on Freedom Square, enjoying the warmth of the sun on his face. The day was still warm but cooled by a pleasant breeze. Freedom Square was a long oblong, with grass in the middle and landscaped garden areas on both sides, and two playgrounds at the far end. It was also a microcosm of Hungarian history: at one end, the grandiose Soviet war memorial, clad in white stone with a metal relief of fighting troops, marking the liberation of Budapest from the Nazis, stood a few yards from the grey metal fence and security posts around the American embassy. At the other stood a kitsch statue of an angel being menaced by an eagle. The angel represented an innocent Hungary, the eagle the Nazis. An impromptu Holocaust memorial of photographs, stones and mementoes had sprung up in front of it, protesting at the travesty of history in a country where the authorities had speedily handed over half a million citizens to be murdered.

Two policemen walked by on patrol duty. One of them, a stocky man in his fifties with heavy jowls, saw Balthazar. They both walked over, shook his hand and congratulated him. He stood up and thanked them. The policeman walked on across the square. Then two more appeared. Balthazar took out his phone and quickly called Sandor Takacs.

'Are you having me tailed?'

'Protected, Tazi,' said Takacs. 'Protected. Just for a while. Enjoy your evening with your son. Sanyi *bacsi* is keeping an eye on you.'

Balthazar smiled. 'Thanks.'

Shouts and laughter spilled over from the nearby playgrounds. He looked over at the children clambering on the wooden train and one boy in particular building an elaborate castle in the sandpit. He glanced at his watch: it was a few minutes after seven o'clock. Sarah was supposed to be here at seven. Normally she would never let Alex meet him so late on a Sunday. But even Sarah knew that this was not a normal day. That had been a close call with the gunman. A very close call and a tricky shot. He had a very good idea who it was. So, he thought, did Sandor Takacs.

A black Toyota SUV with tinted windows pulled up on the corner of the square. For a moment his stomach flipped. Was this a Gendarmerie vehicle? The SUV pulled in to the pavement. He looked at the windscreen to see that Sarah was driving. She waved at Balthazar. The door opened and Alex jumped out, running as fast as he could to his father. Balthazar swept him up in his arms, breathing in his very essence, his fresh, boyish smell, ignoring the pains shooting around his body from Friday's beating, feeling his son's skinny ribs close against his chest and the love and excitement that poured from him. He was holding Alex so tightly that his son started laughing, 'Daddy, I can't breathe!'

Balthazar put him down as Sarah walked over. She wore a baggy white cotton top and light-blue trousers and carried Alex's red-and-black school rucksack. Her frizzy brown hair was tied back and her face was pink from the sun. She was smiling with genuine warmth that lit up her brown eyes. For a moment he was back in the library at the Central European University, surreptitiously watching the new American student, until she said, loud enough for everyone to hear, 'If you keep on staring, you had better buy me a coffee.'

She looked at him, as though re-assessing the man to whom she had once been married, the father of her child. 'That was quite something today. It's all over the news. Are you OK?'

'I'm fine.'

Alex said, 'Daddy, you saved that lady. Are you going to get a medal?'

'I don't think so. I don't need a medal.'

Alex frowned for a moment, thinking. 'Are we still having PBF?'

'Park, yes, burger, yes, but no film tonight.'

His small face fell, 'But Dad...'

Sarah smiled, 'School tomorrow. Right, Tazi?'

'Right.'

Sarah rested her hand on Balthazar's arm. 'Good. This is his bag. There's a clean T-shirt, socks and underwear. His school stuff is inside. He can stay with you tonight.'

A small ball of joy exploded inside Balthazar. 'Thanks, Sarah. And I'll sort out that trip to the women weavers next weekend.'

Sarah smiled wryly. 'Thanks. But he can stay with you anyway.'

Balthazar watched Sarah kiss Alex goodbye. He took his son by the hand to the playground. 'There are two people I want you to meet. They are coming for burgers with us. I hope that's OK.'

Alex looked up at Balthazar. 'Sure, Daddy. Who are they?'

Balthazar stepped into the playground. Jozsi looked up from his sandcastle and ran over to him. Balthazar introduced the boys to each other. 'Jozsi, meet Alex. Alex, meet Jozsi.' They shook hands with all the gravity of youth then ran off to the playground. After a few yards Alex stopped, turned around and sprinted back. 'Who else are we meeting, Daddy?'

'A lady, but not here, at the burger bar.'

Alex's face lit up with excitement. 'A lady. Is she your girl-friend, Daddy? Will I have three mummies now?'

Balthazar laughed, squeezed his son's shoulder. 'No. I don't have a girlfriend.'

'What's her name?'

'You'll see.'

Balthazar sat on the bench that overlooked the playground. Jozsi and Alex were clambering up the sides of the brightly painted wooden train. He took out his mobile telephone and found the number he wanted. She answered after two rings.

'Nice story,' Balthazar said. 'Your editors must be pleased.'

'They are. Very,' said Eniko. 'How about you? Are you OK?'

'I'm fine. I'm with Alex in the park on Freedom Square. We're going for burgers.' He smiled, stopped talking.

'That sounds nice.' She paused before she spoke. 'I've hardly eaten today.'

Balthazar let the moment draw out for several seconds, listened to the sound of Eniko's breathing before he asked, 'Would you like to join us?'

ACKNOWLEDGEMENTS

District VIII has been many years in the making. I have written about Hungary and its neighbours in Central Europe and the Balkans since the change of system in the early 1990s. I have always been fascinated by the Roma and the near parallel universe in which many live, alongside wider society but not fully part of it, and by the fierce bonds of family and blood that unite them against a frequently hostile outside world.

Too often the stories I wrote were about exclusion: a wall in the Czech Republic to separate Roma people from their neighbours, heart-rending accounts of young Roma women sterilised against their will in Slovakia, Roma settlements with no running water, sewage system or electricity. But there is also good news, as a new generation passes through the education system and finds its voice as activists, politicians or simply in the professions, including the police. I was glad to attend an event several years ago at the British embassy in Budapest in support of the Hungarian Roma Police Union.

As well as my own experience I drew on several books: *I Met Lucky People*, by Yaron Matras, is a lively and informative guide to Roma life and history, while *Bury Me Standing* by Isabel Fonseca, is an evocative journey through the world of the Roma. The European Roma Rights Centre, in Budapest (www.errc.org), is a valuable source of reports and analyses on Roma life. I am grateful to all those who shared their insider knowledge of Roma society, Budapest's police and underworld.

My thanks go to my agents, Georgina Capel and Simon Shaps, for their steadfast support and for their belief in Balthazar Kovacs and *District VIII*. It has been a pleasure to work with the team at Head of Zeus: Nicolas Cheetham, Sophie Robinson, Clémence Jacquinet, Jessie Price, Blake Brooks and Louis Greenberg. Thanks also to Val McDermid and Andrew Taylor, my tutors on a crime-writing course at the Arvon Foundation, who strongly encouraged me to write what would become *District VIII*. I am especially grateful to the Society of Authors for a generous grant from the Authors' Foundation. Thanks to Tamas Varga, Kitti Horvath and everyone at Central Gym in Budapest for lessons in various Krav Maga techniques which helped add realism to the book's fight scenes. Clive Rumbold, a diligent reader and astute critic, read an early draft and made several helpful suggestions. A number of other friends helped along the way, especially Justin Leighton, Roger Boyes, Nick Thorpe, Pablo Gorondi and Peter Green, who accompanied me on several reporting trips in central Europe. My thanks most of all, to my ever supportive, patient and loving family: Kati, Danny, Hannah and my brother Jason.

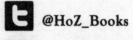
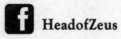